STUDIES IN AFRICAN LITERATURE

▼▼▼▼▼▼▼▼▼▼▼▼▼▼▼▼▼▼▼▼▼

Alex La Guma

Recent Titles in Studies in African Literature

▼▼▼▼▼▼▼▼▼▼▼▼▼▼▼▼▼▼▼▼▼▼▼▼▼▼▼▼▼

▼▼

Alex La Guma

Politics and Resistance

Nahem Yousaf

HEINEMANN
Portsmouth, NH

PR 9369.3
.L3
Z97
2001

Heinemann
A division of Reed Elsevier Inc.
361 Hanover Street
Portsmouth, NH 03801–3912
www.heinemann.com

ISBN 0–325–00189–8 (Heinemann cloth)
ISSN 1351–5713

Library of Congress Cataloging-in-Publication Data

Yousaf, Nahem.
    Alex La Guma : politics and resistance / Nahem Yousaf.
        p. cm.—(Studies in African literature, ISSN 1351–5713)
    Includes bibliographical references (p.   ) and index.
    ISBN 0–325–00189–8 (alk. paper)
    1. La Guma, Alex—Political and social views.   2. Politics and literature—South
Africa—History—20th century.   3. Political fiction, South African (English)—
History and criticism.   4. South Africa—In literature.   I. Title.   II. Series.
PR9369.3.L3 Z97 2001
    823'.914—dc21   00–061332

British Library Cataloguing in Publication Data is available.

Scattered excerpts from Alex La Guma's novels, *And A Threefold Cord* (London:
Kliptown Books, 1988), *In the Fog of the Seasons' End* (London: Heinemann, 1972), *The
Stone Country* (London: Heinemann, 1974), *Time of the Butcherbird* (London:
Heinemann, 1979), and *A Walk in the Night and Other Stories* (London: Heinemann,
1967), are reprinted by permission of the Tessa Sayle Agency.

Printed in the United States of America on acid-free paper.
04 03 02 01 00 SB 1 2 3 4 5 6 7 8 9

Contents

Preface

Alex La Guma was born into a politically active family in District Six, Cape Town, in 1925. His father, Jimmy La Guma, was a member of the executive for the Industrial and Commercial Workers Union of Africa (ICU). By the time Alex La Guma was a year old, his father was also on the central committee of the Communist Party of South Africa (CPSA), the first mass movement in black South African politics with an estimated membership of 100,000 in the 1920s. Jimmy La Guma became Secretary of the Western Cape African National Congress (ANC) and for a four-year period between 1935 and 1939 he was also active with the National Liberation League (NLL), which called for "universal franchise, militant action and working class unity across racial lines."[1] Even after he retired from active politics, Jimmy La Guma was persuaded to head the South African Coloured People's Organisation (SACPO) and did so between 1957 and 1961. It was into this politically committed background that La Guma was born and through which he learned that becoming politically active was both essential in South Africa and extremely dangerous.

Jimmy La Guma's political experience may be read as foundational to his son's burgeoning political and ideological development. As a teenager in the 1930s and early 1940s, La Guma tried to join the International Brigade to fight the fascists in Spain and he attempted to enlist in the army to fight in World War II; both offers were refused. In 1947 he became a member of the Young Communist League, strategically distancing himself from the party three years later when it voted for dissolution before it could be banned by the National Party. La Guma's sharpening resistance and his keen political sense would pervade the journalism with which he started his writing career, and his eclectic and resourceful comprehension of South African struggles would underpin the contexts he went on to create in his novels. It was in writing for *New Age*, a left-wing weekly paper of the Congress Alliance, that he was afforded the scope to comment broadly on events, as in the following bold example, which demonstrates courage and compassion:

> To all the workers and oppressed people of South Africa I extend on this great day [May Day 1956], my sincere greetings and good wishes for a democratic, happy and peaceful future. May Day this year is defiled with increasing oppression by the ruling class and the Nationalist tyrants. Police terrorism and violence is rife. "White baasskap" and "Christian civilisation" marches to the crack of the sjambok, the hose-pipe and the stengun. But on the other hand May Day is greeted and raised to glorious heights by the heroic struggles of the oppressed people against Apartheid, pass laws, removals, deportations and economic exploitation—for the new life of the Freedom Charter.[2]

By the following year he was writing a regular satirical column entitled "Up My Alley" and continued to do so until he became a banned person in 1962.

Alex La Guma was a politically active writer fully committed to the liberation struggle in South Africa. La Guma's credentials as an activist were impeccable. He was a member of the Executive Committee of SACPO in 1954 and was elected in 1955 to its chairmanship. Later that year he was chosen to lead a delegation to the Congress of the People in Kliptown, Johannesburg. Although he never made it to the meeting, having been forcibly and strategically detained to prevent his participation in the refinement and discussion of the Freedom Charter, he had made a bold statement on the impact the Congress would have on resistance struggles with the following words: "The Congress of the People is an historical occasion in the history of the struggle for liberation. There the Non-European and democratic forces will take stock of their forces and plan the final stages of the struggle. I look forward to attending it and hope that the example set by many other Coloured people who are attending will be an inspiration to their people to come closer to the struggle for democracy in South Africa."[3]

Cecil A. Abrahams, La Guma's biographer, has specified the character of La Guma's activism against the restrictive apartheid policies: "He gave leadership in attacking the government's 1955 Race Classification Bill and the 1956 South African [*sic*] Act Amendment Bill, which removed colored voters from the electoral roll . . . he led the bus boycott of April and May 1956."[4] La Guma's high profile in antigovernment agitation led to his being perceived as a potential threat to the State; a counterthreat was made on his life in 1958 and he later received a note with the chilling message "Sorry we missed you. Will call again. The patriots."[5] The government had him arrested along with 154 others in the infamous Treason Trial of 1956–61. After the final acquittal of all the accused, as late as 1960, La Guma was arrested on several more occasions before being placed under house arrest for five years. The removal of his liberty resulted in the writer's virtual imprisonment within the boundaries of his "home" and he was prevented from receiving visitors. It was even required that he obtain government permission in order to have his wife, Blanche, live at home with him. For La Guma the "only oversight of the authorities was that they did not prevent me from using my pen. They have since seen how dangerous this can be and now they won't permit any form of writing."[6]

Writing in South Africa, then, had not only a cathartic and potentially liberatory quality, it also had the potential to threaten governments; in La Guma's case it embodied the power to undermine the State's policies and offered a window to the outside world through which to observe the oppression heaped on the majority South African population. In addition to being placed under house arrest, La Guma was banned under the Suppression of Communism Act (1950) and, finally, his writing was suppressed under the Publication and Entertainments Act of 1963. However, neither measure prevented La Guma from writing or his work from becoming known. He left South Africa on a one-way exit visa in 1966, spending some time in Britain before moving to Cuba where he took on the role of the African National Congress' Latin American spokesperson.

The focus of this book is Alex La Guma's longer fiction. Many of the issues that underpin his journalism and short stories are extensively developed in the five published novels: *A Walk in the Night* (1962), *And A Threefold Cord* (1964), *The Stone Country* (1967), *In the Fog of the Seasons' End* (1972) and *Time of the Butcherbird* (1979). My critical and theoretical position is drawn largely from Frantz Fanon and Mikhail Bakhtin; I provide a Bakhtinian reading of La Guma's fiction while applying Fanon's ideas of liberation from oppressive colonialist practices as an inevitably violent process in *The Wretched of the Earth* to La Guma's narratives of the apartheid era.

La Guma's first attempts at writing fiction were a succession of short stories published in *New Age*, the paper he worked on, and in a range of journals including *New African, Africa South, Modern African Studies, Lotus* and *Black Orpheus*. As important as they are in evoking character, situation and dialogue, the stories function primarily as an apprenticeship to the novels where sustained evocations of context and character find more developed expression.[7] La Guma's professed view on the short story genre was that through this medium he could test his ability to "observe and report interesting anecdotes" and Bernth Lindfors has praised this feature of the writer's *oeuvre*, for the "careful evocation of atmosphere and mood, fusion of pathos and humour, colorful dialogue, and occasional surprise endings."[8] While I do not disagree with Lindfors' analysis, I would suggest that these are qualities made more manifest in the novels, where the scope for elaboration and more detailed examination is integral to the novel form itself. The stories are important precisely because a number of them introduce, prototypically, characters who become intrinsic to the novels: Butcherboy Williams and Yusef the Turk of *The Stone Country* first appear in an early story "Tattoo Marks and Nails" as "the Creature" and Ahmed the Turk; members of the Pauls family, whose poverty underpins the presentation of the township Windermere in *And A Threefold Cord*, are first presented in "On a Wedding Day"; and the Karroo of "Coffee for the Road" is developed so completely in *Time of the Butcherbird* as to render it a character itself.[9]

The significance of La Guma's shorter writings is tangential to my Bakhtinian reading of the novels. Bakhtin provides a critical language with which to discuss the ways in which fictional and political praxis are combined explicitly in La Guma's apartheid narratives. My primary interest lies in the dialogism of the novel in the face of the monologism of apartheid. Whereas the stories inevitably take a single situation or encounter as their focus, in the novels forms of resistance are codified and voiced in a plethora of discourses that question the monologic construction of apartheid. Those individuals and racialized groups who are marginalized and oppressed are able to resist the hierarchical form of their oppression through what Bakhtin's U.S. translators render "heteroglossia," in which manifold ideologies are expressed and interact. Bakhtin's theories of novelistic discourse, most forcefully articulated in "Discourse and the Novel," recognize that different and discordant voices will speak and conflict in the novel form, which is itself dialogic and through which an apparatus may be constructed for communicating the mutable and shifting meanings of political identity and the energy of the masses.[10]

Frantz Fanon's thesis is bound up with an imperative to affirm the humanity of the colonized or nonsubjects as well as to assert their presence via forms of resistance and protest. Alex La Guma's novels are a concerted effort to write marginalized communities back into resistance discourse; he demonstrates their humanity, no matter how flawed or at what stage of political development. La Guma's novels trace the development of political consciousness in his protagonists against what was an unbending apartheid environment. His fiction mirrors the growing disillusionment of the ANC whose policies of peaceful and nonviolent resistance were constantly undermined by the apartheid regime until the only solution or action that was to have any potential impact became a violent one.

In La Guma's politically embedded apartheid narratives questions of resistance to apartheid, political consciousness raising, communitarian politics and identity politics are central. I argue that his novels succeed in demonstrating how resistance is endemic in oppressed communities. In this way, my reading of the novels traces the ways in which unfocused aggression leads to unproductive intraracial violence and the burgeoning of a politicized consciousness moves the representation of conflict toward a dialogics that incorporates the oppressed, whereby aggression might be more effectively channeled towards the overthrow of a racist regime.

I argue that La Guma's fiction is reflective of the African National Congress' policies of nonviolent resistance through to the conception and activities of the ANC's military wing, Umkhonto we Sizwe. Throughout his five novels one detects a growing impatience with the apartheid regime's monologic policies in the face of a dialogically active population. La Guma deploys a dialogic approach in his fiction in order to elucidate the daily realities of the oppressed majority and the various subject positions his characters may adopt in opposition to the monologism of apartheid. In 1996, two years after South Africa's first all-inclusive elections, and nine years after Alex La Guma's death as an exile in Cuba, Barbara Harlow writes in *After Lives: Legacies of Revolutionary Writing* that "'Democracy' and 'negotiation' . . . together with such attendant terms as 'elections,' 'policing,' 'transitions' . . . have . . . in a most important sense displaced . . . 'armed struggle' as the focal point of cultural and political debate."[11] But this does not mean that the work of such writers as La Guma (who does not feature in Harlow's text) is no longer relevant to an understanding of revolutionary writing. Indeed, with the advent of democracy in South Africa, writers of the apartheid era, many of whom gave their lives in the struggles against apartheid, should remain focal; they pitted their voices against the injustices of an inherently unjust system. They remind us of what has only just been consigned to the realms of "history."

I would like to acknowledge the Arts and Humanities Research Board and the University of Hertfordshire for granting me research leave to complete this book.

Notes

1. See Andre Odendaal and Roger Field, eds., *Liberation Chabalala: The World of Alex La Guma* (Bellville, South Africa: Mayibuye Books, 1993), pp. ii–xxx.

2. From *New Age* 2:26, April 26, 1956, p. 3, quoted in Cecil A. Abrahams, *Alex La Guma* (Boston: Twayne Publishers, 1985), pp. 7–9.

3. See Odendaal and Field, *Liberation Chabalala*, p. ix.

4. Abrahams, *Alex La Guma,* pp. 7–8.

5. Odendaal and Field, *Liberation Chabalala*, p.xii.

6. Abrahams, *Alex La Guma,* p. 15.

7. Gerald Moore makes a similar point in *Twelve African Writers* (London: Hutchinson, 1980) and decides that La Guma's interest in form is limited in the stories and tales, p. 110.

8. La Guma quoted in Cecil A. Abrahams, *Alex La Guma* (Boston: Twayne Publishers, 1985), p. 42. Bernth Lindfors quoted in Abrahams, p. 22.

9. "On a Wedding Day," pp. 81–95 in Cecil A. Abrahams, *Memories of Home: The Writings of Alex La Guma* (Trenton, NJ: Africa World Press, 1991); "Tattoo Marks and Nails," pp. 97–107, in Alex La Guma, *A Walk in the Night* (London: Heinemann, 1967); "Coffee for the Road," pp. 70–79, in Jane Leggett and Roy Blatchford, eds., *It's Now or Never* (London: Unwin Hyman, 1988).

10. Mikhail Bakhtin, *The Dialogic Imagination,* ed., M. Holquist, trs. Caryl Emerson and M. Holquist (Austin: University of Texas, 1981), p. 263.

11. Barbara Harlow, *After Lives: Legacies of Revolutionary Writing* (London: Verso, 1996), p. 6.

Chapter 1

▼▼▼▼▼▼▼▼▼

Writing and Resistance

When one considers the South African novel and its form and function, it becomes clear that, with the exception of the missionary-sponsored literature of the early twentieth century, there was little indigenous literary production until the apartheid years, and what there was tended to be bowdlerized and sanitized in order for it to be acceptable to a predominantly white audience. As a result, Marx's oft-quoted sentiment—"*Sie können sich nicht vertreten, sie müssen vertreten werden*"—came to have a chilling significance.[1] White South African writers from Sarah Gertrude Millin to Wilbur Smith often represented the majority population in a derogatory manner in an effort to bolster a racist ideology that echoed the earlier colonial idea of a civilizing mission. Abdul JanMohamed has described the effects of such writing: "The European writer commodifies the native by negating his individuality, his subjectivity, so that he is now perceived as a generic being that can be exchanged for any other native (they all look alike, act alike and so on)."[2] With the denial of individuality all blacks become nonsubjects who gain their subjectivity through literary representation, and the form and content of these representations becomes of paramount importance. Edward Said suggests that representation is significant "not just as an academic or theoretical quandary but as a political choice." He contends that an anthropologist represents a context according to personal, local and historical contingencies shaped by social affirmation or approbation: "The point is that anthropological representations bear as much on the representer's world as on who or what is represented."[3]

Like the anthropologists in Said's discussion of colonized peoples, white South African writers had a choice: sympathetic representations or the

perpetration of racist representations in their literary productions. Both
choices had political ramifications that implicated a writer's position *vis-à-vis* the state. Christian-inflected liberal humanist texts like Alan Paton's
Cry, the Beloved Country, published in 1948, the year of the National Party
victory with "apartheid" as the slogan of the election, deploy the senti-
mental novel form as oppositional to the developing hierarchy of oppres-
sions in South Africa. The subtitle to Paton's first novel is "A Story of
Comfort in Desolation" and while the effort with which he exerted his
social conscience is unquestionable, such a liberal vision would inevitably
risk undermining the radical agendas of black writers in the 1950s: the
Reverend Stephen Kumalo could prove as much of an embarrassment as
Harriet Beecher Stowe's unquestioningly Christian "Uncle Tom" had been
to African American agendas in the 1850s.[4] Homi Bhabha reminds us that
the category of "literature" is itself a form of representation, when he
recognizes "its reality is not given but produced; its meanings transforma-
tive, historical and relational rather than revelatory; its continuity and
coherence underscored by division and difference."[5]

The study of representation is further complicated by the recognition
that the term "representation" is itself semantically unstable and the cultural codes that underlie representations prompt a kind of intellectual ar-
chaeology on the part of the writer or critic. Ezekiel Mphahlele attempted
to work through this issue in preparing his M.A. thesis on the representations of blacks by whites in South African fiction, focusing on Olive
Schreiner, Sarah Gertrude Millin, William Plomer and Alan Paton:

> Non-whites live in locations, or in the Reserves, or work for whites
> in towns and on farms, where there are either labour tenants or
> squatters. There can hardly be a healthy common culture in con-
> ditions that isolate whole communities and make social and eco-
> nomic intercourse difficult or impossible. And the problem of a
> national culture is *per se* the problem of a national literature. It
> must remain sectional and sterile as long as such conditions pre-
> vail.[6]

Mphahlele went on to read Peter Abrahams and novels like *Mine Boy*
(1946) and to understand "what it must have meant to him to want to
justify himself."[7] The inescapability of race relations as the impetus for
South African writing about South Africa is stark and immutable and has
remained a vexed problematic.

However, Alex La Guma's project was not one in which he required
himself to critically evaluate or subvert those negative representations that
went before, as Mphahlele reads Peter Abrahams's South African works or

as Chinua Achebe attempted to do in the Nigerian context with his earliest novel *Things Fall Apart* (1958). Rather, La Guma sought to reclaim a place and a subjectivity for blacks—and specifically "coloureds" in apartheid classification—in creative writing. Deploying Bakhtin's ideas of dialogism, heteroglossia and carnival helps to elucidate some of the ways in which he succeeds in this: recording the everyday speech of his characters, interpreting them through a range of burgeoning politicized discourses, and opening the novel to include opposition to the discourse of apartheid from within the communities that suffer under its monolithic structure. William Plomer learnt a Bantu language in order to represent his black characters in *Turbott Wolfe* (1925) but in La Guma the elements of carnival that directly oppose the official from *inside* marginalized communities enlarge the scope of the novels in ways that combine the aesthetic and the political, and issues of reality and representation. La Guma's black characters are not heroes in any conventional sense, but rather composite characters whose flaws serve an ideological purpose.

Despite the ideology that underpins the power of novels like *The Stone Country* and *In the Fog of the Seasons' End*, critics such as Felix Mnthali believe that La Guma's first novella, *A Walk in the Night*, remains his most successful and that with later works "the greater the revolutionary fire inspiring La Guma's work, the weaker it is aesthetically."[8] For Mnthali "aesthetics" appear to involve the use of imagery and symbolism, but his assessment sees literary aesthetics and revolutionary commitment as discrete, even contradictory, facets of a fiction. Mnthali places linguistic tropes over political commitment in a way that marginalizes that commitment, an anomalous position to take in regard to La Guma. His series of articles "The Time Has Come" alone are evidence enough of the equation between La Guma's politicized revolutionary stance and the fictions he creates. In them he is scathing as to the "mock rights" of colored people, as scathing as he is in *In the Fog of the Seasons' End* in the depiction of Mrs. Bennett, a colored woman with middle-class pretensions, who rejects political involvement out of hand. He also exposes the United Party's[9] manifest treatment of the colored community as "a sort of orphan or retarded child who must receive some kind of seperate [*sic*] and special treatment in the same way as SPCA cares for homeless animals."[10] This rage against people being treated as animals is reflected across his fictions, as is the condemnation of anything other than a clear coalition between African and colored peoples in the face of the apartheid machine. He celebrates what he calls the "ever-increasing political consciousness" of the oppressed.[11] With controlled despair he writes that crime and drunkenness, juvenile delinquency and poor educational facilities proliferate as a direct result of

Nationalist oppression and the poverty that it provokes: "The pattern of apartheid spreads into all spheres of life, and the spheres of culture and education are as important to the White Supremacists as that of politics."[12]

The preoccupations that underpin his novels can be detected in articles such as "The Time Has Come" and "The Condition of Culture in South Africa," which tackles Mnthali's problematic assessment head-on. In this piece La Guma is resignedly categorical in his statement that the idea of "art for art's sake" with "the impression that art, culture, the level of civilisation of a people, have nothing or little to do with socio-economic and political forces" is untenable in South Africa.[13] At the end of the 1970s, he continued to emphasize this fact, reiterating in the article "Culture and Liberation" that responding to what he terms the "life" and "artistic merit" of a cultural product involves responding also to the struggle for "higher levels of civilisation, of social, economic and cultural status" that are encoded within that product, so that "art cannot be separated from the desire for liberation."[14] La Guma takes up Cabral's ideas of how to resist culturally whereby literature, together with the other arts, reflects the colonizeds' level of resistance and "the various stages of development of an anti-imperialist movement."[15]

For La Guma fictions are inevitably works of political resistance. *In the Fog of the Seasons' End* incorporates a sickeningly evocative description of the "big strike" that evolves into the Sharpeville massacre, which is on par with Eisenstein's cinematic evocation of the White Guards' massacre of the workers on the Odessa Steps in *Battleship Potemkin*.[16] The scene is a violent one; in fact, one critic proposes that the entire plot of *In the Fog of the Seasons' End* rests on violence.[17] My contention throughout this book is that it is impossible to understand either La Guma's narratives of apartheid or the anti-apartheid struggle itself without recognizing the use of violence as a factor in the politicization of South Africans and the liberation of South Africa. La Guma claimed that as a South African writer he was "prepared to run guns and to hold up radio stations, because in South Africa that is what we are faced with, whether we are writers or whether we are common labourers."[18] La Guma's call to armed resistance in the two novels that feature prisons, and indeed in *Time of the Butcherbird*, crosses class demarcations; the doctor in *In the Fog of the Seasons' End* supports revolution, as does Flotman the college lecturer and Isaac the errand "boy."[19] La Guma is specific, though, as to the channeling of guerrilla violence, demonstrating that misdirected violence will not ultimately effect change. His characters are frequently "the wretched of the earth," living as they do under the overarching systematic degradation of apartheid. But, in the closing paragraphs of *In the Fog of the Seasons' End* and his final published novel, *Time of the Butcherbird*, La Guma leaves his South Africans on the threshold of a future that will forcibly engender their freedom from degradation. Beukes reflects on the oppressors who "persist in hatred and humiliation" but who must prepare for the revolution that will be their apocalypse. With the words, "Let them prepare hard and fast—they do not have long to wait," Beukes turns his thoughts to the children of South Africa who gather in the sunlight.[20] Similarly, at the close of *Time of the Butcherbird* "the land bends and sags" and, as the winds of apartheid begin to lessen, "the difference in the air makes life possible again."[21]

Writers in apartheid South Africa had for a long time occupied a space that was dangerous and incredibly necessary. It was dangerous because the writers' words were on a par with the actions of those who were politically active, and important because they might help to give a voice to those who had been beaten into silence, but not into submission. As Annamaria Carusi points out in her discussion of the writings of Don Mattera, there is a "structural similarity between what writers do in their poetry and stories and what political or trade union activists do in the political and economic fields."[22] Censorship, banning, detention, house arrest, solitary confinement, shooting, torture—such were the royalties that awaited the writer/activist who dared to write/act against the State during the apartheid years. The writer was crushed by the white racist regime because he or she dared to "express a sensibility and an outlook apart from, and independent of, the mass direction."[23] However, the Nigerian Wole Soyinka's sentiments, as applied above to "The Writer in a Modern African State," cannot be uncomplicatedly attributed to the South African situation since "the mass direction," or common consensus among the people, specifically wished to see the dismantling of the apparatus of apartheid and subsequent liberation for *all* to speak with voices that would represent the "sensibility" of the *mass*, not the minority. Although the anti-apartheid South African writer may not have expressed particularly different views from those of the "mass direction," writers still found themselves in a precarious position *vis-à-vis* a State that Ngugi has labeled a "nervous fascist outpost."[24] Allied to the removal of liberty is the banning of an author's works, whereby nothing that the author said or wrote could be reproduced in apartheid South Africa as a direct result of the Suppression of Communism Act of 1950 and the Publication and Entertainments Act of 1963.[25] Politically active African, colored and Indian South African writers inevitably found themselves in positions where they could not produce "art for art's sake." They felt politically obliged as well as empowered to produce work that would provide the outside world with a detailed exposé of the daily oppression faced by the black majority at the hands of the white minority that exploited it. Consequently, the act of writing can be understood to be a form of resistance against the rulers of that same "fascist outpost."

Ngugi, in a Marxist analysis of the function of the writer, identified three ways in which a writer is affected by the prevailing political environment: (i) the writer is inevitably a product of history, time and place; (ii) the writer's subject matter is history; and (iii) the product of a writer's imagination becomes a reflection of society.[26] These three factors lead to the production of the "realist" novel, with the realist novel being understood in this context as a product of novelists "look(ing), historically, at the crises of their own immediate time" and producing in a mimetic mode "knowable communities" that allow the novelist to delineate "people in essentially knowable and communicable ways."[27] Alex La Guma constructs knowable communities that are recognizably marginalized, black in character and "real" in apartheid South Africa, and it is no accident that his fiction is located, predominantly, in urban environments as these are the arenas that allow the novel to become an instrument for examining lives lived in the ghettos of apartheid.[28]

So, writers reflect what is happening in their society in order to demonstrate their commitment to liberation struggles. A writer espouses politicized literary strategies that move beyond essentialist notions of a precolonial idyll when his or her country is in the grips of colonial or neocolonial domination.[29] Wally Serote in his address to the African Writers' Conference of 1986 stated that a writer should aim to produce work that would: "record the story of the people of South Africa, to portray the people of this country, to contribute to the betterment of their lives, to inspire these same people to reach their aspirations, and to give lasting, sustaining hope, so that their lives can be ruled by optimism."[30] If this sounds like a utopian function, it is because Serote was, at the time, cultural secretary of the ANC and found himself in a sensitive political position whereby advocating out-and-out violent resistance was a final resort. Nevertheless, it is important to acknowledge that the ANC could not dismiss violent action as a means of resistance to the State's racist policies and had adopted armed struggle as early as 1961. Nelson Mandela clearly expressed the difficulty of arriving at a strategic decision about defiance as translated into physical violence at the Rivonia trial when he faced charges of sabotage and revolution. In his statement to the court on April 20, 1964, he did not deny that he had planned sabotage but pointed out that he did so "as a result of a calm and sober assessment of the political situation that had arisen after many years of tyranny, exploitation, and oppression of my people by the whites." Mandela was instrumental in the founding of Umkhonto we Sizwe because violence had become inevitable and responsible leadership was required "to channel and control the feelings of our people," and to prevent the kinds of terrorist activity that would intensify an already volatile national situation. Like many others, by the 1960s Mandela had articulated his antipathy with the political impasse created by white supremacists:

> All lawful methods of expressing opposition . . . had been closed by legislation, and we were placed in a position in which we had either to accept a permanent state of inferiority, or to defy the government. We chose to defy the law. We first broke the law in a way which avoided any recourse to violence; when this form was legislated against, and the government resorted to a show of force to crush opposition to its policies, only then did we decide to answer violence with violence.[31]

In his testimony at the Rivonia trial Mandela spoke of the effects of an unremitting legislative process on the African people: fifty years of nonviolent negotiations had resulted only in the tightening of the repressive structures. Of the forms of violence the ANC considered—sabotage, guerilla warfare, terrorism and revolution—sabotage was the first hesitant step. La Guma's politics followed the ANC's line. His fiction—in particular *The Stone Country* and *In the Fog of the Seasons' End*—follows the development of a policy that first advocated the nonviolent organization of boycotts, "stay-at-homes" and strikes through the distribution of pamphlets and training for an armed struggle against an unbending regime's belief in its superiority over the majority population. Frantz Fanon had categorized pamphleteering within what he terms "the philosophico-political dissertations on the themes of the rights of peoples to self-determination,"[32] associated with political parties and movements that do not advocate violence. Peaceful political activity might elicit sympathy for the anti-apartheid cause but, as La Guma indicates, actively initiating change required a more channeled form of resistance: physical violence and armed struggle in addition to political resistance.

La Guma writes specifically of anti-apartheid defiance and resistance, while Fanon writes more generally of decolonization but the two positions are inextricably interwoven with a philosophy of violence, as a way to open up the possibilities for successful opposition to white supremacy and force, as Mandela outlines. Resistance can be understood as a precondition of decolonization. The moment that initiates the decolonization process is a moment of undiluted resistance for Fanon: "at the moment he [the colonized] realizes his humanity . . . he begins to sharpen the weapons with which he will secure its victory."[33] This is the point at which the colonizer loses the power to project otherness onto the colonized subject.[34] It is human to resist and assertion of that humanity through resistance practices involves the colonized in a potentially violent struggle. Indeed, in Alex La Guma's novels this process is inextricably linked to political consciousness raising as an inevitable precursor to an ideological understanding of self and humanity.

Fanon's ideas may help to elucidate the ways in which violence is endemic within societies dominated by white settler communities. He has noted the characterization of soldiers and police officers as the upholders of colonial order and as the public representatives of colonial systems. These intermediaries are central to Fanon's thesis upon how the colonizers effect control, just as their presence—initiating raids, detaining activists— is an essential component of the narratives that writers construct as reflective of the systematic oppression that is apartheid. Fanon has articulated the complexity of the roles of police officers and the military in their effects upon the quotidian reality of the colonized. They are the grammar of the discourse of apartheid: for Fanon these "agents of government speak the language of pure force" but that force of aggression co-exists alongside their brief to "protect" the natives from their own "infantilised" selves. Their role is crucial for an oppressive regime since they bring "violence into the home and into the mind of the native."[35] State violence erupted with volcanic force in Soweto in 1976, and copies of Fanon's *The Wretched of the Earth* circulated among those student organizers whose commitment to revolution involved ideas of revolutionary theory.[36]

La Guma's first published novel, *A Walk in the Night*, coincides with the point in South Africa's history of apartheid when, as activist Albie Sachs encapsulates, "the Government had, in word and deed, made it plain that it was determined to defend apartheid with the gun," and passive resistance was deemed ineffective as a means to bring about change.[37] Furthermore, writing has the power to offer ideas to the people; it may help to represent the people's choices and potential routes to rebellion. Words have a political function, a task to perform, as Lewis Nkosi, who proved most vocal on this issue, has explicated: "Sometimes words by writers help to bring into clear focus feelings of frustration and resentment which have long remained inchoate and unfocused for the general mass of the public."[38] The revolutionary power that literature may contain is a feature that did not go unnoticed by the apartheid regime, and La Guma himself pointed to the fact that by 1969 the South African government had banned some 13,000 books and was in the regular habit of altering posters advertising American films that showed black and white people together.[39] In a discussion at the African Writers' Conference of 1967, La Guma responded to Soyinka's address on "The Writer in a Modern African State" with a statement about South African writing as expressly a literature "which concerns itself with the realities of South Africa." He endeavored to unravel what that might mean for the writer of apartheid narratives:

> When we sit down to write a book, I or any of my colleagues around me . . . are . . . faced with the reality that 80% of the population lives below the bread-line standard; we are faced with the reality that the average daily population of prisoners in South African prisons amounts to 70,000 persons. We are faced with the reality that half the non-white population who died last year were below the age of five. These are the realities.[40]

La Guma spoke authoritatively and emotively to the need to write from an informed position, of an unswerving allegiance to commentary and reflection on the daily reality of those oppressed under the apartheid regime. In his analysis, there is little meaning behind literature that neither reflects the suffering of the masses nor works to persuade the government to alter its oppressive legislation. La Guma expressed no surprise at the sheer number of prisoners in captivity. After all, he had stated elsewhere that "a society based on suppression, violence, armed force, poverty and unemployment creates violence, bloodshed, gangsterism and murder,"[41] indicating that the apartheid system creates a new grouping of residents, a cross-racial grouping of blacks prepared to use violence against a violent regime.

Lewis Nkosi, in his reading of several South African authors including La Guma, has claimed that black South African writers could not afford the luxury of writing about a pre-colonial past or the luxury of drawing on indigenous cultures; their focus was the apartheid present because "the present exerts its own pressures which seem vast, immanent, all-consuming."[42] These pressures induced by the apartheid system exerted themselves upon writers since, unlike other territories in the African continent, South Africa had not yet achieved "independence." However, Nkosi's analysis is marred by some oversimplifications in relation to the subject matter of apartheid narratives. He believes writers are "unable to contemplate any kind of human action without first attempting to locate it within a precise social framework of racial conflict" because "colour differences provide the ultimate symbols which stand for those larger antagonisms which South African writers have always considered it their proper business to explain."[43] In an apartheid situation, which larger or more important issues supplant the issue of racial conflict? Nkosi's argument is momentarily clouded by his nonclarification of those "larger antagonisms." Nkosi fails to acknowledge that the controlling force behind narratives by black South Africans was the engine of apartheid itself with the somewhat cryptic statement, "To put it bluntly nothing stands behind the fiction of black South Africans."[44] The apartheid system provided authors with their knowable communities and afforded them the opportunity to produce work that, in the words of Miriam Tlali, herself a writer of protest fictions like *Amandla* (1980) banned on publication, allowed them to "determinedly and furiously voice their protest against the detentions without trial, shootings by the police and army, disappearance of leaders and others, the torture of people in detention."[45]

Despite the precise political significance of writing in South Africa, Njabulo Ndebele, tracing the history of the writers' movement in South Africa, notes that writers' organizations tended to be shortlived for a number of reasons; the predominant being access, or more specifically the right to membership based on skin color. He notes, for example, that the Writers' and Artists' Guild of South Africa, established in 1974, developed a policy that Lionel Abrahams describes as an effort to "welcome . . . black writers to its ranks." However, the Guild discovered that its membership remained white, and this in a period when the Guild claimed to "protect the interests of writers and artists against the interference of the State or censorship."[46] The refusal of blacks to join this Guild may be attributed to the rise of the Black Consciousness Movement and the proliferation of black cultural groups in the mid-1970s, all of which were exclusively black in membership. Black Consciousness advocated a particular attitude and way of life, as Steve Biko famously outlined:

> Its essence is the realization by the black man of the need to rally together with his brothers around the cause of their oppression— the blackness of their skin—and operate as a group to rid themselves of the shackles that bind them to perpetual servitude. It is based on a self-examination. . . . thinking along lines of Black Consciousness makes the black man see himself as a being complete in himself. It makes him less dependent and more free to express his manhood. At the end of it all he cannot tolerate attempts by anybody to dwarf the significance of his manhood.[47]

Such a profound philosophical and political conviction in the integrity of black people—albeit couched in masculinist terms—led some members of the Black Consciousness Movement to shun white liberals and radicals who, they argued, were integrally bound up in the structures of white supremacy. It should come as no surprise that black South Africans expressed little or no faith in whites in the 1970s following the Sharpeville massacre in 1960, the subsequent banning of the ANC and the Pan-Africanist Congress, and the Soweto uprisings in the 1970s. Sharpeville acted as a catalyst for the world's coming to consciousness of the specific atrocities occuring in South Africa and it, together with related cultural clashes, was fundamental to blacks' resolve to shun writers' groups that had any white connection. Refusal to combine artistic endeavors at this time may also signal a tacit assumption that black and white writers ultimately espoused different writerly projects under apartheid. The Afrikaner Breyten Breytenbach imprisoned in South Africa and exiled in Paris, writing in 1970, noted that writers of Afrikaans books had not yet been prosecuted.[48] He draws on Fanon in his contention that the alienation of whites and white artists in apartheid South Africa was a direct result of apartheid policies, which had the effect of alienating white artists in general from the popular revolutionary struggle integral to writing by black South Africans.

The dominant tool in literary production by South Africans has been the English language. The use of English can be traced back to the missionary education system implemented by the British. In South Africa the medium of educational instruction was, until 1955, English, and this resulted in black writers utilizing this language. The use of English served and continues to serve a number of purposes, not all of which enabled the colonialist project: In South Africa it united a polyglot population, speaking in, for example, Xhosa and Zulu, and provided the means by which they might communicate the "terrible uniformity" of the oppression "forced on black South Africans" to a world audience.[49] It placed readers—particularly those within South Africa who managed to obtain banned literature—in a politically empowered position since reading is itself a political activity, a form of resistance to a government-sanctioned "official version" of South African reality. In a move to stem the development of English language usage, the ruling political party banned the teaching of English through the Bantu Education Act of 1955 and advanced a policy—in line with its ideology of separate development—of vernacular language education. This move resulted in what Ezekiel Mphahlele has described as the desire to "wrench the tools of power from the white man's hand: one of these is literacy and the sophistication that goes with it. We have got to speak the language that all can understand—English."[50] Similarly, Herbert Dhlomo commended the fact that English enabled writers to "speak to a greater audience than many a politician."[51] However, writing in an "official" language did not evade the consequences for the writer whose punishment could be death. Disturbingly, as Mishra and Hodge have noted "to write in the language of the colonizer is to write from within death itself."[52] Examples of this metaphor in action abound in South Africa for having one's words banned is a form of creative and communicative "death," as is being forced into exile, which has the consequence of distancing the writer from the political and social locus of his or her work.

Exile may prevent the black writer from "writ[ing] from the 'inside' about the experiences of the black masses" and therefore may mitigate the urgency that exists in literature created "inside" apartheid. This is the accusation leveled against La Guma and his novel *Time of the Butcherbird* by David Maughan-Brown, who claims that the exile's experience is inevitably fragmentary, based on memory, news items, articles, letters and contact with other exiles. For this critic, *Time of the Butcherbird* suffers from an impressionistic lack of cohesion.[53] Certainly there is evidence of a disconnectedness in La Guma's final work. This may be the result of locating *Time of the Butcherbird* in the Karroo and of La Guma's focus upon characters who live out experiences different from his own in South Africa. It may also be due to the exiled writer's alienation and disjunction: banned from returning to the homeland, he or she is forced into an ambivalent relationship with the country of exile. Lewis Nkosi has spoken specifically of the plight of black South African exiles in England—where La Guma spent some of his time—and asserted that they were hardly welcomed in the same way as white South African exiles. Indeed, on arrival in England, La Guma could find no other work than as an agent for an insurance company, while Nkosi points to "second rate" white South African writers employed on such reputable newspapers as the *Guardian* and the *Observer*. Such a situation inevitably leads to black individuals becoming marginalized as "outsiders" twice over; a situation further complicated by the much-documented hostility towards black people in Britain in the 1950s and 1960s. Issues of "unbelonging" and rootlessness are critical for the writer in exile.

In *Home and Exile*, Nkosi's exegesis on rootlessness evokes the context in which the homeland becomes more dear and simultaneously more alien.[54] Ezekiel Mphahlele, like many exiled writers, found it difficult to write while distanced from his primary subject matter: "The problem for me as a writer was that as long as I refused to strike roots, I was going to continue to write about home, but at the same time I was away from home."[55] For some writers the price of exile was too high and the distance from the struggle too great, and they succumbed to suicide, a notable example being Nat Nakasa. To the host country the writer would always retain South African identity and, in many ways, this proved to be no bad thing during the apartheid years when the writer's work could provide what Nkosi calls "a point of contact between the defiant victims of apartheid and many men and women of goodwill all over the world" who express solidarity.[56] However, this does rather beg the question as to why writers of apartheid narratives, like La Guma, have not also been appropriated as British when other writers such as the Rhodesian (now Zimbabwean) Doris Lessing and the Indian Salman Rushdie have, and appear in various anthologies to attest to the fact.[57] I am not suggesting that this type of literary critical appropriation operates as a means of expressing solidarity with a particular writer's political affiliations, but posing the question, rather, whether there may be something inherently disturbing in the literature of apartheid that the British found indelicate. A guilty political connection perhaps? Certainly Kenneth Parker has argued that South Africa was an "ever-present and intrusive presence" in the British consciousness during the decades following World War II.[58] The dominant images of South Africa in Britain have been those created by white South African writers; Alan Paton and Nadine Gordimer are pertinent examples. La Guma himself, outlining a history of apartheid as editor of the documentary collection called *Apartheid,* posited that the "legal cornerstone of racism in South Africa was laid when Britain vested all the political power in the hands of the White minority in 1910. The constitution legalised racism and prepared the ground for all the aspects of national oppression, exploitation, humiliation and brutalisation of the non-White people."[59] La Guma does not flinch in his portrayal of violence and brutality in all its forms. In this context Fanon's position on violence as liberatory informs my elucidation of the anti-apartheid struggle in South Africa, and the politicized position of South African writers like Alex La Guma with regard to that struggle.[60] My deployment of Fanon is not indiscriminate: Frantz Fanon was actively involved in resistance struggles both as a theoretician and as a member of the Algerian National Liberation Front (FLN). In fact, his increasing involvement with the FLN led to his resignation from the post of Clinical Director of the Blida-Joinville Hospital in Algiers in 1956 since this gave him the opportunity to devote more time to the resistance movement. It should be apparent from his background, in psychoanalytical theory and practice and as a political activist, that Fanon was well placed to witness the horrors inflicted upon the colonized peoples of Algeria under French rule. Fanon, consequently, devised a theory that does not oppose violence, in the vein of Gandhi,[61] but welcomes it as a means to achieve liberation. It is a theory echoed by the ANC in their shift from nonviolent defiance campaigns to armed struggle and integral to my reading of La Guma's fiction.

Fanon's thesis on violence is controversial; it has been compared to Hitler's *Mein Kampf,*[62] on the one hand, while there are counterclaims on the other for Fanon's violence being that of a "non-violent man . . . the violence of justice, purity, of intransigence,"[63] all of which goes to complicate the interest in Fanon's writing. The philosopher Hannah Arendt, for example, mounted a pointed attack on Fanon in *On Violence*, accusing him of glorifying "violence for violence's sake." She suggested that Fanon "was motivated by a much deeper hatred of bourgeois society and (was) led to a much more radical break with its moral standards than the conventional Left, which was chiefly inspired by compassion and a burning desire for justice."[64] For my purposes, though, the salient point is that Fanon wrote "Concerning Violence" as a warning to the newly "independent" states ruled by petit-bourgeois elites against complacency and against falling into colonialist traps. Yet it also operates as a manifesto for those who found themselves subjugated by totalitarian regimes, offering as it does a model for liberation in the context of South Africa under apartheid.

Violence is a notoriously difficult word to define, but it is imperative to try to do so in the context of La Guma's work. Taken simply, it can mean physical abuse inflicted by an individual or group upon another individual or group that results in physical injury or death. But violence may also be inflicted in other more insidious ways where the results are not so easily discernible; these types of violence may include subjugation, the removal of liberty and the suppression of the views and opinions of an individual or group. Despite Fanon's predilection for metaphors of war and weaponry, which gives the impression that he advocates only physical violence, and has even earned him the dubious label of "apostle of violence,"[65] his thesis also addresses nonphysical forms of violence. For the purposes of this text, I would concur with Hussein Abdilahi Bulhan's Fanonian extrapolation on forms of violence: *"any relation, process or condition by which an individual or a group violates the physical, social, and/or psychological integrity of another person or group.* From this perspective, violence inhibits human growth, negates inherent potential, limits productive living, and causes death."[66] However, linguistic, cultural and "epistemic" violence should be added to Bulhan's definition in order for it to more fully encompass both physical and nonphysical violence and for it to act as a model for my discussion of the violence that underlies the apartheid structures in South Africa and complicates the lives of La Guma's protagonists.

Fanon's assertion that "decolonization is always a violent phenomenon"[67] is premised on his recognition that decolonization will involve a "disordering" of the structures and hierarchies that the colonizers have secured in place through violent means. Decolonization, then, involves a confrontational encounter between the forces of the colonizer and the colonized, just as the initial process of colonization was predicated on violence and the knowledge of having superior armaments, training in warfare, and the protection—if required—of the mother country with her desire to protect her potential economic investment. Fanon's exposition of his ideas also works rhetorically in its reliance upon the images of violence and weaponry—"searing bullets and bloodstained knives"[68]—that operate metaphorically to underscore the polemical force of his argument. Fanon recognizes that the oppressor is not satisfied with dominating the people through militarism, he actually wants to make history: "His life is an epoch, an Odyssey. He is the absolute beginning: 'This land was created by us'; he is the unceasing cause: 'If we leave, all is lost, and the country will go back to the Middle Ages.'"[69]

As Fanon writes generally of the position of the colonized and their lived experience, one becomes aware that the conditions that he goes on to contextualize within the Algerian situation might also be exemplified through a study of the very particular situation of South Africa that La Guma describes. Indeed, Mazisi Kunene recognized a connection between the Algerian and the South African situations as early as 1973 in his paper "Revolutionary Challenges and Cultural Perspectives" delivered at the first Pan-African Festival in Algiers. Kunene acknowledged "on behalf of the fighting forces of South Africa . . . [a] sincere and honest appreciation to the people of Algeria" and he attached significance to the FLN's fight for liberation as relevant to South Africa in his call for a united Africa.[70] Fanon's contention that for the native subjected to colonial constraints, it becomes clear very early on "that this narrow world, strewn with prohibitions, can only be called in question by absolute violence"[71] is also relevant here. South African writers have echoed Fanon, calling attention to the right to knowledge and education largely withheld in South Africa from the people who lived in the "narrow world" of the townships and ghettos of apartheid. La Guma puts it this way: "The people have taken up arms in order to exercise their right to reconstruct and rehabilitate the personality of the South African people."[72] He pursues this issue in his novels as closely as in his political speeches.

Fanon identifies three stages that the colonized subject passes through. These are the assimilationist stage, the stage of being distressed and disturbed, and the fighting stage or stage of resistance.[73] These stages correspond to the awakening of the colonized subjects' consciousness. Initially the colonized want to be *recognized* as sentient beings. This is a reaction to the dehumanizing process that is inherent within the colonialist project. Judging what is human is itself problematic when, as Paulo Freire has suggested, the colonizeds' "ideal is to be men [*sic*]; but for them to be a 'man' is to be an oppressor. This is their model of humanity."[74] It is also made problematic by the discourse of colonialism. When the very recognition of selfhood is denied, the colonized subject becomes self-questioning. This struggle for ontological and epistemological certainty involves tautological questioning as to why "citizens" have been systematically denied autonomy until the point at which the oppressed peoples, in Freire's terms, "see examples of the vulnerability of the oppressor so that a contrary conviction can begin to grow within them. Until this occurs they will continue disheartened, fearful, beaten."[75] The final stage is the one in which the colonized subjects understand that in order to attain the power of self-determination, they must adopt the same method that the colonizers used to attain their power, namely, violence. This position is unavoidable, as La Guma demonstrates in his 1967 series of articles "The Time Has Come," in which he urges the colored community in South Africa to support Umkhonto we Sizwe and an armed resistance: "The people can no longer stand subservient to tyranny and rule by force and violence. Violence can only be fought with violence. There is no alternative in South Africa today."[76] It can be argued, then, that the colonizer is not only the oppressor but is in some senses the teacher, underlining the conscious desire in the native to fight to possess all that has been denied him or her. This final stage cannot, I would argue, be achieved individually but must be enacted collectively. Fanon identifies individualism and its egocentricity as a feature of colonial indoctrination. His words, on this occasion, appear at their most polemical: "Brother, sister, friend—these are words outlawed by the colonialist bourgeoisie, because for them my brother is my purse, my friend is part of my scheme for getting on."[77] This sentiment expresses rancor at the success of what Fanon reads as a policy to divide the communities of the oppressed, to ensure their implosion. Fanon even posits that intraracial violence—for example, tribal hostility—may ostensibly be a means for operating as if colonialism did not intervene in African history, as if engaging in tribal battles and those disagreements *within* the communities relegates the colonizers' influence to the periphery of the natives' existence and delimits colonial control. Of course, this is not to deny the codifying of intraracial violence within colonial discourse and most specifically within the mindset that seeks to justify apartheid. The colonizer/settler can validate oppressive violence as suppressive violence intended to defuse an "inherently" criminal and violent culture and people.

Just as violence can be effective at psychological and social levels as well as the physical, resistance, too, may take many forms. In the context of this book, therefore, to resist is to refuse; this can be a refusal to obey orders or instructions or it can be a refusal to conform to, and therefore confirm, racist stereotypes. Colonialist discourse constructs stereotypes that are both knowable and repellent, stereotypical caricatures that require civilizing or, since they elicit fear, quashing. Edward Said in his study *Orientalism* demonstrates how representations of the other can become realities that exist in the actual world. Through what he calls "radical realism," regions and characteristics are named, designated and fixed.[78] The problem that Said's analysis uncovers is that in colonial discourse the representation of the colonial subject is fixed and stable when in actuality it is not. In this way colonialist discourse is structurally similar to realism.[79] But while realism demands that "Every event, every phenomenon, every thing, every object of artistic representation lose(s) its completedness, its hopelessly finished quality and its immutability that had been so essential to it in the world of the epic 'absolute past,'"[80] colonialist discourse is still locked in the representation of fixed, unshifting images. So notions of blacks and coloreds as lazy and conniving are propagated and perpetuated through an occidental store of "knowledge," a store that provides a library of discourse that allows the "native" to be known—even without direct contact—and reproduced.[81] However, such erroneous notions can be and are being reworked by oppressed groups who are subverting, at an implicit, often barely susceptible level, the stereotypical personality traits attributed to them. They use these purported traits as screens from behind which they may effectively resist the orders and assumptions that rain down upon them.

La Guma creates characters who resist apartheid and contexts in which resistance—nonviolent and violent—becomes possible. The chapters that follow read La Guma's novels for the ways in which individuals and communities come to consciousness of the repressive State apparatus that functions to withhold both civil rights and political agency. Incrementally, the novels coalesce to provide a searing critique of apartheid from within that continued beyond La Guma's banning and subsequent exile. The dismantling of apartheid makes it all the more essential to reevaluate this important writer's apartheid narratives.

Notes

1. Karl Marx quoted in Edward Said, *Orientalism* (London: Penguin, 1991), p. 21.
2. Abdul JanMohamed, "The Economy of Manichean Allegory: The Function of Racial Difference in Colonialist Literature," *Critical Inquiry*, vol. 12, 1985, p. 64.

3. Edward Said, "Representing the Colonized: Anthropology's Interlocutors," *Critical Inquiry*, vol. 15, 1989, p. 224.

4. Alan Paton, *Cry, the Beloved Country* (London: The Reprint Society, 1949). See Michael Chapman, "Identity and the Apartheid State, 1948–1970," for a note on how Lewis Nkosi and the *Drum* journalists saw Paton's character as an embarrassment. In *Southern African Literatures* (London and New York: Longman, 1996), p. 239. See also, Marva Banks, "*Uncle Tom's Cabin* and Antebellum Black Response" in James L. Machor, ed., *Readers in History: Nineteenth Century American Literature and the Contexts of Response* (Baltimore: The Johns Hopkins Press, 1993), pp. 209–227.

5. Homi Bhabha, "Representation and the Colonial Text: A Critical Exploration of Some Forms of Mimeticism," in Frank Gloversmith, ed., *The Theory of Reading* (Brighton: Harvester, 1984), p. 96.

6. Ezekiel Mphahlele, *Down Second Avenue* (London: Faber and Faber, 1971), p. 196. Mphahlele quotes from the M.A. thesis he submitted to the University of South Africa in 1956.

7. Mphahlele, *Down Second Avenue*, p. 195.

8. Felix Mnthali, "Common Grounds in the Literatures of Black America and Southern Africa" in Andrew Horn and George E. Carter, eds., *American Studies in Africa* (Lesotho: University Press of Lesotho and the Ford Foundation, 1984), p. 47. Paradoxically in the light of this statement, Mnthali goes on to praise *The Stone Country*.

9. The United Party was the official white "opposition" party.

10. Alex La Guma, "The Time has Come: New Forms of Struggle Face the South African Coloured Community." First of a series of four articles in *Sechaba*, vol. 1, pt. 3, 1967, p. 15.

11. La Guma, "The Time has Come," pt. 5, p. 15.

12. La Guma, "The Time has Come," pt. 5, p. 14.

13. Alex La Guma, "The Condition of Culture in South Africa," *Presence Africaine*, vol. 80, 1971, p. 8.

14. Alex La Guma, "Culture and Liberation," *World Literature Written in English*, vol. xviii, 1979, p. 26.

15. La Guma, "Culture and Liberation," p. 29.

16. Alex La Guma, *In the Fog of the Seasons' End* (London: Heinemann, 1972), Chapter 9.

17. Omar Sougou, "Literature and Apartheid: Alex La Guma's fiction," *Bridges: A Senegalese Journal of English Studies*, December 1992, p. 42.

18. Alex La Guma, "The Writer in a Modern African State" in Per Wastberg, ed., *The Writer in Modern Africa* (Uppsala: Scandinavian Institute of African Studies, 1969), p. 22.

19. See, for example, Piniel Viriri Shava, *A People's Voice: Black South African Writing in the Twentieth Century* (London: Zed Books, 1989), pp. 59–68, for a fuller discussion, and Alex La Guma "African Culture and National Liberation," p. 58 for the importance of awakening the masses to revolution.

20. La Guma, *In the Fog*, pp. 180–181.

21. Alex La Guma, *Time of the Butcherbird* (London: Heinemann, 1979), p. 119. Theodora Akachi Ezeigbo notes that this final passage is written in the present tense and argues that "In my own view, this can only be because of the prophetic properties of the author's vision." In "'A Sign of the Times': Alex La Guma's *Time of the Butcherbird*," *Literary Half-Yearly*, 32, 1, 1991, p. 112.

22. Annamaria Carusi, "Post, Post and Post. Or Where Is South African Literature In All This?," p. 97. In Ian Adam and Helen Tiffin, eds., *Past the Last Post: Theorizing Post-Colonialism and Post-Modernism* (Hemel Hempstead: Harvester Wheatsheaf, 1991).

23. Wole Soyinka, "The Writer in a Modern African State," p. 16. In his *Art, Dialogue and Outrage: Essays on Literature and Culture* (London: Methuen, 1993).

24. Ngugi wa Thiong'o, *Writers in Politics* (London: Heinemann, 1981), p. 73. See also Etienne Balibar's essay "Racism and Nationalism" in Balibar and Wallerstein, *Race, Nation, Class: Ambiguous Identities* (London: Verso, 1991) in which he equates South African apartheid with German Nazism: "Let us emphasize here the paradigmatic fact that South African apartheid intimately intermixes the traces of the three formations which we have mentioned (Nazism, colonization, slavery)," p. 40.

25. T. T. Moyana, "Problems of a Creative Writer in South Africa" in Christopher Heywood, ed., *Aspects of South African Literature* (London: Heinemann, 1976) has shown the insidious nature of apartheid-constructed legislation designed to restrict the creative output of the artist: "The following carry the most restrictive provisions: the Bantu Administration Act (1927), Riotous Assemblies Act (1956), Entertainment (Censorship) Act (1931), Suppression of Communism Act (1950), Criminal Law Amendment Act (1953), Customs Act (1955), Extension of University Education Act (1959), Prisons Act (1959), Unlawful Organizations Act (1960), Publication and Entertainments Act (1963), General Law Amendment Act (1963), Criminal Procedure Act (1965), Terrorism Act (1967), General Law Amendment Act (1969)," pp. 87–88.

26. Ngugi, *Writers in Politics*, p. 72.

27. Raymond Williams, *The English Novel From Dickens To Lawrence* (London: Hogarth Press, 1984), p. 14.

28. In this context, see also David Rabkin, "Ways of Looking: Origins of the Novel in South Africa," *The Journal of Commonwealth Literature*, vol. xiii, no. 1, 1978, pp. 27–44.

29. See, for example, Fanuel Sumaili, "Literature and the Process of Liberation" in Emmanuel Ngara and Andrew Morrison, eds., *Literature, Language and the Nation* (Harare, Zimbabwe: Association of University Teachers of Literature and Language and Baobab Books, 1989) where Sumaili suggests that: "Given our collective history, all literature that aspires to have a role in

liberation should address itself directly to the necessity of people reclaiming their history and identity from the cultural terrorism and depredation of the colonial period" (p. 8). This can clearly be seen as a fallacy and generalization as it suggests that the colonized peoples are a homogeneous mass with a shared "history" and "culture," and the assertion also carries undertones of essentialism with the call for a return to a precolonial past as some sort of redemptive process.

30. Wally Serote, "Power to the People: A Glory to Creativity," p. 194. In Kirsten Holst Petersen, ed., *Criticism and Ideology* (Uppsala: Scandinavian Institute of African Studies, 1988).

31. Umkhonto we Sizwe (Spear of the Nation) launched an armed struggle in 1961. See Rob Davis, Dan O'Meara, Sipho Dlamini, *The Struggle for South Africa: A Reference Guide, Volume One* (London: Zed Books, 1984), pp. 178–186. See also Donald Woods, *Biko* (London: Penguin, 1987), pp. 25–26. Mandela's statement at the Rivonia trial is reproduced in full in Nelson Mandela, *The Struggle Is My Life* (London: International Defence and Aid Fund for Southern Africa, 1986), pp. 161–181. Mbulelo Vizikhungo Mzamane locates this speech historically in his "Sharpeville and Its Aftermath: The Novels of Richard Rive, Peter Abrahams, Alex La Guma, and Lauretta Ngcobo" in *Ariel*, vol. 16, no. 2, April 1985, pp. 31–44. The Rivonia trial is examined in Hilda Bernstein, *The World That Was Ours: The Story of the Rivonia Trial* (London: SAWriters, 1989).

32. Frantz Fanon, *The Wretched of the Earth* (London: Penguin, 1990), p. 46.

33. Fanon, *The Wretched of the Earth*, p. 33.

34. For a discussion of related issues, see Stuart Hall, "Cultural Identity and Diaspora" in Jonathan Rutherford, ed., *Identity: Community, Culture, Difference* (London: Lawrence and Wishart, 1990), pp. 222–237.

35. Fanon, *The Wretched of the Earth*, p. 29.

36. See Lou Turner and John Alan, eds., *Frantz Fanon, Soweto and American Black Thought* (Chicago: News and Letters, 1986), p. 51.

37. See, for example, Albie Sachs, *The Jail Diary of Albie Sachs* (London: Paladin Books, 1990), pp. 102–103.

38. Lewis Nkosi, "Art Contra Apartheid: South African Writers in Exile," p. 94. In his *Home and Exile and Other Selections* (London: Longman, 1965).

39. Alex La Guma, "The Condition of Culture," p. 119. In *Presence Africaine*, vol. 80, 1971.

40. Per Wastberg, ed., *The Writer in Modern Africa* (Uppsala: Scandinavian Institute of African Studies, 1968), p. 22.

41. Cecil A. Abrahams, *Alex La Guma* (Boston: Twayne Publishers, 1985), p. 12.

42. Lewis Nkosi, "Southern Africa: Protest and Commitment," p. 79. In his *Tasks and Masks: Themes and Styles of African Literature* (London: Longman, 1981).

43. Nkosi, *Tasks and Masks*, p. 76.

44. Nkosi, *Home and Exile*, p. 131.

45. In Holst Petersen, *Criticism and Ideology*, p. 201.

46. Lionel Abrahams, "From Shakespeare House to the Laager: The Story of PEN" quoted in Njabulo Ndebele, "The Writers' Movement in South Africa," p. 413. In *Research in African Literatures*, vol. 20, no. 3, Fall 1989.

47. Steve Biko quoted in Shava, *A People's Voice*, p. 97. See also Gail M. Gerhart, *Black Power in South Africa: The Evolution of an Ideology* (Berkeley: University of California Press, 1978).

48. Breyten Breytenbach, "Vulture Culture: The Alienation of White South Africa," pp. 137-148. In Alex La Guma, ed., *Apartheid* (London: Lawrence and Wishart, 1972).

49. See, for example Ursula A. Barnett, *A Vision of Order* (London: Sinclair Browne Ltd., 1983), p. 16, and Martin Trump, ed., *Rendering Things Visible: Essays on South African Literary Culture* (Johannesburg: Ravan Press, 1990), p. 164.

50. Mphahlele quoted in Trump, ed., *Rendering Things Visible*, p. 182.

51. Herbert Dhlomo quoted in Trump, ed., *Rendering Things Visible*, p. 162.

52. Vijay Mishra and Bob Hodge, "What is post (-) colonialism?," *Textual Practice*, vol. 5, Winter 1991, p. 400.

53. David Maughan-Brown, "Adjusting the Focal Length: Alex La Guma and Exile," *English in Africa*, 18, 2, 1991, p. 32.

54. Nkosi, *Home and Exile*, p. 94.

55. Ezekiel Mphahlele, "South African Writers Talking," *English in Africa*, September 1979, p. 18.

56. Nkosi, *Home and Exile*, p. 95.

57. Malcolm Bradbury, ed., *The Penguin Book of Modern British Short Stories* (London: Penguin, 1987) includes stories by both Lessing and Rushdie, for example.

58. Kenneth Parker, "Apartheid and the Politics of Literature," *Red Letters*, vol. 20, 1986.

59. Alex La Guma, *Apartheid*, p. 13.

60. See "Concerning Violence," pp. 27–84, in Fanon, *The Wretched of the Earth*.

61. Ketu H. Ketrak discusses both Fanon and Gandhi's theories on violence and nonviolence (*satyagraha*) in "Decolonizing Culture: Toward a Theory of Postcolonial Women's Texts" in *Modern Fiction Studies*, vol. 35, no. 1, Spring 1989, pp. 157–179.

62. Hussein Abdilahi Bulhan, *Frantz Fanon and the Psychology of Oppression* (New York and London: Plenum Press, 1985), p. 263.

63. The words are Cesaire's and are quoted in David Caute, *Fanon* (London: Fontana, 1970), p. 85.

64. Hannah Arendt, *On Violence* (London: Allen Lane/Penguin Press, 1970), p. 60. Arendt's Eurocentric views are obvious in this book with comments such as: "In America . . . serious violence entered the scene only with the appearance of the Black Power movement on the campuses. Negro students, the majority of them admitted without academic qualification, regarded and organized themselves as an interest group, the representatives of the black community. Their interest was to lower academic standards. They were more cautious than the white rebels, but it was clear from the beginning . . . that violence with them was not a matter of theory and rhetoric." She goes on to say: "The Third World is not a reality but an ideology . . . The case is different with the Black Power movement; its ideological commitment to the nonexistent "Unity of the Third World" is not sheer romantic nonsense. They have an obvious interest in a black-white dichotomy; this too is of course mere escapism—an escape into a dream world in which Negroes would constitute an overwhelming majority of the world's population." See p. 18; pp. 21–22.

65. Lazarus has argued that ultimately Fanon's ideas are phrased in "messianic terms" (p. 12). He critiques the "revolutionary consciousness" that Fanon has been seen to encode while recognizing Fanon's integrity and the fact that his death in 1961, a year before Algeria gained "independence" and *The Wretched of the Earth* was published, meant he never had the opportunity to reassess his own ideas in the light of later developments. Neil Lazarus, *Resistance in Postcolonial African Fiction* (New Haven and London: Yale University Press, 1990).

66. Bulhan, *Frantz Fanon and the Psychology of Oppression*, p. 135. Emphasis in the original. A. Sivanandan, considering *The Wretched of the Earth* and Sartre's introduction to it, declares "violence in our time does not need to be overt and obtrusive to be recognised as violence—poverty is violence, and racism; and the coincidence of poverty and racism is a violence beyond endurance" (p. 65) in his *A Different Hunger: Writing Black Resistance* (London: Pluto Press, 1991).

67. Fanon, *The Wretched of the Earth*, p. 27.

68. Fanon, *The Wretched of the Earth*, p. 28.

69. Fanon, *The Wretched of the Earth*, pp. 39–40.

70. Mazisi Kunene, "Revolutionary Challenges and Cultural Perspectives" in Joseph Okpaku, ed., *New African Literature and the Arts, vol. iii* (New York: The Third Press: Joseph Okpaku Publishing Inc., 1973), pp. 49–56.

71. Fanon, *The Wretched of the Earth*, p. 29.

72. Alex La Guma, "African Culture and National Liberation" in Okpaku, ed., *New African Literature*, p. 59. See also Hilda Bernstein, "Schools for Servitude," pp. 43–79, for an analysis that supports La Guma's view on the way that education for Africans is outlawed in order to secure the maintenance of apartheid, in La Guma, *Apartheid*. For a discussion that seeks to define an African personality see Robert W. July, "The African Personality in

the African Novel" a discussion of *A Walk in the Night* in U. Beier, ed., *Introduction to African Literature* (London: Longman, 1967).

73. Fanon, *The Wretched of the Earth*, pp. 178–179.

74. Paulo Freire, *Pedagogy of the Oppressed* (London: Penguin, 1972), p. 22. See also Albert Memmi, *The Colonizer and the Colonized* (London: Earthscan Publications, 1990), p. 82, where he writes in a similar vein to Freire that the colonized "by choosing to place themselves in the colonizer's service to protect his interests exclusively, they end up by adopting his ideology, even with regard to their own values and their own lives."

75. Freire, *Pedagogy of the Oppressed*, p. 40.

76. Alex La Guma, "The Time Has Come: The Coloured People Must Prepare to Bear Arms for Liberation," *Sechaba*, vol. 1, pt. 6, June 1967, p. 15.

77. Fanon, *The Wretched of the Earth*, p. 36.

78. Said, *Orientalism*, p. 72.

79. Homi Bhabha "The Other Question," *Screen*, 24:6, 1983, p. 23.

80. M. M. Bakhtin, *The Dialogic Imagination,* ed., M. Holquist, trs. Caryl Emerson (Austin: University of Texas Press, 1981), p. 30.

81. Stuart Hall discusses what he calls "the grammar of race" in his essay "The Whites of Their Eyes: Racist Ideologies and the Media" reproduced in Manuel Alvarado and John O. Thompson, eds., *The Media Reader* (London: BFI, 1990), pp. 7–23. He examines the "slave-figure" or loyal retainer, the "native" whose "bad side is portrayed in terms of cheating and cunning" and the "clown" or "entertainer" and notes the ambivalence of these images.

Chapter 2

▼▼▼▼▼▼▼▼▼

Problems of Limited Political Understanding: A Walk in the Night

Alex La Guma's *A Walk in the Night*, first published in 1962 in Nigeria after being smuggled out of South Africa, focuses on the events of one single evening in Cape Town's District Six. District Six is the living embodiment of the apartheid regime's nightmare belief in the savagery of the majority population, as exemplified in its later destruction by that regime. The decaying environment is as much the protagonist of the novella as the coloreds who inhabit it and La Guma pulls no punches in his uncompromising descriptions of the squalor and deprivation of the area. Instead, he constructs heroes and antiheroes who are each victims of their enforced socioeconomic conditions and are either survivors who are prepared to succumb and be shaped by their environment or casualties who drown in the mire of the urban slum.

Writing from a Marxist perspective, La Guma examines the macrocosmic capitalist-sponsored apartheid state's ill treatment of its majority population in microcosmic detail in his first novel. Such an emphasis on verisimilitude has resulted in La Guma being dubbed by one critic "the chief representative of South African Naturalism."[1] However, to label La Guma and his early creative output as predominantly and simply naturalistic is misleading. La Guma certainly displays a naturalistic tendency, and other critics like JanMohamed find *A Walk in the Night* to be "quasi-naturalistic."[2] But it is perhaps more insightful to align La Guma's early fiction with the African American Richard Wright's novels like *Native Son* and *Rite of Passage*—examples of social protest fiction. Critically useful correlations can be made between fiction by African American and South African writers, and parallels posited between urban South Africa and Chicago's

South Side, or South African apartheid and segregation in the American South. Certainly Robert July begins to tease out the similarities between environments in which people live in overcrowded tenements, via Cape Town and Harlem city slums: "amidst dirt and disease, lacking the means for a normal family life with its security, its childhood pleasures and adult satisfactions, constantly brushing against the brutalised amorality of criminals" and police brutality.[3] However, July curiously attempts to deny the significance of race while drawing a clear correlation between Cape Town and Harlem. This could be read as an attempt to deflect the racist assumptions that whites may hold about blacks as inferior and lacking in subjectivity and therefore deserving of their poor living conditions. But, it also serves to ignore the fact that July is incorrect in his assumption that Cape Town is a "negro quarter." It was, in fact, designated a "coloured preference area" for employment purposes under apartheid. July denies another distinct difference that exists between his two sets of "negroes." African Americans had at least the opportunity to move geographically in an attempt to improve their social and economic lot[4] while the restrictive apartheid laws offered no such option to black South Africans. The South African capitalist system required plentiful supplies of cheap labor that could easily be tapped into, and these were provided in the form of those who inhabited the slums on the outskirts of the industrialized centers, and later the townships after the clearance of the slums. July's assertion that inhabitants lack "the means for a normal family life" is also tenuous in that he does not examine the hierarchies of oppression that exist within racial groups. July opens up the space to consider a comparativist reading but fails to pursue literary-critical approaches.

While perceiving a correlation between Richard Wright's African American social protest fiction and Alex La Guma's South African fiction, July—and Felix Mnthali who also follows this line—fails to address a salient point: that Marxist analysis is the basic model for both writers. Both were initially committed to Marxism, both were members of the Communist Party and both deploy ostensibly naturalistic conventions to express this commitment in their writing. As Wright describes it "my heart is with the collectivist and proletarian ideal."[5] Wright described his life as having "shaped me for the realism, the naturalism of the modern novel" but like La Guma he is essentially referring to Marxist concepts of critical and socialist realism with which he sympathised for much of his writing life.[6] Whereas La Guma has not commented directly on the structuring of *A Walk in the Night*, except to say that the "sad story" was precipitated by his reading a short paragraph in a newspaper about a "hooligan" dying in a police van,[7] Wright has delineated the process of constructing *Native Son* in some detail. His comments are illuminating for my reading of La Guma's novel. Wright's intention was to write so that "in the same instant of time, the objective and subjective aspects of Bigger's life would be caught in a focus of prose." His understanding was that "all serious fiction consists almost wholly of character-destiny and the items, social, political, and personal, of that character-destiny."[8] In my reading, and extrapolating from Wright, La Guma constructs Adonis's progress through the novel and the long night of apartheid episodically, as strung along a series of episodes and, most importantly, exchanges with others. In this way, a limited political understanding, dormant until these points of crisis or revelation, is built up incrementally. The structuring of the narrative echoes Wright's idea of providing "test tube situations" through which to chart his protagonist's destiny that comment objectively on wider problems of power, corruption and human welfare.

If the environment is the novella's referencing frame, then the central figure, of arguably three protagonists, is the ironically named Michael Adonis. Michael Adonis with his "pustule of rage and humiliation"[9] is the semi-passive victim of the South African "capitalis' system" (*AW*, p. 17). In his efforts to live within the law, Adonis represents the black, specifically colored, proletariat who attempt to survive by selling their labor and therefore become actively involved in the capitalist enterprise of accumulation and gain. However, Adonis is dismissed from his position at a sheet metal factory for answering back to a white foreman who: "Called me a cheeky black bastard. Me, I'm not black. Anyway I said he was a no-good pore-white and he calls the manager and they gave me my pay and tell me to muck of out of it. White sonofabitch. I'll get him" (*AW*, p. 4). This seemingly trivial verbal exchange is the first of the series of exchanges in which Adonis becomes involved, and it is interesting for two reasons. First, as representative of basic labor relations, it allows La Guma to highlight the quasi-powerful positions that are abused by petty officials due to the existence of a cheap and plentiful labor supply and, allied to this, the management's endorsement of such abuse. The white foreman also sees Adonis as a generic unit rather than an individual, which results in his calling him a "black bastard" rather than admonishing him with being a "coloured bastard." Second, Adonis's rendition of the exchange demonstrates a lack of political awareness that the blacks exhibit in their interaction with the whites and a lack of understanding that stems from the insularity of not interacting with other racial groups. Adonis establishes the incident as particular ("White sonofabitch. I'll get him") rather than as indicative of common social practice. In addressing the above example, Chandramohan suggests that Adonis represents "an attitude of ethnic ex-

clusiveness. Ethnic exclusiveness leaves Adonis in a moral cul-de-sac."[10]
This clearly is the case in that the emphasis on the moral leaves Adonis
bitter at being labeled as something that he perceives himself not to be.
He fails to observe the ways in which his own experience mirrors that of
other disenfranchised individuals and groups.

Adonis is one of the handful of black characters who participate in
wage labor and he attempts to live within the law in an effort to secure
financial and economic gain and its attendant feature of self-worth. However, with his dismissal from the economy of production he is doomed to
become one of the "wasted ghosts in a plague-ridden city" (*AW*, p. 21). La
Guma borrows from Shakespeare's *Hamlet* and the Ghost's speech from
Act I, Scene V, acts as the novella's epigraph:

> I am thy father's spirit;
> Doom'd for a certain term to walk the night,
> And for the day confined to fast in fires,
> Till the foul crimes done in my days of nature
> Are burnt and purged away.

The novella's title is contained within the speech and the essence of the
speech, and the fact that La Guma's characters are indeed doomed to walk
the night, immediately alerts the reader that the novel will involve the
potentially tragic. Just as Claudius cuts down his brother and initiates a
chain reaction of events that culminates in multiple deaths, so too the
South African system of apartheid murdered the inherent hopes of its
mass population. From the first encounter of white Europeans with South
Africa, the country has suffered the destruction of some of its indigenous
races and of their modes of production. The majority population was
forced to accept white domination and its attendant economic practices.
La Guma's characters—and most crucially Michael Adonis in this novel—
slowly inch towards some understanding of the practices that militate against
them, often as an indirect result of the violence and deaths that proliferate
in District Six.

In discussing the disenfranchisement and marginality of blacks,
JanMohamed draws out the distinction between experiencing oneself as a
"significant individual" and as "an insignificant unit of a condemned caste,"
which is itself the springboard for the tension that La Guma creates between self-fulfillment and alienating deprivation. For JanMohamed, La
Guma addresses this tension by "defining various communities within which
his characters can find an optional and fecund balance between personal
freedom and communal obligations."[11] This is of especial significance in
the case of Joe, a character who inhabits the periphery of Cape Town's

"centre" as well as a particularized community that he constructs around the beach and the sea, where he is able to assert himself as a "significant individual." There is no doubt that La Guma's characters in *A Walk in the Night* are units of a "condemned caste" but it is difficult to agree with JanMohamed that they tolerate anything that is remotely connected to "communal obligations." In my view, it is the precise lack of a real, lawful community that La Guma describes as the by-product of apartheid. La Guma ensures that his characters are unable to discover a sustaining community. In attempting to articulate La Guma's political project, JanMohamed has suggested that the predicament of race and rights is elaborated through the tacit assumption that the individual *should* have certain inalienable rights—"the right to elect his own government, to live where he wants, to receive adequate compensation for his labor, to shape his children's education, to marry whomever he wants"—but that this is "not generally articulated in the novels because La Guma, assuming its universal theoretical acceptance, chooses to focus on its absence."[12]

JanMohamed's exposition of the principles for self-fulfillment at first sight appears more applicable to those writers of the 1950s who fell into the category of liberal humanist writers. The liberal humanist doctrine considered the primacy of the individual to be of essential importance and believed that individual fulfillment would inevitably contribute to the overall health and sustenance of society.[13] However, the emphasis on individual rights posits the individual as member of a larger group and so bespeaks La Guma's tendency to focus on the significance of communal action *via* "character-destiny," to use Richard Wright's phrase,[14] and this stems from his affiliation with a Marxist doctrine. The majority of characters encountered, and specifically those who become casualties of the system in *A Walk in the Night*, tend to be self-centered, exhibiting little interest in communal action or communal values, even at their most indirect. It is not simply the absence of the rights of the individual that La Guma decries but the loss of any sense of communitarian network at an ontological level that is most troubling.

The very first introduction of Michael Adonis occurs as he steps off a "trackless tram" oblivious of being "jostled by the lines of workers going home . . . He looked through them, refusing to see them" (*AW*, p. 1). Adonis is the prototypical alienated individual in La Guma's work, and, rather than react to or interact with his peers or his milieu, he concentrates his efforts on "a little growth of anger the way one caresses the beginnings of a toothache with the tip of the tongue" (*AW*, p. 1). Adonis is directionless, driven only by the bitter gall of painful impotence. La Guma's imagery emphasizes this potentially self-destructive hopelessness:

"his thoughts concentrated upon the pustule of rage and humiliation that was continuing to ripen deep down within him" (*AW*, p. 1). In endeavoring to take his mind off the events that led to his dismissal, Adonis walks into the Portuguese restaurant, which enables La Guma to deploy a description of a rundown eating-house and its unfortunate diners. This passage functions metonymically for District Six and its inhabitants:

> Ancient strips of flypaper hung from the ceiling dotted with their victims and the floor was stained with spilled coffee, grease and crushed cigarette butts; the walls marked with the countless rubbing of soiled shoulders and grimy hands. There was a general atmosphere of shabbiness about the cafe, but not unmixed with a sort of homeliness for the unending flow of derelicts, bums, domestic workers off duty, in-town-from-the-country folk who had no place to eat except there, and working people who stopped by on their way home. There were taxi-drivers too, and the rest of the mould that acumulated on the fringes of the underworld beyond Castle Bridge: loiterers, prostitutes, *fah-fee* numbers runners, petty gangsters, drab and frayed-looking thugs (*AW*, p. 3).

Significantly, the inclusivity of the restaurant fails to afford Adonis respite from his anger. Indeed, his conversation with Willieboy—who proudly asserts that "I don't work. Never worked a bogger yet . . . Eff work" (*AW*, p. 4)—only adds a degree of resentment to the already ripening cancer that is Adonis's anger. Despite his meeting with Willieboy and then Foxy and his gang, Adonis's angry desire for revenge against the white foreman, Scofield, remains locked within him where it festers, awaiting an outlet.

Adonis is shown to be a victim of his circumstances; there is little evidence to suggest that he is an inherently violent character. On the contrary, he does not commit any crime or utter any comment that would indicate so. On the surface Adonis appears to be frustrated but, nevertheless, in reasonable control of himself. After leaving the restaurant he shows that he can be charitable and considerate of others, even though he too has become one of the area's unemployed, when he gives money for supper to the destitute Joe. In this action he does not simply demonstrate sympathy but shows that he is capable of valuable human interaction and exchange that is not premised on selfish motives. Adonis genuinely helps a fellow human being, which highlights his ability to participate in a relationship that rests on affiliative rather than filial foundations.[15] This is, however, the only point in the novella where he is shown to be in control and feels able to demonstrate solidarity and equality with a peer. This action affords him the opportunity to subjugate his anger and impotence in a small act of fraternity. The anger ignites again, however, when Adonis encounters two white police officers on his way home from the restaurant. The episode is a significant stage on his walk through the night since it is a strong indication of how his literal and metaphorical progress is delimited by the apartheid regime's circumscription of the civil rights of the majority population:

> They came down the pavement in their flat caps, khaki shirts and pants, their gun harness shiny with polish, and the holstered pistols heavy at their waists. They had hard, frozen faces as if carved out of pink ice, and hard, dispassionate eyes, hard and bright as pieces of blue glass. They strolled slowly and determinedly side by side, without moving off their course, cutting a path through the stream on the pavement like destroyers at sea (*AW*, pp. 10–11).

This description immediately draws attention to the fact that the police officers are little more than automata. There is little humanity in the description: faces are ice and eyes are glass. While the first and third sentences point to a military image of danger and threat, which embodies the violence of warfare and the unthinking (unblinking) public face of apartheid, the composite image serves as a grotesque caricature of the police officers' function. They are hard, inanimate objects driven by an inner essence and unquestioning belief in the apartheid regime's cause. JanMohamed draws attention to La Guma's style, in that he "confines himself to placid and factual descriptions of concrete human behavior and the material surface of society." More importantly, he sees how deceptive such descriptions can be since any pretence of objectivity "masks a powerful and explosive hostility."[16] JanMohamed's point is pertinent in the case of the officers since La Guma's adoption of a concrete style and a straightforward matter-of-factness belies his interest in appearance and reality. The encounter codifies the dialectical relation between social order and violent oppression. If the narrator denies the police officers *human-ness*, then the character of Adonis is deployed to move a stage beyond. He has "learned from experience to gaze at some spot on their uniforms, the button of a pocket, or the bright smoothness of their Sam Browne belts, but never into their eyes, for that would be taken as an affront by them" (*AW*, p. 11). From a metaphysical point of view, Adonis's refusal to look the police officers in the eyes can be read as a denial of their very *existence*. In terms of identity construction, a young child passes through two separate but contingent stages. The first stage is labeled, in Lacan's formulation, as the imaginary order and is the field where the child is able to recognize his/her specular image but, because there exists an "untransversable distance between self and the Other (who is seen as self), the experience is deeply imbued with aggressivity toward the self/Other." In the "'symbolic' order [the second stage] language mediates (and, once again, alienates) the subject's desire, but the specular dynamics of the 'imaginary' phase remain embedded in the 'symbolic' order."[17] Adonis does not look at the officers and therefore does not allow himself to be drawn into a potentially challenging position. It is only when the police officer addresses Adonis that a direct example of the officer's desire to have his authority is realized and the *actuality of presence* acknowledged. In the colonial context "the European settler is able to compel the Other's recognition of him and, in the process, allow his own identity to become deeply dependent on his position as a master."[18]

Adonis finds himself in a position where he actually holds power, *the power of projecting existence*, but is unable to exercise that potential power due to his lack of political consciousness and his own lack of identity. In short, Michael Adonis is unable to construct an identity for himself, nor are any of his peers present who may facilitate such a construction. He is asked if he uses drugs and instructed to turn out his pockets, and he has no option but to comply. Adonis's real feelings, during interrogation, are conveyed in parentheses, which reiterate his impotence in the face of the regime:

> "Where did you steal the money?" The question was without humour, deadly serious, the voice topped with hardness like the surface of a file.
> "Didn't steal it, baas (*you mucking boer*)."
> "Well, muck off from the street. Don't let us find you standing around, you hear?"
> "Yes, (*you mucking boer*)."
> "Yes, what? Who are you talking to, man?"
> "Yes, baas (*you mucking bastard boer with your mucking gun and your mucking bloody red head*)" (*AW*, p. 12).

Here the police officers can be read as displaying patriarchal power, questioning an errant child. Adonis's responses create the impression of his being reduced to a chastized child; the police officer will not allow his authority or presence to be negated or abridged and therefore must be addressed as "baas." So, despite his maturity, Adonis finds himself treated as a child twice in the space of one day—first at the workplace and second in public, on the street. This treatment exacerbates his feeling of anger toward whites, just as a child's anger would increase towards the authoritarian father figure that the apartheid regime may represent. Adonis is unable to operate within the law because his skin color marks him as an easy target within the workplace for a perpetual cycle of abuse and unfair treatment. The filial relationship he has with his white masters, predicated in colonial discourse on "obedience, fear, love, respect,"[19] is no better.

The encounter with the white police officers leaves Adonis humiliated and shaken and emphasizes, yet again, his insignificance in the scheme of apartheid. Such episodes function to indicate the facility Adonis has for keeping his emotions in check but also illustrate the tenuous hold he has over them. His anger, which was originally *only* directed at the white foreman, becomes a thirst that needs to be quenched after his degrading experience with the white law enforcers. In apartheid South Africa, La Guma outlines the fact that the law does not represent the clichéd concepts of truth, honesty and justice, nor can any of these attributes be attached to La Guma's so-called law enforcers. The police officers in *A Walk in the Night* are not interested in the safety or well-being of their black constituency and only demonstrate their agency in petty or corrupt situations. La Guma indicates the predominance of *dagga* use early on when he introduces the characters of Willieboy and Foxy's gang with their yellow eyes—an outwardly visible effect of their habit—and it is this pernicious stereotype that the blacks and criminal classes smoke *dagga* that the police seize upon in their questioning of Adonis, "Where's your dagga?" (*AW*, p. 12). Even though Michael Adonis has not actually committed a crime, the police criminalize and categorize him as a *dagga*-using thief. His integrity undermined, Adonis makes the fatal mistake of entering the pub, which

> like pubs all over the world, was a place for debate and discussion, for the exchange of views and opinions, for argument and for the working out of problems. It was a forum, a parliament, a fountain of wisdom and a cesspool of nonsense, it was a centre for the lost and despairing, where cowards absorbed dutch courage out of small glasses and leaned against the shiny, scratched and polished mahogany counter for support against the crushing burdens of insignificant lives. Where the disillusioned gained temporary hope, where acts of kindness were considered and murders planned (*AW*, p. 13).

The drinking of alcohol endows Adonis with the temporary "dutch courage," which acts as a cushion "against the crushing burdens of [his] insignificant [life]" and, furthermore, prompts him to think of the whites as "Effing sonofabitches" and himself as a "trouble-shooter" and a "mighty tough hombre." However, this is only the effect of the alcohol. The dominant impression remains that Adonis will not, and cannot, take revenge against the whites: he fully understands his own cowardice when the real gangsters of the novella appear and have the effect of wiping "the fantasy" away (*AW*, p. 14). Although Adonis continues to meet people he "knows," they are, in fact, only passing acquaintances and consequently only add to his burden of loneliness. This is a recurring motif that La Guma employs to elicit the perception of the wastefulness of individual intransigence, in contrast to the strength that can be gained from group action or group affiliation that remains *un*represented. In participating in the pub conversation with the taxi-driver, who asserts that "There's mos no colour bar" in the United States, and with Greene, whose counterclaim is that white Americans hang "negroes" for looking at white women, Adonis is once again prompted to feed the anger within him.

Rather than attempt to understand the political and economic system that alienates and abuses him, Adonis's thoughts return to "the little knot of rage," which is likened to the "quickening of the embryo in the womb" (*AW*, p. 16). In choosing to ignore the pub discussion of the "capitalis' system," Adonis exhibits a painful lack of political affiliation or political consciousness, while the inebriated Greene—who wants to "Cut out politics" from the conversation because those who organize meetings and speak to the masses are "bastards [who] come from Russia"—at least demonstrates a limited political understanding. These characters are not intellectually challenged or racially inferior to their white "masters"; they simply bear the stigma of the continually harassed and have consequently cowered into submission. They find themselves wandering aimlessly through the long night of apartheid. For Greene politics are anathema and Adonis cannot or is not prepared to see beyond his personalized and unpoliticized conceptualization of racist affronts to the motives behind South African whites' deliberate subordination of blacks. This is redoubled in his unfounded, because uninformed, belief that American whites "are better than ours" (*AW*, p. 16). In introducing the taxi-driver and his talk of politics, La Guma makes an explicit reference to the need for organized mass action against the political regime, which is overtly responsible for making people like Adonis, Willieboy, and Foxy and his gang what they are. The characters are not motivated by the desire to change or improve the South African situation since they do not fully comprehend the interdependence of their private individual agendas with the overall political agenda that is apartheid.

In *A Walk in the Night*, La Guma links racial positions to a class-based analysis in order to highlight the antagonisms between the blacks and the whites. He achieves this by virtue of the very absence of political analysis on the part of his characters as in the exchange in the pub. The conversation is elliptical: their failure to translate the personal into the political elides their comprehension of both national and class distinctions. For Chandramohan whose project is "trans-ethnicity," this scene could provide an example of La Guma trying to evolve "a set of trans-racial moral and political values based on Marxist ideas of the binary polarisations between exploiting and exploited social groups."[20] Ethnic divisions are intractable in so far as they are underpinned by class divisions. The characters La Guma depicts are not yet able to undertake such a sophisticated analysis of their subaltern positions. But, in extending the hand of friendship to Adonis, Doughty does not predicate his actions on race but, rather, on class, nor does Doughty claim a paternal power relationship with Adonis. Instead, Doughty offers Adonis an affiliation that is premised on the equality of class. This is clearly the case despite Michael Wade's claim that Doughty is representative of a "culture in decay" belatedly attempting to make an affiliative gesture that can only prove confusing and dangerous to a member of a "subservient group." Necessarily, Wade reads Doughty as representative of an English tradition in South Africa and Adonis as resentful of his faded power, hence what Wade sees as a destructive outburst.[21] It is clear that Doughty does represent the faded past of Britain's colonial endeavor in South Africa, but Wade fails to align this with the fact that, being of Irish extraction, Doughty also shares the history of the colonized at the hands of the English. In addition, Doughty seems to have forfeited his role in the so-called cultured society that is supposedly British by marrying a black woman and choosing to live with, and as part of, Wade's "subservient group." Wade's suggestion that Adonis, as a representative of a subordinate group, is unequipped to deal with the change in relationships is also tenuous in that Adonis's actions are predicated on an *exact understanding* of Doughty's "offering." It would be more accurate to suggest that Adonis is unequipped to fully accept the reality of his situation, which is elucidated by La Guma through Doughty and through his rendition of Hamlet's father's speech. It is the articulation of his exact social, political and economic condition as a doomed ghost walking the night that leads Adonis to finally react emotionally to his dismissal that morning. His anger has been held in abeyance until the expansive, derisive and explosive gesture with the port bottle, the arc of which terminates in his accidentally killing the drunkard Doughty. Shock and guilt manifest themselves immediately when he should tell the authorities of his part in the drunkard's death. But La Guma ensures that the possibility of fair treatment within the law is quickly dismissed: "You know what the law will do to you. They don't have any shit from us brown people. They'll hang you, as true as God. Christ, we all got hanged long ago. What's the law for? To kick us poor brown bastards around. You think they're going to listen to your story; Jesus, and he was a white man, too" (*AW*, pp. 43–44).

Adonis begins to understand his subaltern position in direct relation to the crisis in which he finds himself. He realizes that the regime will not respect his honesty, his attempt to live as a law-abiding citizen, because the regime operates in an essentially racist manner in which it encodes blacks as inherently criminal inferiors. It is at this point that Adonis begins to address the larger problem of colonial history when he recognizes himself in conjunction with all the other "poor brown bastards" and painfully acknowledges their anomalous subject-position: "hanged" from the moment of their first bloody encounter with the white races. In his effort to exert his own humanity and selfhood, Adonis accidentally kills another of apartheid's victims and consequently looks to other means of identity construction, outside of the society-victim dichotomy. He finds it in the affiliative relationship he goes on to form with Foxy and his gang.

Adonis's killing of Doughty can be understood as a direct consequence of his frustration with whites like Scofield who operate within the apartheid regime. As the shock subsides, the act releases a temporary sense of elation and signals a rejection of the subordinate status that is his lot as a black South African. In addition, by electing to join Foxy and his gang, Adonis is offering affirmation of his desire to "belong" to a group of similarly frustrated but antagonistic individuals, rather than work and suffer abuse at the hands of white bosses in an environment he cannot control. Ultimately, though, in joining a gang that countenances violence, Adonis succumbs to the environment as enforced by apartheid as it shapes and affects him. La Guma based Adonis on an African schoolfriend whom he recalls as "a cheerful, lighthearted fellow" who, forced to relocate because of his skin color, "had become a gangster, been to prison, and his whole life before him didn't hold any sort of rosy prospects. . . . [He] had become a victim of circumstances which he couldn't cope with."[22] Adonis cannot cope alone and throws his lot in with a group whose antisocial resilience gives them the impression at least of evading victim status. As Said points out, affiliation allows for "consensus, collegiality, professional respect, class"[23] and it is this that Adonis longs for, even if the consensus incorporates criminal violence.

Cecil A. Abrahams, in "The Writings of Alex La Guma," claims that three distinct types of youth inhabit District Six: "the law-abiding, eager-to-work citizens such as Adonis; the deliberately and chronically unemployed, such as Willieboy, who eke out an existence by becoming a ward of their working friends; and those, like 'skollies,' who choose crime and violence to finance their expensive drug and leisure habits."[24] In my reading of *A Walk in the Night* the factors that may initially distinguish one type of young man from the next are gradually elided. Willieboy is without doubt "chronically unemployed" and his attitude is that employment should be avoided wherever possible. His actions are not premised on any overtly concrete political foundation, but one may conjecture that, in his dismissal of employment and the economy of production, he understands the negative attitudes of employers to black employees and the impotent positions that blacks like Adonis are allotted in the working environment—given degrading and demeaning jobs, treated as nonsubjects, left open to abuse and lacking rights to political recourse. Instead of working for a living, Willieboy occupies a middle ground between those who participate in the capitalist enterprise and those who live and operate outside the law, in the shadows of society. In an allegorical sense, then, Willieboy inhabits that space that is available to Adonis, that liminal space that exists between law and order and outright criminality. A fluid interidentification exists between Adonis and Willieboy that has been noted by more than one critic; even though they only encounter each other once in the novella and their actual physical paths appear separate, "they are all the time moving towards one another so that, in the end, they constitute a metaphysical continuity."[25] The interconnection is such that the patterning of Willieboy's experiences becomes the accumulation of Adonis's: the options that are *available* to Adonis are *lived* by Willieboy. Willieboy is presented as one of the District's petty criminals, a character who has spent time in a reformatory and who will ultimately meet with an unpleasant demise:

> Willieboy was young and dark and wore his kinky hair brushed into a point above his forehead. He wore a sportscoat over a yellow T-shirt and a crucifix around his neck, more as a flamboyant decoration than as an act of religious devotion. He had yellowish eyeballs and big white teeth and an air of nonchalance, like the outward visible signs of his distorted pride in the terms he had served in a reformatory and once in prison for assault (*AW*, p. 3).

Willieboy is a petty criminal who parasitically lives off the goodwill of his "friends" and finally dies at the hands of the corrupt Raalt, who happily mistakes him for the killer of Doughty. At this stage, the transference of identity between Adonis, the real murderer, and Willieboy appears to be complete: Adonis is about to embark on his first criminal enterprise with the area's "skollies," Foxy and his gang, while Willieboy is about to die in the back of the police van. Ironically, Willieboy's aspirations are limited to the fantasy world of the celluloid gangster figures he so admires. His wish is to become a "big shot": "He had seen others rise to some sort of power in the confined underworld of this district and found himself left behind. He had looked with envy at the flashy desperadoes who quivered across the screen in front of the eightpenny gallery and had dreamed of being transported where ever he wished in great black motorcars and issuing orders for the execution of enemies" (*AW*, p. 72). Criminal activity and gangsterism constitute a form of "irregular warfare" and the member of the proletariat who performs subversively and brutally effective activities operates as an icon for Frantz Fanon, as well as La Guma, in his contention that colonialism "is violence in its natural state."[26] For Fanon the only possible social upheaval that can end the rule of a colonial regime is *greater* violence than that which initiated and maintained that regime. He explores the idea that the colonized in their community create meaning out of particular episodes, and the actions of particular individuals, in order to maintain the idea of subversive activity at the heart of that community, just as La Guma deploys episodes and exchanges as the focal features of his structuring of *A Walk in the Night*. Fanon offers the example of the gangster "who holds up the police set on to track him down for days on end, or who dies in single combat after having killed four or five policemen, or who commits suicide in order not to give away his accomplices—these types light the way for the people, form the blueprints for action and become heroes."[27] Acting against the colonial authorities invests the antihero with political substance so that in the communities that writers create in apartheid narratives the street criminal may be the archetypal resistance fighter. Certainly, his underworld existence—the need to be alert and opportunistic—is echoed in Fanon's description of the methods of survival of the colonized. It is echoed in his central assertion that "in the colonial countries the peasants alone are revolutionary, for they have nothing to lose and everything to gain. The starving peasant, outside the class system, is the first among the exploited to discover that only violence pays."[28] The peasant may be the guerrilla, a member of an underclass for whom the fight against oppression is a fight for survival. My use of the term "guerrilla" is strategic here in my effort to indicate that fictional characters may be read as revolutionaries who are *inevitably* politicized because, in the South Africa of their experience, their subversive activities signal their involvement in a "people's war." "Guerrilla" means irregular warfare, and my general emphasis at this point lies with the irregularity of criminal resistance rather than with the connotations of an organized military force also contained within the term. According to his wife, Blanche, when interviewed in 1988, Alex La Guma was himself a recruiter of others to the anti-apartheid resistance movement.[29]

So, criminal activities may be appropriated as part of anticolonial and anti-apartheid resistance. In considering characters like Michael Adonis, it is interesting to proffer Fanon's question—"How do we pass from the atmosphere of violence to violence in action? What makes the lid blow off?"[30]—and to examine the way in which these murderers are essentially also victims. Murder is ultimately the mechanism of apartheid that "murdered" the hope in La Guma's old schoolfriend on whom he based Adonis and that can extinguish the inherent human potential within an individual to affirm life in a particular context. The prototypical native town that Fanon describes as "a world without spaciousness," as "a town on its knees" that is "starved of bread, of meat, of shoes, of coal, of light,"[31] foreshadows La Guma's District Six and the streets inhabited by Michael Adonis and his peers:

> He turned down another street, away from the artificial glare of Hanover, between stretches of damp, battered houses with their broken-ribs of front-railings; cracked walls and high tenements that rose like the left-overs of a bombed area in the twilight; vacant lots and weed-grown patches where houses had once stood; and deep doorways resembling the entrances to deserted castles. There were children playing in the street, darting among the overflowing dustbins and shooting at each other with wooden guns. In some of the doorways people sat or stood, murmuring idly in the fast-fading light like wasted ghosts in a plague-ridden city (*AW*, p. 21).

Adonis and Willieboy are not *particularized* victims of such depressed and depressing living conditions. In a later novel, *In the Fog of the Seasons' End*, La Guma has Beukes travel by taxi into a similar urban ghetto that seems strangely surreal and allegorical in the manner of Jean Baudrillard's descriptions of American streets as reminiscent of modern dystopian gangster movies where "it is always turbulent, lively, kinetic and cinematic, like the country itself . . . its violence is the violence of a very way of life."[32] La Guma's streets are also defiantly sociorealistic, though, in that their "cinema" is the documentary footage of a war-torn city: "The sector had the look of a town cleared after battle. Whole blocks had disappeared, leaving empty, flattened lots surrounded by battered survivors."[33] The characters who populate the streets are the "battered survivors" of apartheid politics, hanging on in the face of restrictions and repercussions.

In both *Black Skin, White Masks* and *The Wretched of the Earth*, Fanon has stressed the absolute necessity, for the white oppressor, of a manichean duality that fixes the native as "insensible to ethics" so that he represents "not only the absence of values, but also the negation of values."[34] This negation involves the kind of dehumanization that Paulo Freire has described in conceptually similar terms: "Dehumanisation, which marks not only those whose humanity has been stolen, but also (though in a different way) those who have stolen it, is a distortion of the vocation of becoming more fully human."[35] This "distorted" humanity is evident in the nihilism exhibited by many of the characters in *A Walk in the Night*. But, Freire's observation that the oppressor's humanity is inevitably demeaned and distorted in the process of attempting to dehumanize the oppressed is encapsulated in the portrayal of Constable Raalt, whose "values" privilege calling to buy a pack of cigarettes over any attempt to ensure Willieboy might reach the station in time to have a chance of receiving some sort of medical attention. Raalt has seen the violent encounter between himself and Willieboy in animalistic terms. He is the predator and Willieboy is his prey: "He had his quarry trapped and he was quite sure that he would conclude the hunt successfully. He crouched there in the dark and smiled with satisfaction" (*AW*, p. 85). The idea of Willie's death causes him to curl his lips away from his teeth in a scowl that is wolf-like in its menace (*AW*, p. 91).

Willieboy represents the forgotten majority ignored by white society until scapegoats are required. Despite Willieboy's attempts at bravado, he remains "something less than nondescript, part of the blurred face of the crowd, inconspicuous as a smudge on a grimy wall" (*AW*, p. 72). However, at the end of the novella he also understands his predicament as a victim of apartheid's unfair and cruel treatment of individuals who are fated to participate in a cycle of intraracial violence. This cycle of violence is at times instigated in the family home by the tyrannical fathers who assert their frustrated manhood by beating their wives who, in turn, respond by thrashing their children. Indeed, Willieboy is a product of one such home. After being abused by the American sailors and being forcibly removed from the illegal brothel-*cum*-drinking-den, Willieboy proceeds to attack the elderly Mr. Greene in a vain effort to obtain some money and, more importantly, to reassert his manhood to prove that he is a survivor, despite the adverse conditions he faces. The impact of his upbringing is foregrounded in his delirious childhood remembrances of his mother who "slapped his face" and his father whose "leather belt whistled and snapped through the air, its sharp edge ripping at his legs and buttocks" (*AW*, p. 89, p. 92). But Willieboy is very clear as to who places people like him and his parents in such brutalized circumstances with his final words: "They's always kicking a poor bastard around" (*AW*, p. 93). Apartheid denies subjectivity by othering the black individual and this results in what Frantz Fanon has called a "manichean delirium" whereby the individual asserts his subjectivity—and it is usually the male in a patriarchal setting—in the form of dominance over his subordinates; his wife or partner, and children who may grow up to be Willieboy.

In *A Walk in the Night* La Guma shows how the master/slave dialectic must be enforced at all times, that is the (white) master must never allow the (black) slave to forget his or her identity position, for to do so would lead to a potential reconfiguration of the dialectic, which could, conceivably, favor the majority population. La Guma presents the reader with a glimpse of the fragile power positions the whites hold when the crowd— the mass tenement community—confronts Raalt and his driver, Andries. The crowd demonstrates that it has "no desire . . . to cooperate with these men [the law]" (*AW*, p. 58) while Raalt senses that "They hate us" (*AW*, p. 58). The driver acknowledges his fear: "the people had little regard for the authority of the law, and he was not sure that he would have been able to handle this thing" (*AW*, p. 63). Despite this tangible antagonism, John Abrahams, with his ingratiating smile, steps forward and proceeds to "inform" Raalt of the events that have taken place and, in so doing, implicates the innocent Willieboy in Doughty's murder. The tenement community, led by Franky Lorenzo, condemns Abrahams's actions. This is a powerful indicator that it *is* possible to resist the regime by withholding information and by demonstrating solidarity and class reserve in the face of police harassment. Indeed, J. M. Coetzee has suggested that through his actions, Franky Lorenzo may be the novella's "potential hero."[36]

To dismiss *A Walk in the Night* as simply a "profoundly pessimistic"[37] novella, as JanMohamed does, is to risk ignoring the complexity of La Guma's political reading of the South African situation and his attempt to show how individuals, no matter how defeated they are, may move beyond the narrow boundaries that exist to restrict their political growth. Political awareness—if we leave aside his stance *vis-à-vis* employment— comes too late to Willieboy. But in his dying moments, like a revelation, he understands that his real enemies are not those of his own racial background but the whites in power who label him less than human. The characters presented in *A Walk in the Night* are shown to have a limited political awareness that requires organizing on a mass scale. In discussing the title of the novella, La Guma allowed that "in my mind the coloured community was still discovering themselves in relation to the general struggle against racism in South Africa. They were walking, enduring, and in this way they were experiencing this walking in the night until such time as they found themselves and were prepared to be citizens of a society to which they wanted to make a contribution." He professes that his intention was to create "a picture of a people struggling to see the light, to see the dawn, to see something new, other than their experiences in this confined community."[38] La Guma's black characters begin to create communities from within which they can operate. They may be walking, or stumbling, in the dark and they may only make small steps and small contributions, but these can be read as sufficiently important breakthroughs in terms of burgeoning political awareness. JanMohamed eschews this interpretation, however, believing La Guma's "answer to the oppression of the white authoritarian government is emotional and apolitical." In an effort to clarify cause and effect, JanMohamed is finally reductive in his analysis: "For the deprivation and degradation that apartheid society imposes on his characters, La Guma can only provide a reaction in the same terms. To the arbitrary persecution of apartheid, the characters reply with equally arbitrary and emotional violence; to the exclusionist legal and economic monopoly of apartheid, the characters can only respond with crime and theft."[39] What JanMohamed's reading fails to acknowledge is that the actions of these protopolitical characters are represented as forms of political resistance. Foxy and his group live outside of the law in order to maintain a certain freedom of choice and autonomy of action. Within the gang there exists a communal code calling for each member to trust and protect the others: the gang shares a common enemy and that is white people, whether they represent the law or are simply members of the wider white society. JanMohamed also fails to acknowledge precisely the ways in which violent action may prove effective in resisting the authority imposed upon blacks. The police violence and, indeed, the violence of apartheid must be met with equal violence in order to disrupt the status quo, to demonstrate that subaltern subject positions are no longer tenable or viable. In a similar vein, Felix Mnthali incorrectly suggests that "*A Walk in the Night* is the one work where political committment [*sic*] is peripheral."[40] Political commitment need not be explicated in an overt manner. In portraying the urban slum that is District Six, the inhuman brutality of the police force, and the stunted growth of political awareness in the characters, La Guma makes a powerful political statement. The characters may not be as politically aware or committed as those encountered in La Guma's later fiction,[41] but their concerns remain political even if, at this stage, they are ill formed and unfocused.

Notes

1. V. Klima, et al., *Black Africa: Literature and Language* (Prague: Czechoslovakian Academy of Sciences, 1976), p. 257.

2. Abdul JanMohamed, *Manichean Aesthetics: The Politics of Literature in Colonial Africa* (Amherst: University of Massachusetts Press, 1983), p. 229.

3. Robert July, "The African Personality in the African Novel," in Ulli Beier, ed., *Introduction to African Literature: An Anthology of Critical Writing* (London: Longman, 1967), p. 221. See also Felix Mnthali, who argues that *A Walk in the Night* bears "an uncanny resemblance" to *Native Son*, and goes on to say that "in both works the central characters live in the most desolate parts of the city. Both characters are hemmed in by racism and poverty and both are haunted by the spectre of police brutality." In Andrew Horn and George E. Carter, eds., *American Studies in Africa* (Lesotho: University Press of Lesotho and the Ford Foundation, 1984), p. 41. See Richard Wright, *Native Son* (London: Penguin, 1986) and *Rite of Passage* (New York: Harper Collins, 1994). Wright began the latter novel in 1945 though it was not published until 1994. His Johnny Gibbs is very like Adonis: He becomes involved in mugging an innocent man and joins a gang who mug Harlem whites.

4. Harlem became an African American urban center after 1909 and from the period following World War I to the Civil Rights era of the 1950s and 1960s was one of the main destinations of those Southern blacks who moved North as part of what has come to be known as the Great Black Migration. Harlem was a sought-after area of Manhattan Island and it was not until after the Depression that its tenements came to signify decay and representations of Harlem started to include descriptions of poverty and criminalization. See James de Jongh, *Vicious Modernism: Black Harlem and the Literary Imagination* (Cambridge: Cambridge University Press, 1990).

5. Richard Wright, "How Bigger Was Born." Introduction to *Native Son*, p. 25.

6. Bernard W. Bell, *The Afro-American Novel and Its Tradition* (Amherst: University of Massachussetts Press, 1987) p. 167. Bell discusses Wright and his contemporaries at length under the title "Richard Wright and the Triumph of Naturalism" and consequently examines Wright's relation to European Naturalism and the African American tradition of social protest, pp. 150–187.

7. Alex La Guma in Cecil A. Abrahams, *Alex La Guma* (Boston: Twayne Publishers, 1985), p. 48.

8. Richard Wright, *Native Son*, p. 35–66.

9. Alex La Guma, *A Walk in the Night* (London: Heinneman, 1967), p. 1. All further references to this novella will be abbreviated as *AW* and included in the text.

10. Balasubramanyam Chandramohan, *A Study in Trans-Ethnicity in Modern South Africa: The Writings of Alex La Guma* (Lampeter: Mellen Research Press, 1992), p. 82.

11. JanMohamed, *Manichean Aesthetics*, p. 228.

12. JanMohamed, *Manichean Aesthetics*, p. 227.

13. Chandramohan also makes this point stating, "The writers of the 1950s appealed to the liberal conscience of their readers," *A Study in Trans-Ethnicity*, p. 15.

14. Kathleen Balutansky in *The Novels of Alex La Guma: The Representation of a Political Conflict* (Boulder, Colorado: Lynne Rienner Publishers, Inc., 1990) also argues that La Guma valued the "collectivity" over the "individual," p.15.

15. See Michael Wade who believes that Adonis's act of generosity "liberates him momentarily from his isolation and consequent anonymity," p. 179. For a fuller discussion of Adonis's actions in specific relation to Joe, see Wade's "Art and Morality in Alex La Guma's *A Walk in the Night*," in Kenneth Parker, ed., *The South African Novel in English* (London: Macmillan, 1978), pp. 164–191.

16. JanMohamed, *Manichean Aesthetics*, p. 229.

17. JanMohamed, "The Economy of Manichean Allegory: The Function of Racial Difference in Colonialist Literature," *Critical Inquiry*, vol. 12, 1985, p. 86.

18. JanMohamed, "The Economy of Manichean Allegory," p. 66.

19. Edward Said, *The World, the Text and the Critic* (London: Vintage, 1991), p. 20.

20. Chandramohan, *A Study in Trans-Ethnicity*, p. 27.

21. Wade, "Art and Morality in Alex La Guma's *A Walk in the Night*," pp. 187–188.

22. Abrahams in *Alex La Guma*, p. 4.

23. Abrahams in *Alex La Guma*, p. 20.

24. Cecil A. Abrahams, "The Writings of Alex La Guma," in his *Essays on Literature* (Toronto, Canada: AFO Enterprises, 1986), p. 87.

25. See, for example, Wade, "Art and Morality in Alex La Guma's *A Walk in the Night*," p. 173.

26. Frantz Fanon, *The Wretched of the Earth* (London: Penguin, 1990), p. 48.

27. Fanon, *The Wretched of the Earth*, p. 54.

28. Fanon, *The Wretched of the Earth*, p. 47.

29. Blanche V. La Guma states in interview that "Basil February is a Coloured young man whom Alex had recruited in fact to join the *Umkhonto we Sizwe*. He was the first man of the ANC to fall," quoted in Chandramohan, *A Study in Trans-Ethnicity*, p. 212.

30. Fanon, *The Wretched of the Earth*, p. 56.

31. Fanon, *The Wretched of the Earth*, p. 56.

32. Jean Baudrillard, *America* (London: Verso, 1988), p. 26.

33. Alex La Guma, *In the Fog of the Seasons' End* (London: Heinemann, 1972), p. 26.

34. Fanon, *The Wretched of the Earth*, p. 32.

35. Paulo Freire, *Pedagogy of the Oppressed* (London: Penguin, 1972), pp. 20–21.

36. J. M. Coetzee, "Alex La Guma and the Responsibilities of the South African Writer," in Joseph Okpaku, ed., *New African Literature and the Arts: Vol. III* (New York: The Third Press, 1973), p. 124.

37. JanMohamed, *Manichean Aesthetics*, p. 238.

38. Abrahams, *Alex La Guma*, p. 49.

39. JanMohamed, *Manichean Aesthetics*, pp. 237–238.

40. Felix Mnthali, "Common Grounds in the Literature of Black America and Southern Africa," p. 47.

41. Samuel Asein makes a similar point about Adonis when he argues that, even though Adonis "is not led into organized action because he is yet to be fully enlightened on the larger issues of social and political restructuring of his society, he does pursue, in his own private and rather simplistic way, the cause of justice . . . in the prevailing circumstances," p. 61. See S. O. Asein, *Alex La Guma: The Man and His Work* (Ibadan: New Horn Press/Heinemann, 1987).

Chapter 3
▼▼▼▼▼▼▼▼▼▼

Border-Crossings:
The Germination of a Political
Consciousness in And A Threefold Cord

Alex La Guma's *And A Threefold Cord*, originally published in 1964, can be seen as his first attempt at writing a novel rather than a "long story," as was the case with *A Walk in the Night*. During 1963, the apartheid state instigated further measures of oppression in an attempt to stem the flow of the ANC's underground activities and, in particular, the work of its military wing, Umkhonto we Sizwe. To this end, a number of the ANC's prominent members were arrested, and it was from the position of incarceration that La Guma began work on *And A Threefold Cord*. Published in East Berlin by Seven Seas Publishers, it is immediately apparent that La Guma and his publishers made a number of concessions for an overseas readership, the most notable of these are the inclusion of a "glossary of terms" and a long foreword by the Communist activist and former *New Age* editor Brian Bunting.

And A Threefold Cord continues La Guma's project of proletarian consciousness raising, which formed part of the subject matter of the earlier *A Walk in the Night*. La Guma once again focuses on dual protagonists: the unemployed colored Charlie Pauls and the unremitting rain that permeates every aspect of his protagonists' lives in a manner that is redolent of apartheid itself. Indeed, Brian Bunting described *And A Threefold Cord* as "drenched in the wet and misery of the Cape winter, whose dreary tones Alex La Guma has captured in a series of graphic prose-etchings"[1] and La Guma has himself stated that he wished to "correct" the holiday-brochure impression that an overseas readership might hold about South Africa: "I am contesting the official propaganda of South Africa's natural beauty and trying to show the world that the tourist poster world of wonderful beaches and beautiful golf links is not the total picture."[2] From this one may conclude that La Guma's intention was to rewrite the popular preconceptions that a non-South African might hold about South Africa and concomitantly to reinsert, into literature, the daily reality of those who did not form a part of the privileged white minority. Furthermore, the rain functions as a metaphor for the regime's relentless incursions into the lives of those it oppresses. La Guma was not unaware of the role played by capitalism in the racist ideology that forced certain sections of the South African population into squalor and degradation. Writing in *Sechaba,* he asserts that "in the face of increasing forms of apartheid and racial discrimination in politics and economics, it is not surprising that the physical and social life of the Coloured community is deteriorating at an alarming degree. . . . Social problems which might exist under 'normal' capitalist conditions are aggravated seriously by racial discrimination."[3]

On first reading, *And A Threefold Cord* appears to be a simple story following Charlie Pauls' attempts to maintain the shack that functions as home for Ma and the dying Pa Pauls and their sons Charlie, Ronald and Jorny. But while this might initially appear to be a reasonable summary, it is somewhat reductive in that the Pauls represent only one family in a community that encompasses Africans as well as other colored inhabitants whose plights are shown to be markedly similar. The idea of community is of central ideological importance in this text as it functions to elucidate the proposition that group action is far more effective than the random acts of individuals. Indeed, the title of the book is taken from Ecclesiastes IV: 9–12 to indicate this position:

> Two are better than one; because they have a good reward for their labour. For if they fall, the one will lift up his fellow: but woe to him that is alone when he falleth; for he hath not another to help him up. Again, if two lie together, then they have heat, but how can one be alone? And if one prevail against him, two shall withstand him; and a threefold cord is not quickly broken.

La Guma stated in an interview that he intended to show that "while people have got their own problems, or what they believe to be their own problems, these problems are not actually entirely their own but they are shared by other people."[4] The issue of solidarity is an ideologically salient one, and the novel incorporates a number of incidents and sequences that speak directly to this feature of La Guma's efforts to raise awareness of context and consciousness. We are informed that the Pauls moved to Windermere—the ironically named settlement, when one remembers the Wordsworthian pastoral of the lakes—from the country in an effort to find better housing. It is to be assumed that this was also an effort to increase their opportunities in the job market, since in the years preceding the 1960s, the Western Cape was one of the biggest industrial areas in South Africa. Housing shortages and rapidly expanding urbanization led to what has been described as "a mushrooming of squatter settlements in the Peninsula, especially at Windermere and Retreat."[5] These in turn led to the development of disenfranchised communities in which groups were forced to live in appalling conditions with little support from white authorities but a great deal of hindrance, since the apartheid state's insistence on separate development demanded that Africans and coloreds live separately. It is in one of these communities that the Pauls find themselves, with Pa Pauls renting a piece of land on which to build his *pondokkie*, the description of which bears quoting:

> Dad and Charlie had scavenged, begged and, on dark nights, stolen the materials for the house. They had dragged for miles sheets of rusty corrugated iron, planks, pieces of cardboard, and all the astonishing miscellany that had gone into building the house. There were flattened fuel cans advertising a brand of oil on its sides, tins of rusty nails which Charlie had pulled from the gathered flotsam and jetsam and straightened with a hammer on a stone; rags for stuffing cracks and holes, strips of baling wire and waterproof paper, cartons, old pieces of metal and strands of wire, sides of packing-cases, and a pair of railway sleepers (*AATC*, p. 17).

The effort of accumulating the materials belies Charlie's efforts to maintain the "upkeep" of the shack. In the rainy season it takes all his energy to prevent the place from flooding or being swept away in the high winds. In fact, H. Britten, in his *Report of the Commision of Enquiry into Conditions Existing on the Cape Flats and Similarly Affected Areas in the Cape Division*, was prompted to conclude in 1943 that the pondokkie "owes nought to any school of architecture." Its design, the report states "is determined entirely by the scraps of material which go into its structure" in the way La Guma describes, and, "piece by piece, scrap material is bought, begged or filched and added to make room for a growing family. There are no windows, ceilings, and very often no door. Sanitation is non-existent. Many of these hovels would do a disservice to animals."[6] Most significantly the *pondokkies* are considered unfit for animals, yet the racist system that relegates blacks to the status of animals prevents them from earning adequate wages that would allow them to rent the only slightly improved council accommodations. We are informed that Alfy, Caroline Pauls's husband, works hard, yet he is unlikely to qualify for, or be in a position to afford, council housing, although he and his pregnant wife live in an old "pack-ing-case." To compound matters, research into the context La Guma de-scribes uncovers that "the cost of living in Cape Town was consistently higher than in other industrial areas. Despite the higher wage rates in the peninsula, conditions of living in the squatter camps nevertheless reveal serious poverty and squalor. Socioeconomic surveys reveal that between 50–70 percent of all African households in the Cape Peninsula lived below the poverty datum line (PDL) between the 1940s and 1960s."[7] The back-drop La Guma creates in this novel is tied carefully and consciously into a reality that he had left behind; hidden from the tourist, it preoccupies the writer in exile.

In the South Africa of the 1950s the colored community are either unable to participate in wage labor or forced to accept a meager return on their labor power. In *And A Threefold Cord* we discover that of Ma Pauls's four children only Ronny works and, on closer examination, only three other characters in the novel—Alfy, Freda and Uncle Ben—are in employ-ment. Of these characters, Alfy is in regular employment, the nature of which is not specified, while Ben's employment as a painter is reliant upon the weather, and Freda is in poorly paid work as a maid to a white family. Yvonne Muthien has analyzed the coordinating factors that contributed to the vast majority of colored people being unemployed. She explains that employers preferred African to colored labor, believing Africans to be physi-cally stronger and more reliable when compared to their colored counter-parts who they stereotyped as unwilling, even alcoholic, absentees, prone to be generally inefficient.[8] The predominance of this level of stereotypical thinking underscores the paradoxical nature of apartheid: on the one hand it is a capitalist system that relies on cheap black (African) labor in order to function, yet on the other it constructs strategies to prevent the fair employment of—in this context—the doubly marginalized coloreds. To this end the coloreds depicted in *And A Threefold Cord* are forced to live below the poverty datum line, which results in their existence as an underclass. Free from the measures of the pass system, they are neverthe-less restricted in their movements in economic terms and in specific rela-tion to the Group Areas Acts. This last point is somewhat lost on Ursula A. Barnett, who mistakenly argues that in La Guma's fiction characters may support a Marxist cause but that class struggle is relegated to back-ground. In emphasizing white victimization of blacks, she asserts: "Al-though La Guma does not believe in thinking in colour, he makes it clear in his fiction that the conflict is not identical with the class struggle."[9] While it is true that some of La Guma's characters support a Marxist cause, Barnett is grossly oversimplifying her discussion of capitalists as a close reading of *And A Threefold Cord* makes clear. The white regime represents capitalist interests and to this end the police are also representative of capitalist orthodoxy, despite the fact that they may dress their activities in the guise of protection from and security against subversive elements. Indeed, Marx himself emphasized this factor when he explained security as "the supreme social concept of civil society."[10] In the South African context, the workers' struggle was part of the popular struggle and as trade unionist Joe Forster, for example, has pointed out, an "important effect of this development was that capital could hide behind the curtains of apartheid and racism."[11] South African apartheid and capitalism operate as interchangeable practices. The long-term effects of the process ensure that apartheid "nestled into a pragmatic accommodation with capitalism," to borrow Muthien's phrase. For Muthien the empirical confirmation is the formation of a black working class who were treated inequitably in a system where capitalists did not need to pay labor at the cost of reproduction.[12] The question that one should ask is whether the black population is aware of its exploitation and, if so, what it intends to do about it. In *And A Threefold Cord* La Guma points explicitly to the concomitant relationship between wage labor and living conditions: the two are reflected in the regime's less than equal treatment of blacks both inside and outside the workplace. The desire for equal rights is not voiced in this text in an overtly theorized manner. But, as I will show, the germination of consciousness, away from the fatalistic trope displayed by certain characters, is nevertheless present in the character of Charlie Pauls.

The limited choices open to those forced to inhabit the area are clear. Either they follow the communitarian line and become active agents in an effort to maintain community, despite the obstacles of unemployment and harassment at the hands of the security forces, or they become pseudo-capitalists and attempt to maintain a livelihood at the expense of their neighbors. La Guma juxtaposes these two options in the preparations for Pa Pauls's funeral. We are presented with Missus Nzuba, who is willing to let Ma Pauls have water in order to wash the dead body before burial and in so doing represents what La Guma sees as a vital element in any resistance to apartheid: a communitarian spirit, and a desire to support one another intracommunally. La Guma underlines this feature of extrafamilial support by making Missus Nzuba an African who, therefore, may be understood to be in a worse position in relation to apartheid law than her (colored) neighbors. In contrast to this woman, he presents an unnamed man whose racial background is unspecified and who profits from the sale of water to the community. The torrentially heavy rainfall, and the problems that ensue for the settlement dwellers who struggle to combat its deleterious effects in their fragile homes, functions as a metaphor for the oppressive elements of apartheid rule. But La Guma adds another dimension to the life-sustaining function of water, namely, its use in capitalist enterprise: "Water is profit. In order to make this profit, the one who sells the water must also use it to wash his soul clear of compassion. He must rinse his heart of pity, and with the bristles of enterprise, scrub his being sterile of sympathy. He must have the heart of a stop-cock and the brain of a cistern, intestines of lead pipes" (*AATC*, p. 72). Kathleen Balutansky sees these two episodes—Missus Nzuba's offer of water for the washing of the dead body and the unnamed man's selling of water—as reflective of La Guma's desire to show how the devastating effects of poverty divide the community, "preventing it from achieving the togetherness necessary for its survival."[13] I would argue that his intention is much more strategically posed than this abstraction implies. La Guma, in juxtaposing these two episodes, is attempting to demonstrate that capitalism has no strategic place in a community that is voiceless and marginalized. The first incremental steps towards opposing apartheid lie within the practices of the community itself, not outside of it, and certainly not in emulating white capitalist practices. In this last point, I concur rather with JanMohamed, who writes that "the merging of the man and the product does perfect justice to the moral transformation necessitated by the economic exploitation of others."[14] The man is a man no more; he has in effect become the product—the heartless water pump—which is of more value to him than the needs of the community. JanMohamed believes that in the limited community of *And A Threefold Cord* individuals are at best partially aware of their victimized status and are, consequently, self-pitying.[15]

But we also need to bear in mind that La Guma's nascent community is itself in a state of flux and change. In the context of the novel, apartheid regulations do not allow Africans, coloreds and Indians to live together, and the reader cannot fail to be aware that it was only a matter of time before the law would separate this mixed community. I would argue that rather than indulging in self-pity, La Guma's characters are, on the whole, distrusting of one another and that it is this that prevents them from uniting. To compound matters, the security forces are in such an unassailable position of power that the community can neither escape them nor stand up to them. In a Fanonian sense, the "the settler-native relationship is a mass relationship":

> The settler pits brute force against the weight of numbers. His preoccupation with security makes him remind the native out loud that there he alone is master. The settler keeps alive in the native

an anger which he deprives of outlet; the native is trapped in the tight links of the chains of colonialism.[16]

In *And A Threefold Cord* the unannounced security and police raids that the community is subjected to exemplify the dialectic Fanon describes. The rule of surveillance promotes what Fanon calls "auto-destruction,"[17] where "the settler or the policeman has the right live-long day to strike the native, to insult him and to make him crawl to them." In turn, the native is capable of "reaching for his knife at the slightest hostile or aggressive glance cast on him by another native; for the last resort of the native is to defend his personality vis-à-vis his brother." So, by "throwing himself with all his force into the vendetta, the native tries to persuade himself that colonialism does not exist," and Fanon concludes that "on the level of communal organizations we clearly discern the well-known behaviour patterns of avoidance."[18] This is most clearly the case with Roman, who in his efforts to assert his masculinity—an attribute that is inherently undermined by apartheid—finds that the most convenient victim for his violent rage is his wife. Fanon's paradigm does not, however, apply to Charlie. Charlie is not avoiding the immediate problem of apartheid, and this is best exemplified through his growing political consciousness and his awareness of the helpless plight of those around him, most particularly Freda and Ronny. In defending Ronny against Roman, Charlie is simply fulfilling a familial obligation that is indicative of his realization that two are indeed better than one.

A number of criticisms have been leveled against *And A Threefold Cord*. For example, Abdul JanMohamed believes that, if we judge the novel purely on the basis of its plot, it is "a weak and paltry affair," only lifted out of such a negative reading by the strength of the descriptive passages which, in his view, are more important than the narrative itself.[19] In a similar vein, Vernie February suggests that a "concentration on external forces occurs at the expense of individual characterization."[20] What these critics fail to acknowledge is that La Guma is not necessarily intent on providing a mimetic representation. The characters are not intended to act as his mouthpiece, but as autonomous individuals who act according to their own motives and principles, which are inevitably shaped by the overarching impact of apartheid on their lives. In my reading, once Charlie Pauls is established as the novel's hero, for the hero to function as such there must exist the conditions for his self-consciousness to be expressed outside of the authorial function. For Bakhtin, self-consciousness is salient in breaking down "the monologic unity of an artistic world." In the world of the novel, this only comes about when the hero's "self-consciousness" is "represented and not merely expressed, that is, does not fuse with the author, does not become the mouthpiece for his voice; only on condition, consequently, that accents of the hero's self-consciousness are really objectified and that the work itself observes a distance between the hero and the author. If the umbilical cord uniting the hero to his creator is not cut, then what we have is not a work of art but a personal document."[21] Charlie Pauls functions as a hero in the Bakhtinian sense precisely because La Guma does not interfere in his coming to consciousness. Even though the exploiter of the community—the water seller—functions as an example of the lack of community spirit, Charlie does not see him or comment on him in the way that the reader might.[22] Rather, Charlie needs the memory of a conversation that took place outside of the community to spur him towards a critique of his own and his neighbors' living conditions. Charlie has advanced from the position held by Michael Adonis in *A Walk in the Night* to become a more developed example of an individual whose perspective echoes that of Franky Lorenzo from that novel.

In the essay "Culture and Liberation" La Guma argues that "life is the stimulation of artistic endeavour" and "man's struggle to reach higher levels of civilisation." For La Guma, art should address "the central questions that involve life."[23] His ideas encompass the need for art to reflect life experiences ideologically rather than mimetically. In my context, his politicized aesthetic coincides with Medvedev's assertion that "all the products of ideological creation" are material, "having significance, meaning, inner value. But these meanings and values are embodied in material things and actions. They cannot be realized outside of some developed material."[24] *And A Threefold Cord* is that developed material. In this novel La Guma deliberately draws attention to the inequities that exist between his black and white characters in order to demonstrate that the prevailing material conditions are responsible for creating a totally disenfranchised underclass. Consequently, Medvedev's assertions as to the realization of an ideological reality are played out in this text, "realized in words, actions, clothing, manners, and organizations of people and things—in a word: in some definite semiotic material."[25] In this way social criticism and political belief are enmeshed in La Guma's organized attempt to place his nascent community in a position of understanding, rather than passive acceptance, of its lived condition. Charlie Pauls is his primary semiotic material.

Charlie Pauls is surrounded by people who exist in a condition of helplessness and ignorance, apparently devoid of the desire to resist their allocated status. For example, Ma Pauls and Uncle Ben are both drowning in the quagmire of their religious beliefs, advocating the view that their subordinate position is not a result of apartheid at all. Ma Pauls, in talking about life with her husband, opines: "He worked for his family and when he couldn't work no more, he lay down and waited for the Lord Jesus to take him away. Now he's gone away to the Lord and he's away from sickness and hunger and gone to rest from his work. He carried his cross, too, like Our Lord Jesus, and now the burden is taken from off his shoulders" (*AATC*, p. 67).

This kind of stoical resignation is also present in Uncle Ben with his "We got to trust in the Lord" (*AATC*, p. 49). It is arguably such abject reliance on an otherworldly power, with resignation bordering on defeat, that prompts Charlie to recall the words of a pipe-laying workmate he met while working in Calvinia: "Always reading newspapers and things. He said to us, the poor don't have to be poor. . . . This burg say, if the poor people all got together and took everything in the whole blerry world, there woudn't be poor no more. Funny kind of talk, but it sounded awright. . . . Further, this rooker say if all the stuff in the world was shared out among everybody, all would have enough to live nice. He reckoned people got to stick together to get this stuff" (*AATC*, pp. 49–50). Although it is easy for Uncle Ben—like old Greene in *A Walk in the Night*—to dismiss this as "communis' things. Talking against the govverment" (*AATC*, p. 50), Charlie cannot finally dismiss the words, which are symptomatic of the growing consciousness that has taken root in him. The pipe layer functions to initiate Charlie's politicization. Vološinov explores this idea in terms of a linguistic exchange: "I give myself verbal shape from another's point of view, ultimately, from the point of view of the community to which I belong. A word is a bridge thrown between myself and another. If one end of the bridge depends on me, then the other depends on my addressee. A word is territory shared by both addresser and addressee, by the speaker and his interlocutor."[26]

In participating in the conversation about the pipe layer's words, Ben unconsciously allows Charlie the opportunity to address an essential issue, namely, the question raised earlier in this chapter, why are blacks marginalized under apartheid, and what can they do to ease their oppression? In this act of dialogue, Charlie reaches a new understanding of his poverty-ridden situation. For him it cannot simply be that the good Lord deems it so; it is rather that whites will not allow blacks equality of opportunity and equal rights. Charlie considers the *burg's* comments and concludes that they "sounded awright," which indicates that he has not yet fully assimilated the meaning behind the words of his interlocutor. However, he has reached a level of understanding that Bakhtin describes as "active," whereby the word is assimilated into "its own conceptual system filled with specific objects and emotional expressions, and is indissolubly

merged with the response, with a motivated agreement or disagreement."
In this way, "primacy belongs to the response, as the activating principle:
it creates the ground for understanding, it prepares the ground for an
active and engaged understanding. Understanding comes to fruition only
in the response. Understanding and response are dialectically merged and
mutually condition each other; one is impossible without the other."[27] To
this I would add that the word is not finalized at the point of utterance,
but has the potential to live in the memory of its intended recipient, the
ability to be recalled at another, opportune moment. Charlie recalls and
reworks the words he heard uttered at Calvinia, as an initial stage in his
approaching understanding of his condition and context.

La Guma shows that a gradual cumulative understanding of one's environment is possible, but that it will be a slow process if it is left in the
hands of one individual rather than in the hands of the community. Marx's
statement that liberation is an "historical and not mental act" brought
about by "historical conditions, the development of industry, commerce,
agriculture" but most importantly by "the conditions of intercourse," is
given resonance in this context.[28] In the first instance the marginalized
community is denied equal access to labor, and is therefore victim to the
ideas of the ruling class that are "at the same time its ruling intellectual
force." This entails a recognition that the class that controls material production also controls mental production so that "the ideas of those who
lack the means of mental production are subject to it."[29] La Guma identifies the victims of this ideological brainwashing as ordinary people like Ma
Pauls and Uncle Ben. Religious indoctrination acts as the ideology controlling the ordinary people, the people who cannot or will not contemplate political action as a means of altering their lived conditions. Those
who privilege the teachings of the church above all else also place their
trust outside of the political community that has the potential to help
them in concrete ways.

Skepticism about political action is clearly presented in the notion that
community, in this case predicated on Christianity, is "better" than individualism, which is misunderstood as politics. Charlie's idea that the poor
people should form a union is dismissed by Uncle Ben with, "Sound
almost like a sin, that. Bible say you mustn't covet other people's
things"(*AATC*, p. 50). Ben's mind-set is as rigid and unbending—and as
unworldly—as a missionary-education statement: "It is our belief that with
the spread of better understanding in Church and college circles the future
of South Africa is one we can contemplate with a fair degree of optimism
in the hope that Christian influences will dispel illusions, transcend the
mistaken political expedients of pseudo-segregationists and usher in a South

Africa of racial peace and goodwill."[30] Uncle Ben and Ma Pauls firmly represent the type of thinking characterized by one Christian spokesperson in the belief that Communism should be rejected because it "stood for violence" and a "crass, materialistic . . . outlook on life which rejects all religious and moral idealism."[31] But La Guma is not suggesting that religion and politics are not commensurate with each other, and this is best exemplified through Charlie's response to Ben: "Bible say love your neighbour, too" (*AATC*, p. 50). La Guma's point is simply that one should use any means necessary to educate the masses into understanding the ramifications of the oppressive conditions they endure. While it is true that Charlie Pauls will not follow his parents' lead and trust in the Lord, he is capable of understanding that unity is an essential element in mass resistance, and can discern that the Church might have a role to play, even if, at this stage, it is aimed at the older generation who need to be educated out of their current monologic mindset.

Marx's oft-quoted idea that "the mode of production of material life conditions the social, political, and intellectual life process" and that it is the social that determines the population's consciousness has a significant impact on the unemployed Charlie.[32] He is gradually coming to the realization that, in order to maintain its hegemonic position, the regime "strives to impart a supraclass, external character to the ideological sign, to extinguish or drive inward the struggle between social value judgements which occurs within it, to make the sign uniaccentual."[33] This is the process of silencing the majority, and beating it into submission. It is a process of reinforcing the monologic nature of apartheid. The war that Charlie initially has to wage is centered within his community; he has to demonstrate that the real enemy is the white apartheid regime, and that it is the regime that is responsible for characters like the drunken Ria, the prostitute Susie, and the bully Roman. By denying these characters subjectivity, the apartheid structure devalues their self-worth and self-esteem, leaving them locked in the petty lives they lead, without the option to escape its ever-tightening grasp.

Charlie's growing political awareness functions to exemplify the fact that, in order to break free of the manicheanism that is the lot of the majority population, individual antagonisms need to be left to one side since a degree of solidarity is required to smash the regime. In recalling the words of his pipe-laying mate, Charlie understands that mobilization of the people at events other than funerals and celebrations is not only necessary, but is essential if things are to change for the better. The ruling ideology curtails individual thinking and prevents La Guma's characters from realizing that there is another way of life, a way of living that is not predicated on the laws of apartheid. Medvedev's statement that "the ideological environment is the realized, materialized, externally expressed social consciousness of a given collective" is particularly pertinent in the apartheid context where the epistemic violence that *is* apartheid has taken root in the minds of the community. Medvedev bases his analysis in the belief that the ideological environment is determined by political and economic pressures that constrain individual consciousness. These are the decisive factors in the articulation of collective consciousness.[34] Curtailed in this way, Charlie finds himself pitting his wits against his community, precisely because he has come to the specific realization that black people are not inferior to whites. The introverted violence in which blacks turn their anger against each other is sanctioned by the regime precisely because it deflects attention away from the regime's oppressive constraints on all blacks. This is a point that I will return to in my discussion of the border metaphor in *And A Threefold Cord*.

The highway that cuts across the South African landscape in this novel encapsulates the division between the whites who enjoy all the social benefits and the blacks who are forced to inhabit the squalor of the shanty towns dotted around the Cape. The physical presence of the border marks off those who are economically, socially and politically powerless. The border is more than a physical presence in that it functions as a powerful metaphor for the South African apartheid situation. In the case of George Mostert, whose garage nestles on just the right side of the highway, the border functions to signify a division between purity and impurity: in his thinking and that of his two white customers, crossing the border into the shanty town will result in inevitable pollution and contamination. The narrator glosses this situation with indications that Mostert is "trapped in his glass office by his own loneliness and a wretched pride in a false racial superiority" (*AATC*, p. 38). Conversely, the blacks who inhabit the shanty town are forced to trek across the highway in search of discarded materials in order to maintain their *pondokkies*. Charlie Pauls's crossing the highway is likened to a cockroach crossing the floor, indicating the belittling humility he feels in his honest task. Once in the presence of Mostert, Charlie is forced to play the role of the subservient other:

> "I say, Mister George, I must ask you another pleasure. Other time you give me some scrap to fix up the house. Now the blerry roof is leaking. Rain coming into the blerry house. Well, I reckon, you *mos* give me that stuff last time—" George Mostert sensed the praise and he cut in, "You want some more scrap?" (*AATC*, p. 39).

This occurs even though Mostert appears to look forward to the visits from the shanty dwellers; they sporadically alleviate his loneliness while also serving to reestablish his superior position. The issues that La Guma exposes here are interesting: Mostert is not ill judged; he is presented as a simple man, living a simple life—not completely dissimiliar to old Doughty in *A Walk in the Night*—yet the subject position that Charlie adopts is called into question. Why, for example, does he feel the need to present a humble, groveling demeanor? The reason seems obvious: the colored man has been conditioned into thinking that this is the appropriate way to address whites. It is only after Charlie recalls his conversation in Calvinia and later hits out at a police officer that his attitude towards whites changes and, consequently, his awareness is heightened as to the effects such debilitating role-playing and border crossings wreak on his internal coherence.

Kathleen Balutansky equates the shanty town and Mostert's garage, believing each of them to be victims of progress left to rot in the face of the highway that passes them by. She believes the descriptions of each "make a clear statement about their similarity in status: they are both wretchedly poor and they are both left behind by the fast developing wealth of the city." In her view, the highway "may separate Mostert's garage from the shantytown, but it passes them both as its smooth asphalt leads the shining cars and loaded trucks to the prosperous bustle of Cape Town."[35] I would argue that these two physical locations are, in fact, antithetical: Windermere faces Mostert's garage across the highway, which acts as the border. La Guma describes the setting in this way:

> The highway from the city unreeled like dark, wet adhesive, pasted like a strip across the country, curving in places where it seemed to have come unstuck from the moist surface of the land. The Service Station and Garage stood just off one of these curves in the road where it navigated a bulge of gum, green portjackson wood and wattle, as it by-passed a string of suburbs.
> Like a lone blockhouse on a frontier, it stood against the dark-green background of trees, with an air of neglect surrounding it, as if deserted by its garrison and left to crumble on the edge of hostile territory (*AATC,* p. 36).

The border/frontier metaphor is most appropriate when one considers issues of transgression and punishment; white George Mostert can leave whereas the coloreds cannot. This last point is made in opposition to Barnett, who unthinkingly reproduces apartheid-speak by stating that "George Mostert . . . is as much a victim of poverty as the *brown* and *black* people in the shanty-town around him."[36] This is precisely the equation that La Guma erects in order to refute; Mostert's false pride in his superiority might make him a victim but, as a white man, he is neither inescapably marginalized nor voiceless like the people around him. In this context, Medvedev's assertion that "ideological creation and its comprehension only take place in the process of social inter-course" has particular resonance.[37] The ideology that underpins apart-heid is reinforced for George Mostert in his connection to the white world, particularly through his conversation with the white customer who stops for petrol:

> He . . . gazed across the road. Beyond the opposite edge and the growth of brushwood, the roofs of the shantytown were scattered like grey and brown rocks along a coastline. A cloud of smoke was dwindling in the white-grey air above it.
> "What's that?" he asked George Mostert. . . .
> "That?" George Mostert said, . . . "Oh, jus' one of those slum places."
> "Christ, I bet it's mucky as hell. Wonder why the authorities don't clear the bloody lot out. Just brings disease and things." He stared out across the road. "If I had any say, I'd pull down the wholly bally lot and clear 'em out." He shook his head and the wisps of hair, like straw, fluttered. "I don't know what we poor buggers pay taxes for." (*AATC*, pp. 106–107)

At a simplistic level this conversation may appear one-sided, with the white, possibly English, customer doing all the talking and instigating the negative comments. But, George Mostert is complicit in such racist thinking by virtue of his silence, which is further compounded when one remembers that an earlier conversation with Charlie evolved into one that was predicated on an almost equal footing. One also notes the fear that the customer expresses towards the shanty community, seeing the men and women as the harbingers of diseases, which aligns his thinking with the fear of "miscegenation" that lurks in the mind of George Mostert. Charlie extends an invitation to Mostert to have a "wake up time" with the inhabitants of the settlement, and this familiarity prompts Mostert's initial response of "I don't want any trouble," before he succumbs with the thought that "Nobody would see." He is most concerned that no *white person* should see him fraternizing with the *pondokkie* inhabitants. But, when Charlie continues—"I tell you, I was in Egypt with the war. Had me a French goose in Alexandria. *She* didn't min' what colour men she took in. All the blerry same to *her*"—the reaction is aversion: "George

Mostert looked a little shocked and ashamed at hearing a white woman talked about in this way" (*AATC*, p. 40).

Charlie's efforts at inclusivity prompt Mostert swiftly to change the subject in order to regain the upper hand, which epitomizes Homi Bhabha's theory that issues of cultural difference emerge at points of social crisis, so that questions of identity are agnostic; "identity is claimed either from a position of marginality or in an attempt at gaining the centre: in both senses, ex-centric."[38] It is important for Mostert to demonstrate his *difference* from Charlie, while at this stage, Charlie might be seen to represent Fanon's notion that the black man has a choice either to turn white or disappear, he would seem to emulate a white man in his action of sleeping with a white woman. Bhabha disagrees with Fanon's assertion that the choice remains restricted to two options when he posits that there is "the more ambivalent, third choice: camouflage, mimicry, black skins/white masks."[39] Bhabha's assertion involves making a *political* choice, and I would argue that Charlie, in choosing to retell this event, is making a partially veiled political point: Why shouldn't black and white people live together in some sort of harmony? This is further reinforced by La Guma in his delineation of the shanty town that comprises Africans and coloreds who are prepared to share their limited resources in an effort to instil an egalitarian community spirit.

In discussing the geopolitical environment patterned to include the Susie Meyers, Roman and Ronny Pauls triangle in the novel, it has been suggested that La Guma negates hope in their future since they turn their anger on each other and "wallow in their failure and despair."[40] Balutansky describes Ronald as a "delinquent adolescent who commits murder out of spite," which risks the implication that blacks inherently translate their emotions into violence and perpetrate acts of violence without logical foundation or motive. More troubling still, she seems to accept and even endorse a belief in inexorable degradation. Balutansky aligns her thinking with Cecil A. Abrahams's equation that the poor living conditions forced upon the *pondokkie* dwellers result in their allegiance to "cheap liquor, prostitution, family quarrels and violence."[41] This betrays a deterministic analysis. Instead, I would argue that La Guma is intent on demonstrating that it is possible to survive *and* to contribute to the community *despite* the living conditions dictated by apartheid ideology. To this end he presents a much more balanced picture of Windermere's inhabitants than previous critics allow. On the night of the police raid the reader is introduced to feisty Aunty Mina who is not prepared to stand any nonsense from the police officers. This woman, "thick and dark as an oak" stands her ground and uses her anger as a platform for protest:

> "Look here, captain, I'm not giving a damn what you say about it, but what for I'm standing in this rain? You tell me."
>
> The officer laughed. He was arrogantly cheerful, and thought this fat old aunty was rather fun. He had had altercations with her before. He laughed, "Alright, Mina. We'll give you a nice dry van all to yourself. Then you can have a private cell until you appear before the magistrate."
>
> Aunt Mina poked the umbrella at him. It had broken in the wind and rain and now consisted of a handle, a flap of cloth, and several frightful spikes, dangerous as some medieval instrument of torture. The officer reared backwards, fearful of his eyes.
>
> "I'm not frighting for your magistrate, colonel. I paid seven fines awready and I can pay seven more. There! What I'm wanting to know is what for in this rain, hey? You tell me." She possessed the ferocity of an old African buffalo (*AATC*, p. 90).

Aunty Mina is in trouble not because she does not have a pass, but because she brews and sells beer in order to remain economically independent, an illegal act under a government that refused to promote the selling of alcohol in a community-organized way, preferring the promotion of beer halls that were easier to raid and control.[42] Roman and Ronny's behavior may seem to exemplify a dissipated and disaffected lifestyle but others like Freda and Missus Mbuza and even the irascible Aunty Mina, herself the proprietor of a shebeen, avoid reacting in this way.

In the heterogeneous community he creates, La Guma also demonstrates the hybrid nature of language in the context of black South Africa and illustrates the ways in which such language can be commandeered to resist the dominant apartheid-sanctioned Afrikaans. Vernie A. February in *Mind Your Colour: The "Coloured" Stereotype in South African Literature* argues that La Guma uses "the language of the poor, that peculiar mixture of English and Afrikaans, which I shall refer to as *Englikaans*. This type of language seems to define the oppressive circumstances as well as the tragic-comic position of the poor."[43] Although, of course, English was hardly a nonoppressive language, given British colonization, February's "Englikaans" is more usefully reflective of Bhabha's assertion that the natives challenge "the boundaries of discourse and subtly changing its terms by setting up another specifically colonial space of the negotiations of cultural authority." Since this takes place under the surveillance of the authorities, they "change their conditions of recognition while maintaining their visibility;

they introduce a lack that is then represented as a doubling of mimicry."[44] Aunty Mina's refusal to give up her economic freedom and her vociferous resistance to apartheid laws and protocols—such as avoiding eye contact with the whites—points the way forward for the other inhabitants, most notably Charlie who watches her confront the policeman, in their fight against the regime.

For Balutansky and Abrahams, Ronald is little more than a violent thug who kills Susie out of "spite," but the reality of the event is carefully bound into representation of the colonized as a tightly wound spring. In Fanon's terms, "the surface of his skin like an open sore which flinches from the caustic agent; and the psyche shrinks back, obliterates itself and finds outlet in muscular demonstrations which have caused certain very wise men to say that the native is a hysterical type."[45] This is as true of Roman, who fights with Charlie and regularly beats his wife, as it is of Ronny who, in his blind desire for Susie, unthinkingly murders her and therefore inevitably commits himself to a death sentence. La Guma posits the notion that the political development of certain characters is stunted primarily because of their individualism. For example, Roman is described in the following terms: "Between terms of imprisonment, he took to drinking and blamed all his miseries on his wife. Having no capacity for any sort of advanced thought, he struck at those nearest to himself, and he went for them like a drowning man clawing madly over the heads of other drowning shipwrecks, in order to reach the dubious safety of a drifting oar" (*AATC*, p. 64). Roman's instinct for survival is paramount, regardless of the cost to his family. Indeed, having fathered eleven children, he shows little interest in their welfare or well-being. The implicit aim of *And A Threefold Cord* is the need for community values over individual needs, but La Guma ascertains that these will only be met once self-worth replaces self-loathing. Roman, for all his apparent strength, finds it easier to massage his bruised masculinity by beating up his wife than facing the reality of his situation, that is, his emasculation in the face of the politics of apartheid, a politics that refuses to see black people as better than animals. The respite offered by beating his wife's head "with faggots, or her face with his fists," or whipping the children, is shortlived because, in the longer term, the only way to disentangle himself from the situation he finds himself in is to focus his anger against the regime.

Like Roman, Ronny is caught in an economy of individualism where "violence is a cleansing force" that has the potential to "free" him, in Fanon's terms, "from his inferiority complex and from his despair and inaction; it makes him fearless and restores his self-respect."[46] After losing his fight with Charlie, Roman "went back to his hovel and bludgeoned her [his wife], as a sort of compensation for his own defeat" (*AATC*, p. 65), and after hearing the friendly taunts from his brother about his relationship with Susie, Ronny is rejected by her. It is disbarment from her house that promotes feelings of hatred: "The blerry bastard bitch, she better not mess me around . . . She better not bogger around with other *jubas* or I'll give her what for. He stumbled away through the oozing muck and strewn bricks, rage and disappointment mingling with the unravelling knots of hatred" (*AATC*, p. 60). The reason these two related incidents are of particular relevance to this reading is, quite simply, that any understanding of the psyche of the ordinary inhabitant of the shanty town must take into account desire; whether it be desire for a relationship or desire for a better life. Desire for equal treatment as an inalienable right is dismissed by apartheid, which, in turn, fuels petty squabbles and promotes intraracial violence between those who have a little more than those who have nothing. For Susie Meyers, existence is the simple pleasure of escaping the reality of living in poverty in a dilapidated house: "The house had been four-roomed once, long ago, but one side and the back had collapsed, leaving a rambling pile of wet rubble and the gaping interior, like the scene of a bombing. All that was left were a front room and the kitchen," leaving it resembling a "haunted house in a movie picture" (*AATC*, pp. 59–60). Through the lyrics of Bing Crosby and others singing of moonlight and roses, she momentarily transcends the house and the limits of her physical existence. Susie is not averse to befriending men in an effort to exploit them for monetary gain and more concrete hopes of escape. This is precisely the relationship she engenders with Roman, who can offer her money and drink—ephemeral release—while Ronny can offer her nothing but his affection.

Desire for Susie provokes Ronny into killing her. He is warned by Charlie to avoid Susie but the warning goes unheeded and Ronny is drawn to her like a moth to a flame. Susie understands her power over Ronny and sends him away in order to see Roman, which fires the feelings of anger and humiliation in Ronny. But Ronny realizes that he is not strong enough to fight Roman and overcome his rival: "When unappeased, violence seeks and always finds a surrogate victim. The creature that excited its fury is abruptly replaced by another, chosen only because it is vulnerable and close at hand."[47] The rivalry between Roman and Ronny over Susie can best be expressed as the microcosm of the macrocosm that is Charlie's thinking about the oppressive regime. Indeed, Rene Girard's assertions in *Violence and the Sacred* are as relevant to black South Africans in crisis as to this love triangle in particular: "The rival desires the same object as the subject, and to assert the primacy of the rival can lead to only one conclusion. Rivalry does not arise because of the fortuitous convergence of two desires on a single object; rather, the subject desires the object because the rival desires it. In desiring an object the rival alerts the subject to the desirability of the object."[48] In desiring freedom from objectification, blacks look to what the whites have and demand the same things and the same treatment in society as whites receive. This is the first step that Charlie has taken through repeating the ideas of another.

To augment Charlie's dawning politicization, La Guma shows how characters like Freda may only be deemed worthy of their employer's cast-offs, but may turn their employment to advantage through stealing odds and ends to supplement their meager wages. The employment of maids remains common practice in South Africa, and the poor treatment of those in this type of employment under apartheid mirrors the treatment of blacks in general. In an extensive survey, Jacklyn Cock discovered that the majority of white employers believed their maids to be intrinsically inferior, thus mirroring apartheid policy of the superiority of whites. She discovered that white employers did not trust their maids and consequently treated them as little more than ill-paid servants who might undermine the situation at any opportunity. In an effort to counter the problem of low pay, many of Cock's respondents said that they paid their maids with cast-offs and leftover food. Freda finds herself in a position where she needs to work in order to support her children: "domestic servants are most accurately to be viewed as trapped workers. They are trapped in a condition of subjugation and immobility within which they are subject to intensive exploitation."[49] Susie Meyers, on the other hand, is more akin to Willieboy in *A Walk in the Night* since she has no visible means of income and spends much of her time drifting from place to place in order to find chance opportunities for financial support. Her chief interests appear to be music, drink and men. In this sense, she is presented as the "other" to the hard-working and responsible mother, Freda.

The border that is the highway on the edge of Windermere is a dangerous zone for Susie Meyers, who is shown to transgress the mores of apartheid by attempting to prostitute herself with George Mostert in order to get a drink of his brandy, and access to his motor car and money. And while George is tempted by the thought of a sexual encounter with Susie, the thought is quickly pushed away with "One didn't go with coloured girls; it was against the law" (*AATC*, p. 82), reiterating an ingrained belief in his inflexible superiority over the colored girl. It is Susie's desperation for acceptance into a society where her poverty and position are not an issue that finally leads to her death. George Mostert's rejection of her makes her bitter and angry, which leads her to taunt Ronny into believing that she slept with George, and he kills her. In a highly ironic and convoluted sense, the white man is implicated in the death of Susie and the eventual death of Ronny for her murder: his alien presence in the locale is implicitly related to the demise of these two unfortunate characters. In contrast to the circumstances surrounding Susie Meyers's death, La Guma shows how poor housing is directly responsible for the death of Freda's children. In an effort to stave off the cold and to dry the shack, Freda is forced to keep the poorly functioning primus stove lit, but it topples over and sets the *pondokkie* on fire, burning the children. The tragic deaths of the children along with Susie and, subsequently Ronny, might have been avoided had the oppressed been afforded equality of opportunity with whites rather than felt the presence of whites as an infringement.

On the night of Mostert's aborted visit and Susie's death, the shanty town is raided by the security forces searching for dagga and pass law violators. The security police violate the privacy of innocent inhabitants: they disturb Caroline giving birth, label Freda a "whore" and round people up in a superficial show of strength. It is on this night that Charlie hits the police officer:

> "You got any business here, man?"
>
> "Just looking," Charlie said, and feeling suddenly malicious, grinned at the policeman through the wet stubble on his face. "Move off" the policeman said. "Go home. Eff off." Something smouldered inside Charlie and now he said stiffly: "I'm just looking. Can't a man watch his own people being effed off to jail?"
>
> "Oh," the constable said, his moustache moving as he spoke. "Oh, a hardcase bastard, *ne*?" His hands started to grope for the handcuffs on his belt while his shadowy eyes watched Charlie. Charlie said, his voice surly: "Okay, I'm a hardcase. Now what then?"
>
> "Bet you're one of those Communist troublemakers. I'll show you."
>
> Charlie grinned insolently through his surliness. His eyes watched the constable's hands. They were big and red, the colour of wet ham, as they fumbled with the handcuffs. Then the policeman turned his face slightly, to call for assistance, and Charlie hit him suddenly on the exposed jawbone. It was a hard snapping blow, with all his weight behind it, and the policeman's feet left the ground and his back struck it with a hard, muddy, plopping sound,

as if he had been dropped from a great height. Then Charlie was
off, past the flaying khaki-clad legs, heading for the darkness (*AATC*,
p. 91).

This is a crucial incident in the narrative as it is the second time
that Charlie and his thinking are named "communist." This is especially significant since Charlie now has a name for his burgeoning political thinking, as exemplified through his inclusive terminology of
"our people" rather than the narrower focus on self that is displayed by
characters like Roman and Ronny. The individualistic approach of
Michael Adonis is replaced by the kind of community affiliation represented by Joe in *A Walk in the Night*. And, in direct contrast to Adonis
who was unable to stand up to the police officers he encountered,
Charlie takes the step of speaking to the constable as an equal. When
this fails, he strikes him.

Abrahams argues that *And A Threefold Cord* is "more devastatingly pessimistic" than *A Walk in the Night*, since it does not offer Charlie Pauls "a
way out of the nightmare of poverty and terror."[50] Balutansky believes that
while Charlie's hitting the police man offers him "a large measure of personal relief . . . it remains clear that its personal political repercussions are
still very remote."[51] What these critics and others like Ursula Barnett[52] fail
to recognize is that Charlie is now set firmly on the road to understanding
that, in order to stand up to the regime, selfish individualism must be
replaced by a communitarian ideology in which people help each other in
the overthrow of the racist government. Charlie's growing awareness and
his interest in Marxist politics and their potentially liberatory effects is at
the forefront of his mind when he hits the figure of spurious authority.
The act of hitting the policeman is not the futile gesture that the murder
of Susie proves to be, but rather an opportunity for Charlie Pauls to demonstrate his acquisition of what in discussions of resistance has been called
"intellectual penetration."[53] Charlie discerns what lies behind the illusion
of unassailable authority. Initially displaced into violence on behalf of "our
people," the desire for unity overrides the transitory relief in violent ends.
It is in a new condition of selflessness that he proposes marriage to Freda
after she has been labeled a whore by the security officer on the night of
the raid.

In the final analysis, *And A Threefold Cord* represents La Guma's belief
that only as a united community of people can the oppressed begin to
fight against the apartheid regime. The desire for communitarian politics
fulfills an essential need in a narrative that attempts to substantiate a community, "substantializes cultural difference" and that "constitutes a 'split-

and-double' form of group identification . . . through a specifically 'anti-colonialist' contradiction of the public sphere," as Bhabha has it.[54] Only when the oppressed are politically aware will they come to the realization that they are subjects rather than objects. *And A Threefold Cord* might only present the reader with an embryonic community, a community developing out of an underclass, but it produces characters like George Adams in *The Stone Country,* who is prepared to risk imprisonment for his beliefs.

Notes

1. Brian Bunting, "Preface" to Alex La Guma, *And A Threefold Cord* (London: Kliptown Books Ltd., 1964, 1988), p. viii. All further references to this work will be included in the text as *AATC*.

2. Cecil A. Abrahams, *Alex La Guma* (Boston: Twayne Publisher, 1985), p. 72.

3. Alex La Guma, "The Time Has Come," *Sechaba*, 1:IIII, 1967, p. 14.

4. Abrahams, *Alex La Guma*, p. 71.

5. Yvonne Muthien, *State and Resistance in South Africa, 1939–1965* (Aldershot: Avebury Press, 1994), p. 17.

6. H. Britten, *Report of the Commision of Enquiry into Conditions Existing on the Cape Flats and Similarly Affected Areas in the Cape Division,* p. 14. The quotation comes from Muthien, *State and Resistance*, p. 38.

7. Muthien, *State and Resistance*, p. 28.

8. Muthien, *State and Resistance*, p. 75.

9. Ursula A. Barnett, *A Vision of Order* (London: Sinclair Browne Ltd., 1983), p. 132.

10. Marx goes on to say that " . . . the concept of *police*, the concept that the whole of society is there only to guarantee each of its members the conservation of his person, his rights and his property. In this sense Hegel calls civil society "the state of need and of reason." The concept of security does not enable civil society to rise above its egoism. On the contrary, security is the *guarantee* of its egoism." See Karl Marx, "On the Jewish Question" in *The Early Writings* (Harmondsworth: Penguin, 1992), p. 230.

11. Joe Forster, "The Workers' Struggle—Where does FOSATU Stand?," *South African Labour Bulletin*, vol. 7, no. 8, pp. 71–73, quoted in Michael Vaughan, "Literature and Populism in South Africa: Reflections on the Ideology of *Staffrider*," in Georg M. Gugelberger, ed., *Marxism and African Literature* (Trenton, NJ: Africa World Press, 1986), pp. 195–220.

12. Muthien, *State and Resistance*, p. 31.

13. Kathleen Balutansky, *The Novels of Alex La Guma: The Representation of a Political Conflict* (Boulder, Colorado: Lynne Rienner Publishers, Inc., 1990), p. 36.

14. Abdul JanMohamed, *Manichean Aesthetics: The Politics of Literature in Colonial Africa* (Amherst: University of Massachusetts Press, 1983), p. 240.

15. JanMohamed, *Manichean Aesthetics*, p. 243.

16. Frantz Fanon, *The Wretched of the Earth* (London: Penguin, 1990), p. 42.

17. Fanon, *The Wretched of the Earth*, p. 42.

18. Fanon, *The Wretched of the Earth*, p. 42.

19. JanMohamed, *Manichean Aesthetics*, p. 239.

20. Vernie February, *Mind Your Colour: The "Coloured" Stereotype in South African Literature* (London: Kegan Paul International, 1981), pp. 154–155.

21. Mikhail Bakhtin, *Problems of Dostoevsky's Poetics,* trs. Caryl Emerson (Manchester: Manchester University Press, 1984), p. 51.

22. This point is lost on Gerald Moore who argues, in a contradictory manner, that "La Guma has sought to show in Charlie the dawnings of an ideological consciousness, but he has weakened this by making it only a recollection of some half-understood words spoken by a 'slim rooker' with whom he once worked." Moore goes on to say that "La Guma could equally well have shown Charlie as coming to certain decisions by himself (as in his striking of the policeman and his taking in of Freda), without the aid of these rather adventitious appeals to the rooker and his opinions." See Gerald Moore, *Twelve African Writers* (London: Hutchinson, 1980), p. 112.

23. La Guma, "Culture and Liberation," *World Literature Written in English*, 18, 1979, p. 27.

24. P. N. Medvedev, *The Formal Method in Literary Scholarship: A Critical Introduction to Sociological Poetics,* trs. Albert J. Wehrle (Baltimore and London: Johns Hopkins University Press, 1978), p. 7.

25. Medvedev, *The Formal Method*, p. 7.

26. V. N. Vološinov, *Marxism and the Philosophy of Language,* trs. Ladislav Matejka and I. R. Titunik (Cambridge, MA, and London: Harvard University Press, 1973), p. 86.

27. Mikhail Bakhtin, *The Dialogic Imagination,* ed., M. Holquist, trs. C. Emerson and M. Holquist (Austin: University of Texas, 1981), p. 282.

28. Karl Marx and Frederick Engels, *The German Ideology* (London: Lawrence and Wishart, 1989), p. 61.

29. Marx and Engels, *The German Ideology,* p. 64.

30. From DDT Jabavu, *The Segregation Fallacy and Other Papers* (Alice: Lovedale Press, 1928, p. 24), quoted in Gail M. Gerhart, *Black Power in South Africa: The Evolution of an Ideology* (Berkeley: University of California Press, 1978).

31. R. Philips "Communism or Christianity, the Present Day Question for Native Youth," *South African Outlook*, 1 August 1929, p. 148, quoted in Gerhart, *Black Power in South Africa*, p. 38.

32. Karl Marx, *Selected Writings* (Oxford: Oxford University Press, 1990), p. 389.

33. Vološinov, *Marxism and the Philosophy of Language*, p. 23.

34. Medvedev, *The Formal Method*, p. 14.

35. Balutansky, *The Novels of Alex La Guma*, p. 40.

36. Barnett, *A Vision of Order*, p. 132. Emphasis added.

37. Medvedev, *The Formal Method*, p. 7.

38. Homi Bhabha, *The Location of Culture* (London: Routledge, 1994), p. 177.

39. Bhabha, *The Location of Culture*, p. 120.

40. Balutansky, *The Novels of Alex La Guma*, p. 43.

41. Abrahams, *Alex La Guma*, p. 91. From a historical perspective, see also D. Welsh, who in "The Growth of Towns" says "it should be understood that the town is a European area in which there is no place for the redundant Native, who neither works nor serves his or her people but forms the class from which the professional agitators, the slum landlords, the liquor sellers, the prostitutes and other undesirable classes spring." In Monika Monica Wilson and Leonard Thompson, eds., *The Oxford History of South Africa*, vol. 2, quoted in Gerhart, *Black Power in South Africa*, p. 23.

42. See, for example, Elizabeth Thaele Rivkin, "The Black Woman in South Africa: An Azanian Profile" in Filomena Chioma Steady, ed., *The Black Woman Cross-Culturally* (Cambridge, MA: Schenkman Publishing Company, 1981), pp. 215–229, for her discussion of the beer demonstrations of the late 1950s.

43. February, *Mind Your Colour*, p. 156.

44. Bhabha, *The Location of Culture*, p. 119.

45. Fanon, *The Wretched of the Earth*, p. 44.

46. Fanon, *The Wretched of the Earth*, p. 74.

47. Rene Girard, *Violence and the Sacred*, trs. Patrick Gregory (Baltimore and London: Johns Hopkins University Press, 1977), p. 2.

48. Girard, *Violence and the Sacred*, p. 145.

49. See Jacklyn Cock, *Maids and Madams: A Study in the Politics of Exploitation* (Johannesburg: Ravan Press, 1980), p.124. See also Chapters 4 and 5 for a detailed exploration of Cock's findings.

50. Abrahams, *Alex La Guma*, p. 92.

51. Balutansky, *The Novels of Alex La Guma*, p. 50.

52. Ursula A. Barnett sees this incident as "a gesture of protest for his own satisfaction," *A Vision of Order*, p. 135.

53. Richard Bjornson in Christopher L. Miller, "Nationalism as Resistance and Resistance to Nationalism in the Literature of Francophone Africa," *Yale French Studies*, 82, 1993, p. 79.

54. Bhabha, *The Location of Culture*, pp. 230–231.

Chapter 4

Resistance from Within the Prison of Apartheid: The Stone Country

The action of *The Stone Country* takes place in a prison. The novel tells the story of colored George Adams, a political agitator, who is arrested along with his African colleague Jefferson Mpolo for attempting to distribute "subversive literature." The "stone country" of the title is the unnamed prison where we witness, through the subjectivity of George Adams, the confined lives and narrow expectations of his fellow incarcerated and his attempts to converse with them in order to politicize them. The prison setting does not delimit La Guma's political vision or action, but rather enhances it, allowing the prison and its community to function as a powerful metaphor for the situation in South Africa in general; the prison is a microcosm of apartheid South Africa. One critic, Dieter Riemenschneider, approaches this idea when he posits that *The Stone Country* is an example of a South African text that succeeds in blending "the celebration of life and the expression of protest," a reading with which it is easy to concur. But his argument rests on a premise very different from my own, in its focus on Yusef the Turk's assertion that prison is where "people settle their own business and don't have nothing, or little, to do with the white man as possible."[1] This may appear to be the case in the fight between Yusef and Butcherboy to settle their business, but whereas Riemenschneider goes on to argue that "everyday confrontation with South African reality is reduced in these novels," I would emphasize the prison as microcosmic, not of "the interrelationship of black South Africans on the one hand and the confrontation of man with himself on the other hand,"[2] but rather of the interrelationship between apartheid structures and everyday life. As well as exploring the identity of the prisoners existentially, I am interested

in the ways in which the apartheid regime invades even the smallest cor-
ners of characters' lives, whether they sit, for example, in a cell on the
inside, or outside on a park bench. I am interested in the specific ways in
which characters attempt to resist the restrictions of apartheid in a variety
of circumstances.

In cells prisoners are segregated on the same lines as the Group Areas
Act operating across the "Republic." The ID cards that they carry at all
times to exhibit their "name, number and offence" (*SC*, p.23) operate
similarly to the pass books that are mandatory for Africans outside the
prison walls. Elias Tekwane in *In the Fog of the Seasons' End* recalls being
given his passbook, and consequently his "coming to identity" in South
Africa as humiliation, and his cell in the barracks of the location is little
different from those in the prison described in *The Stone Country*. With its
"warren of cells, cages, corridors, and yards"(*SC*, p.17), the description of
the building could serve equally as a description of any location or shanty
town. Even a walk in the park is dictated by the laws of apartheid or
"South African reality" in Riemenschneider's terms. For example, at the
beginning of *In the Fog of the Seasons' End* the black domestic Beatie Adams
has to push far into the park before she is able to find a bench that is not
marked "Whites Only."[3]

With reference to the identity of the South African people, the apartheid State applied the nomenclature of "Bantu," "Coloured" and "Indian" to what it considered to be the three main groups of "Black"
people; the "Europeans" formed the fourth and, in their own eyes, the
primary group. The four groups were subjected to separate laws and
forced to inhabit different geographical positions. With this desire to
divide and rule, the government aimed to prevent mass mobilization of
people and could play different ethnic groups off against one another.
This is the construction of the four pillars to which Robin Cohen
refers[4] and it is predicated divisively and indisputably on race. It rests
on a belief in the superiority of the white/European race over the black
race, in the way that David Lloyd has claimed racism is the attribution
of "essential" characteristics "structured in the first place by the cultural determination of a public sphere and of the subject formation
that is its condition of existence."[5] What this claim encapsulates, then,
is that racism is never "simply" a product of inherent biological differences (skin color, for example) but is a product of a culture, in this
case the culture that claims universality, the culture of the West. Balibar
extends this idea further in his extrapolation of the present as "bound
to the singular imprint of the past" whereby "the heritage of colonialism is, in reality, a fluctuating combination of continued exterioriza-

tion and 'internal exclusion.'" This recognizes that stereotypes of difference are produced and reproduced through colonialist discourse and
orientalist projects. These allow the majority population to be "known"
and allow internal racism to continue on the basis of the colonizer's
superiority to the native. In other words, the "interiority-exteriority
configuration" forms one of the structuring dimensions of racism.[6] It is
this configuration that La Guma deploys in the structuring of prison
life in *The Stone Country*. Blacks, already geographically constricted
within the public institution of the prison, are further separated by
partitioning within the organization of cells according to racial classification.

Since South African apartheid was predicated on the separation of
races, as a structure, it had its roots in the desire of Afrikaners to make
South Africa a "White man's country."[7] One significant method employed in achieving this end was in claiming that South Africa was a
nation of white—specifically Afrikaner—people who identified with
each other and shared similar cultural and ethnic characteristics. Indeed, Dr. D. F. Malan, in his professed effort to promote solidarity
and a feeling of belonging through the usage of Afrikaans as a national
language, asserted that "A living powerful language is born from the
soil of the People's history (*volksgeskiedenis*) and lives only in the mouth
of the People (*volksmond*) . . . Raise the Afrikaans language to a written
language, make it the bearer of our culture, our history, our national
ideals, and you will raise the People to a feeling of self-respect and to
the calling to take a worthier place in the world civilization."[8] Nation-
hood is rooted in ethnic pride, borne out in cultural practices and
productions. We might take Said's description of a State community to
illustrate a further dimension of Malan's call: "To be for and in culture
is to be in and for a State in a compellingly loyal way. With this
assimilation of culture to the authority and exterior framework of the
State go as well such things as assurance, confidence, the majority sense,
the entire matrix of meanings we associate with 'home', belonging and
community."[9] The National Party achieved election to office in 1948
on a platform specifically set against the equality of races: the "natives"
did not belong, South Africa was not their "home."

Apartheid, then, which can be seen as a means of making the mass
population "home"-less (although prison, like the locations, may function
as an alternative "home") in their own country, was a form of colonization
that disenfranchised the majority while ensuring that the white minority
maintained economic and political power. Apartheid was linked to capitalism[10] so that those blacks not prepared to function as cheap labor found

themselves further removed from "accepted society" and were forced to become outcasts with little choice but to steal in order to survive. By living outside the law they were subject to arrest and harassment in the same way as those whom the authorities considered to be politically subversive. *The Stone Country* examines this criminalized population, where political and nonpolitical prisoners are allowed to interact despite the discrepancies in their so-called crimes. La Guma's focus in this novel is on the section of the prison population on remand and awaiting trial. Although the different races are separated, the remand prisoners are allowed to mix freely—that is, no distinction is made at this stage between crimes. The South African prison system enforced a rigorous policy of keeping political and nonpolitical prisoners in separate cells in an effort to avoid potentially subversive situations, and to minimize the possibilities of dissent that so interest La Guma.

The prison, then, functions as a temporary—although at times temporary may become long-term or permanent—"home" for those who are "guilty" of being black. But it is a "home" that mirrors and reflects all that occurs beyond its boundaries. La Guma, himself an experienced prisoner, based *The Stone Country* on his own experiences and those of others who spent time behind bars and professes that "Most of it is completely authentic, but, of course, from my point of view."[11] We are given a firsthand account of prison life, life that is as regulated and restricted for blacks on the "inside" as it is for those on the "outside," in the form of "prison writing" as resistance literature, as I shall argue. The African Jefferson Mpolo highlights the pervasiveness of the segregationist policy of the South African government when he explains to George Adams that "this jail is a small something of what they want to make the country. Everybody separate, boy: White, African, Colored. Regulations for everybody, and a white boss with a gun and a stick" (*SC*, p. 20). This analogy is, in fact, echoed throughout La Guma's fiction. In *Time of the Butcherbird*, for example, Mma-Tau sadly reflects that "We are all in prison, the whole country is a prison. Our people die all the time, of starvation diseases, of murder, of shooting and hanging."[12]

The prison is the forum in which the deranged and dangerous can enact, with impunity, violent and torturous acts upon those who are less powerful than themselves. In *The Stone Country* characters like Butcherboy Williams are described in such animalistic terms that they function to embody the dehumanization process that is apartheid: he is "half-naked, revealing an *ape-like* torso covered with tattooed decorations . . . emblems consistent with his *barbarism*" (*SC*, p. 31 emphasis added). Butcherboy strives to become the aggressor, and temporarily the oppressor, an act that is wryly sanctioned by the white prison officer Fatso, and that ensures that those prisoners who are either new or physically weaker than Butcherboy recognize him as the "cell boss." In this hegemonic relationship power is, albeit briefly, ostensibly wrested away from the whites and vested in Butcherboy who proceeds, in mimetic form, to organize mock courts in which he has the "authority" to mete out punishment, punishment that invariably involves violence and often results in death. In the prison the most violent are encouraged in their violence if it serves to oppress their own peers.

A particularly powerful description of such violence occurs in a novel that does distinguish between "politicals" and "nonpoliticals," D. M. Zwelonke's prison novel *Robben Island* (1973). The nonpolitical prisoners are those he labels "convicts" as they are the "common-law criminals."[13] A distance and lack of comradeship is set up between the two groups whereby the convicts are malicious and readily accepting of the oppressors' methods of torturing the political prisoners. It is worth quoting at length:

> Mr. Mlambo, a twenty-year-stretch man, a short man, was made to dig a pit big enough to fit him. Unaware of what was to follow, he was still digging on when he was suddenly overwhelmed by a group of convicts. They shoved him into the pit and started filling it up. He struggled to climb out, but they held him fast. When they had finished, only Mlambo's head appeared above the ground. A white warder, who had directed the whole business, urinated into Mlambo's mouth [the same kind of humiliation experienced by Elias Tekwane in La Guma's *In the Fog of the Seasons' End*]. The convicts tried to open his tight-locked jaws, but could not. They managed only to separate his lips. The warder pissed and pissed; it looked as if he had reserved gallons of urine for the purpose. From far off we could see showers of urine blown from Mlambo's mouth, as he fought off the torrents of ammoniac liquid, trying to prevent them going down his throat. When the warder had finished, his face was covered with piss. Then vicious blows of fists and boots rained around the defenceless head sticking out of the ground.[14]

In participating in this disgusting act the convicts, it may be argued, are deflecting attention from themselves and are, therefore, less likely to suffer abuse at the hands of the warder. But, by participating, they are also demonstrating that they too would relish the position of power that the warder holds. The spectacle of "punishment" further functions as a warning to those who see it perpetrated that it could be a fate that awaits them too, if they step out of line. This example from *Robben Island* corresponds on one level to the spectacle of the cat cornering the mouse and *almost* beating it to death in *The Stone Country*:

> The mouse, small and grey, had no intention of being devoured, but there, in the hot glare of the sun that practically blinded it, and dizzy from the blows it had received from the cat's great paw, there seemed little hope. . . . A clubbed paw reached out and nudged it. To the mouse it was like the charge of a rhinoceros. Pain quivered through the punched muscles and the hide rippled, but it remained balled up, waiting with tiny, beating heart for another chance to escape the doom that waited for it with horrid patience. . . . Then the cat made a mistake. It rose up on all fours. Without hesitation the mouse streaked straight forward, under the long belly and out past the swishing tail. There was a vast roaring sound in its ears. It was the laughter of the onlookers (*SC*, pp. 124–126).

On one, obviously symbolic, level the mouse represents the black population of South Africa—constantly alert and occasionally beaten down—while the cat is the system of oppression that is enforced by, for example, the prison warders who "felt a natural association with the feline sadism" (*SC*, p. 124). Kathleen Balutansky sees this metaphor as wholly pessimistic as it is juxtaposed with "the narration of Solly's attempt to pass the saw blades to Gus"[15] and Gus's subsequent escape attempt is unsuccessful. But on a deeper level the allegorical meaning of the cat and mouse episode relates directly to the issue of punishment. Punishment is enforced by those who have the authority and, through that authority, power. The spectacle of punishment allows punishment to cascade, directed as it is at all the potentially guilty, as Foucault has elucidated.[16] Watching the punishment, then, may act as a deterrent, but in a prison environment where the warders may behave inhumanely, the desired result of punishment is not deterrence but sadistic pleasure on the part of the warders and those convicts who, like Butcherboy Williams, are complicit in the perpetuation of violent acts.

Although writing in a different context, Foucault has succeeded in summarizing the very mechanisms that have allowed apartheid to operate so emphatically in twentieth-century South Africa. With reference to eighteenth-century Europe, he demonstrates evidence of "an adaptation and refinement of the machinery that assumes responsibility for and places under surveillance their [the people's] everyday behaviour, their identity, their activity, their apparently unimportant gestures; another policy for that multiplicity of bodies and forces that constitute a population."[17] This same "machinery" was very apparent in apartheid South Africa with the repressive state apparatus, in the form of the army, the police force and the secret service, monitoring the movements of the majority population. Foucault acknowledges the power of surveillance, as does Bhabha in "Signs Taken for Wonders" as a means of social control,[18] and La Guma emphasizes its power repeatedly in *The Stone Country*, with the eye in the door "always watching and peeping" (*SC*, p. 41).

As I have noted, in *The Stone Country* the prisoners are not separated according to the nature of their crimes. This is why George Adams, a political prisoner, finds himself contained in a cell of thirty-nine others comprising "petty thieves, gangsters, rapists, burglars, thugs, brawlers, dope peddlars." Of this "human salad"(*SC*, pp. 80–81), Adams is considered to be an intellectual who demands his rights and in so doing offends Fatso who, in his turn, allows Butcherboy to attack him. Yusef the Turk comes to Adams's defense which results in the mock court and the subsequent fight between Butcherboy and Yusef. Butcherboy, for all his physical strength, does not understand that he is merely a pawn in the system of apartheid. He follows the model outlined by Paulo Freire of those who given power use it against their oppressed peers because essentially the context remains one of oppression. In his model Freire argues that the oppressed witness the power of the oppressor and use that power as a yardstick by which to measure humanity. The violence of Butcherboy and Yusef the Turk is not consciously the "auto-destructive" or "horizontal violence" of Fanon or Freire but violence intended to determine leadership or assert equality with that "leader" in the microcosm of the prison. Neither character is politically motivated against apartheid and Yusef's dismissive statement, "Ah, the Resistance. Read about it" (*SC*, p. 38), signals the limited parameters of his political vision.

However, in *The Stone Country*, one can detect a potentially political space that allows for carnivalesque activity to take place. This space is not the carnival square but rather the enclosed prison cell within which all "the laws, prohibitions, and restrictions that determine the structure and order of ordinary, that is noncarnival, life are suspended." According to Bakhtin, what is suspended initially is the "hierarchical structure and all the forms of terror, reverence, piety, and etiquette connected with it—that is, everything resulting from socio-hierarchical inequality or any other form of inequality among people (including age)." In this way, socially constructed distances between people are suspended and "a special carnival category goes into effect: *free and familiar contact among people.*"[19] In the prison cell all pretense of conformity to the white master's sociohierarchical code is suspended and, paradoxically, in the divide-and-rule system of apartheid governance, political and nonpolitical prisoners are allowed to mix freely with one another. Furthermore, the carnivalesque atmosphere opens the door to a world that "unifies, weds, and combines the sacred with the profane, the lofty with the low, the great with the insignificant, the wise with the stupid."[20] In short, this is a world where strategies of resistance can be worked out and plans of escape and overthrow hatched. However, it would be incorrect and misleading to assume that carnival is a totally liberatory practice for it is sanctioned by authority as Terry Eagleton, for example, has argued "Carnival, after all, is a *licensed* affair in every sense, a permissible rupture of hegemony, a contained popular blow-off as disturbing and relatively ineffectual as a revolutionary work of art."[21] Eagleton's note of caution is necessary (and one to which I shall return later), but keeping it in mind, one may proceed carefully with Bakhtin's general formulation of carnival in literary analysis of *The Stone Country*.

An interesting function of the carnival act is the "*mock crowning and subsequent decrowning of the carnival king* . . . Carnival is the festival of all-annihilating and all-renewing time."[22] This is an important feature in that it exposes that authority is never truly invested in the "mock" king and that his position is, at best, tenuous. This is a point that is most keenly illustrated in the fight between Butcherboy Williams and Yusef the Turk. Butcherboy Williams is the cell king by virtue of his reign of terror and brute strength while he has the support of his henchmen. But their support belies their own desires to ascend to the position of cell king or boss and is expressed by the narrator in the following terms: "Brakes Peterson, Pinks, Moos and Squinteye Samuels, flanked him, all demonstrating their allegiance with admiring grins, which however, on closer scrutiny, would have revealed certain elements of hatred and mockery" (*SC*, p. 33). In order to reinforce his position, Butcherboy attempts to set up the "mock trial" in the carnivalesque cell, with the would-be-defendant the Turk. The mock trial not only implicates the other cell occupants but also serves to highlight Butcherboy's role as sovereign law giver and enforcer. However, his authority is further tested when the prisoners demand a "fair fight," one that he must win in order to remain king. Despite the spectacle of a hard-fought and fair fight, Butcherboy is stabbed in the back by an on-looker, the Casbah Kid, who desires revenge following his earlier humilia-tion at the hands of the prison bully. The death of Butcherboy stuns the inmates into silence and swift preparations for sleep immediately follow—each man shuns discussion of the murder even to clarify who committed the deed. Indeed, in his naivety, Adams states that, if questioned, he would tell the authorities that he witnessed the fight, but did not see the murderer. His urge is towards honesty and efficiency in clearing up the situation but it is also misplaced since the authorities would certainly torture him into confessing more than he actually knows, which would inevitably bring their wrath down on Yusef the Turk. He is finally prevented from speaking by the unspoken threat of torture either by the guards or Butcherboy's ex-henchmen.

Foucault claims that torture inevitably affects those who enact it as well as those at the mercy of a system that countenances its barbarism: "It is ugly to be punishable, but there is no glory in punishing. Hence that double system of protection that justice has set up between itself and the punishment it imposes. Those who carry out the penalty tend to become an autonomous sector; justice is relieved of responsibility for it by a bureaucratic concealment of the penalty itself."[23] This results not only in punishment becoming purportedly hidden, in that it is usually removed from the prying eyes of the general public, but also in the birth of organizations that are willing to enforce this insidious "punishment." With the removal of public punishment arrives government-sanctioned oppression in the form of intelligence organizations like the Bureau for State Security, nicknamed BOSS. That apartheid South Africa is a special case is not in doubt: the authorities employed those methods of punishment that had often been outlawed in many other areas of the world. The crux of Foucault's argument becomes clear in this context when he states that the body "serves as an instrument or intermediary: if one intervenes upon it to imprison it, or to make it work, it is in order to deprive the individual of a liberty that is regarded both as a right and property." Therefore, punishment mutates from "an art of unbearable sensations" into an "economy of suspended rights."[24] In South Africa, under the apartheid regime, the daily existence of the majority was that of a people who *lived* the "economy of suspended rights." Take, for example, the lone figure of Joe in La Guma's *A Walk in the Night* who is homeless and has, apparently, only one pleasure, the beach. But the beach will soon be out of bounds to him because he happens to be black, "they're going to make the beaches so only white people can go there. . . . It's going to get so's nobody can go nowhere."[25] In the world of La Guma's novels the only way to survive is to abjure the limited rights offered by the State and to go "underground," joining the network of outlawed criminals that is wholly removed from the realm of white law, or to join the network of political activists opposing white law.

The prison is "very much a place where eveyone takes care of himself," as Cecil A. Abrahams has specified in his discussion of the Casbah Kid and Butcherboy Williams.[26] Taking care of oneself may involve killing another person or remaining silent to hide one's guilt and to prevent consequent reprisals. Abrahams, however, does not appear to take into account a number of other important factors, the most obvious being the way that the Casbah Kid, surreptitiously, and Yusef the Turk, more explicitly, also take "care" of George Adams, protecting him from the treacherous Butcherboy Williams. The second and perhaps more significant factor is that Abrahams ignores, just as the judge does, the social background of the Casbah Kid, the circumstances that lead him to shield his emotions, including those of reciprocal or communitarian feeling. The practices of apartheid permeate the whole fabric of society in this novel and therefore deny autonomy and personal development, resulting instead in an abrogation of self-worth. This lack of integrity in turn promotes a hierarchy of violence that is bolstered by cheap wine and poor familial relations. The circumstances of the Casbah Kid—like those of Willieboy in *A Walk in the Night*—are such that he is a victim of physical abuse at the hands of his father at home: "In a corner, flung there like a rag doll, lay the pinched and stunted body of a boy. He was not dead, but suffering from a savage blow on the head, a broken arm, a blackened eye and various bruises and abrasions. These apart from signs of malnutrition and probable tuberculosis" (*SC*, p. 141). Locked into an existence where self-worth is consistently negated and constantly undermined by comments such as "One kaffir looks just like another,"[27] the oppressed individual is forced to assert his selfhood and sheer existence through violent exploitation of those who are generally weaker than himself, whether in the prison or outside of it. The presence of Adams in *The Stone Country* draws out an empathetic feeling in Albert March that Samuel Asein has outlined as an ideological as well as a humanitarian connection, which "reveals the latter's indifference to the struggle and his helpless resignation to the situation" but progresses towards the Kid's more sensitive response to the "reformist hopes of George Adams."[28] The Casbah Kid is not finally devoid of humanity and, his deep-seated desire for connection with another bears out Bakhtin's claim that the novel "always includes in itself the activity of coming to know another's word, a coming to knowledge whose process is represented in the novel."[29]

The Stone Country is a prison fiction in which politicization under the aegis of common humanity under oppression is as salient as the violence that is clearly, as Ioan Davies has argued, at the center of all prison writing. The locations of prison writings are "precisely those where violence is a prominent feature of resolving social differences, where antagonistic states of mind are manifested in counter-brutalities."[30] For Davies, though, writing of and out of prisons and confronting the reality of violence is finally also a "rearticulation" of humanity.[31] This is, I believe, a significant statement when applied to La Guma's work. His novels attempt to articulate the frustrations of people imprisoned within apartheid who persist in their humanity against all odds. In *In the Fog of the Seasons' End* Elias, resolved upon silence, and consequently tortured to death, discovers that "the amalgam of pain and brutality atomized slowly into the gathering ghosts of his many ancestors which seemed to insulate him from the pain."[32] If he is, in any way, able to transcend the violently persistent pain of electric shocks and beatings, it is through believing the pain to be inchoate and the genealogical human connection to be intensely specific in these his final perceptions. This is not to say that torture, prison and apartheid operate only metaphorically in the context of my reading of *The Stone Country*;[33] La Guma is precise in his rendition of their actualities, and has frequently been described as a "critical realist."[34] Prison is one thing and apartheid another, but prison is an architectural structure that functions to segregate "criminal"—or criminalized—people from the rest of society and apartheid was an "architectural structure" of laws and organizations that maintained a racially segregated society. The two were interdependent since South African prisons, whether Robben Island or the Cape Town prison of La Guma's personal experience, were extensions of the repressive state apparatus of apartheid.

Through the prison in *The Stone Country* and in the prison sections of *In the Fog of the Seasons' End* that serve to bind its structure, La Guma specifies a territory in which the effects of apartheid as an ideology of confinement and containment may be examined. La Guma produces texts about prisons and imprisonment in order to create resistance to the hegemonic "texts" of apartheid culture. His examinations of prison can be viewed in terms of Ioan Davies's definition of prison fiction, which "not only sees the prison experience as part of a criminal subculture, but which sees that subculture as part of an entire dispossessed culture." In this context, "the underground man is underground not simply because he is a criminal but because he comes from an entire society which is underground. This is no imaginary camaraderie of bandits, but a life where prison experience and everyday life intersect."[35] Davies goes on to exemplify his definition through the novels of African American Chester Himes, but his assertion of the predicament of "the underground man" is inclusive of both La Guma's gangsters and his political prisoners, "in the solidarity of the underworld" (*SC*, p. 156). It is the predicament of how to live while incarcerated within the walls of a prison or the boundaries of a "Group Area," which even the judge pronouncing sentence on Albert March the Casbah Kid recognizes.

If some of George Adams's experiences as a colored political prisoner are accepted as commensurate with those of La Guma, Davies's theory that the writer-prisoner identifies with his fellow prisoners politically—and is consequently led to assess his own political attitudes "as they relate to the conditions that place other prisoners in gaol"[36]—may help to specify the way in which the character of Adams functions to provide an analysis of prison life in *The Stone Country*. Riemenschneider sees the character as "catalytic" in the way that he creates an insight into other characters like the Casbah Kid[37] and uncovers their underlying humanity. I would propose that, if catalytic, he is so in that his burgeoning political consciousness in this prison, where even a wink and a grin are seen as rebellious, subversive signals (*SC*, p. 62), is prescient of the commitment of characters La Guma goes on to create in subsequent novels. He foreshadows Beukes and Elias in *In the Fog of the Seasons' End* and the revolutionary consciousness of those soldiers who finally go to war "in the name of a suffering people," and who translate politics into a violent backlash "against an ignoble regime" in the name of "the tortured victims of hatred and humiliation."[38]

The Stone Country also exhibits instances of resistance, an issue that continues to preoccupy La Guma in later works. The character of John Solomons is an indicator of the complexity of resistance in *The Stone Country*. V. A. February describes Solomons as "the clown . . . obsequious, pathetically playing out his role of a 'coloured' buffoon."[39] Solomons, then, recalls earlier representations of blacks in Afrikaans literature, who function as stereotypes. It is possible that La Guma was aware of the existence of such derogatory literary portrayals, since his characterization of Solomons can be rescued from February's negative reading by means of Bakhtin's ideas of dialogism and heteroglossia. Solomons can be accorded a role that serves to demonstrate his particular brand of resistance to apartheid ideology. In a Bakhtinian reading of the novel, the fool has a special function through "not grasping the conventions of society." Strategically, "the prose writer represents a world through the words of a *narrator* who does not understand this world . . . or else the prose writer introduces a *character* who does not understand; or, finally, the direct style of the author himself involves a deliberate (polemical) failure to understand the habitual ways of conceiving the world."[40] La Guma, therefore, introduces a character whose apparent inability to understand is salient in any reading of his resistance to the oppressive nature of apartheid. The narrator informs us that the other convicts "did not bully the little man; he had assumed the position of court jester" (*SC*, p. 122). It is precisely through this subject position that Solomons can be read as a character who, by deliberately feigning ignorance and incomprehension, subverts his allotted position in order to function as the inside man in Gus's escape plan. His stupidity and incomprehension serve to mask his real role. A more concrete example of a Bakhtinian fool is, paradoxically, George Adams himself who fits Bakhtin's elaboration of the fool's function since at its center "always lies a polemical failure to understand someone else's discourse, someone else's pathos-charged lie that has appropriated the world and aspires to conceptualize it, a polemical failure to understand generally accepted, canonized, inveterately false languages with their lofty labels for things and events."[41]

George Adams, then, functions to highlight the incongruities and inequalities in the prison system and his perverse "incomprehension" of the prison rules and regulations serves to demonstrate the monologic nature of prison society, where even the act of asking for blankets can lead to death. Furthermore, in his effort to "educate" his fellow prisoners who have been inculcated into a belief in their own inferiority, Adams's "stupidity" or "incomprehension" is always polemical: "it interacts dialogically with an intelligence (a lofty pseudo-intelligence) with which it polemicizes and whose mask it tears away."[42] Adams is able to demonstrate that the monologic belief system that has taken root in the prisoners can be torn down and overcome. His conversations with the other inmates lead to what Bakhtin describes as "the process of coming to know one's own language as it is perceived in someone else's language," and thereby coming to know one's own belief system via someone else's.[43] This is presented as an essential first step towards coming to self-consciousness. To theorize coming to consciousness in this way is to reveal "Not [only] that which takes place within, but that which takes place on the *boundary* between one's own and someone else's conciousness, on the *threshold*. And everything internal gravitates not toward itself but is turned to the outside and dialogized, every internal experience ends up on the boundary, encounters another, and in this tension-filled encounter lies its entire essence. This is the highest degree of sociality (not external, not material, but internal)."[44]

George Adams succeeds in bringing to *political* consciousness a number of his fellow inmates through conversation and simple acts of generosity on the boundaries of his prison experience. For David Maughan-Brown, George Adams's activism is "notably low-key": "He wins respect by the dignity of example, sharing food and cigarettes and insisting on his rights, rather than by political argument, and the rationale for becoming politically involved presented by the novel is fairly rudimentary."[45] Maughan-Brown's initially helpful analysis is undercut in the respect that these are precisely the first steps to be taken in order to establish political dialogue. Any openly political overture would inevitably result in the authorities hearing about it and subsequently quashing all social intercourse and debate. The act of standing up to the white warder, Fatso, is also politically motivated, because by challenging monologic authority Adams demonstrates that political progress can be made without recourse to violence on this occasion.

I have, through reference to Ioan Davies, considered the extent to which *The Stone Country* as a resistance fiction incorporates conventions associated with prison writings. Sheila Roberts has also attempted to describe the conventions of prison literature, specifically that of South Africa, in other ways. She worries that "it might be more vulnerable to cliché than other kinds because of the very circumstances of the prison environment."[46] But none of the recurrent images she detects—birds as images of freedom, saintly figures, a glorification of life beyond the prison—occur in *The Stone Country* (although in *And A Threefold Cord* a bird flies straight for the free open sky at the novel's end). Roberts's is a general examination of prison memoirs but when she considers fictions, they are those of Nadine Gordimer (*Burger's Daughter*), J. M. Coetzee (*Waiting for the Barbarians*) and Andre Brink (*A Dry White Season*). La Guma and Zwelonke receive no mention, and consequently the breadth of her study suffers. Barbara Harlow's definitions of resistance literature are more useful in locating La Guma's novels in a way that expands the general idea of protest fiction; she differentiates quite sensibly between "prison memoirs" and "prison writing." Her explication of resistance fictions sees them as redolent of liberation struggles that frequently involve armed force and as literature that "calls attention to itself, and to literature in general, as political and politicized activity . . . directly involved in a struggle against ascendant or dominant forms of ideological and cultural production."[47] In other words, this is a literature of *justified resistance* whereby literary theorizing about that literature is inconceivable without reference to the politics that underpin it. Susan R. Suleiman defines the ideological novel as almost inevitably realistic and didactic in validating a political or religious doctrine or philosophical position.[48] Whichever definition one invokes, *The Stone Country* is ideologically grounded. La Guma employs a predominantly realist mode of representation but he is not overtly didactic in intent; rather he leaves gaps and silences that the reader is required to fill. Furthermore, by applying Pierre Macherey's idea that "we always find, at the edge of the text, the language of ideology, momentarily hidden, but eloquent by its very absence,"[49] one can conclude that *The Stone Country* is, on the one hand, a successful exposé of an ideological system that subordinates and oppresses the majority South African population, while on the other an attempt to promote an ideology that counters the dominant one. The power of racist ideology is exemplified through the mind-set of Albert March, who believes that his life is mapped out and that he cannot be anything but a criminal. This belief is reinforced by the judicial system with the judge's speech, which rejects all responsibility as "the State and local authorities are involved in immense expenditure in improving social conditions" (*SC*, p. 166). The judge presiding in March's case firmly upholds apartheid ideology: "It has been advanced, on behalf of the accused, that he comes from a class and from surroundings where violence and drunkenness are an everyday occurrence. This cannot be accepted as an excuse" (*SC*, p. 166). Apartheid ideology, grounded in capitalism, functioned to maintain the divisions in labor which are initially enacted in the domestic setting of the patriarchal home space. For Marx and Engels the division of labor is reliant on the division of the family unit according to specific labor tasks unequally distributed within and across families in which the wife and children are auxiliary to the husband. This leads to what they describe as "latent slavery in the family,"[50] or what Michele Barrett calls the "ideology of domesticity."[51] Indeed, March senior is so entirely caught up in it that he enforces the domestic enslavement of his wife and child with complete violence.

The effect is depressing, and Balutansky believes that *The Stone Country* reveals La Guma's "loss of confidence in the ultimate possibility of the individual activist to have control over his own destiny, let alone to affect that of others."[52] Her point is predicated on the passage where Adams muses:

> You were on the side of the mouse, of all the mice, . . . The little men who get kicked in the backside all the time. You got punched and beaten like that mouse, and you had to duck and dodge to avoid the claws and fangs. Even a mouse turns . . . You were on the side of the little animals, the weak and the timid who spent all their lives dodging and ducking.
>
> Well, that mouse must have been bloody punch-drunk, slap-happy, after that mauling it received. People got knocked slap-happy by life, too, and did funny things. Like that Casbah Kid over there . . . But he's slap-happy. Like he's been in a boxing ring all his life and was slap-happy from it (*SC*, pp. 127–128).

Balutansky believes, then, that Adams' analysis is apolitical and undermines any sense of optimism or any effective political activity. She does not read the escape of prisoner Koppe positively but chooses rather to focus more narrowly on the recapture of Gus and Morgan. She suggests that the Casbah Kid's death "counteract(s) whatever positive elements may have emerged from this episode."[53] I do not share her unrelieved pessimism: George Adams succeeds in politicizing Yusef the Turk, no matter how simply, and he has a profound effect upon the fatalistic young Albert March. Most importantly, this novel also marks the last moments of the ANC's policy of nonviolent confrontation with the white authorities. Therefore, Adams functions to highlight an intermediate stage in the development of political agitators. His belief in a better future and his role in helping to achieve it is wholly unselfish. He has no regrets: "You did what you decided was the right thing, and then accepted the consequences. He had gone to the meetings and listened to the speeches, had read a little, and had come to the conclusion that what had been said was right. He thought . . . there's a limit to being kicked in the backside" (*SC*, p. 74).

Ultimately, through concerted resistance, La Guma foresees that the time will come when South Africa will create new narratives beyond the parameters of apartheid. La Guma's characters witness or participate in the development of a South African revolution as described by Oliver Tambo in "Call to Revolution" and Vincent Goabakwe Matthews, both members of the banned ANC, and in the ANC's own report, which explains the decision taken in 1961 for armed struggle against the police state.[54] That decision involved "sober assessment of the obstacles in our way," as undertaken by George Adams, and "an appreciation that such a struggle is bitter and protracted."[55] Nor was the decision dependent upon a particular episode of resistance like the antipass law march that ended in the Sharpeville massacre in 1960; the ANC's Political Report of 1969 notes the importance of the Defiance Campaign of 1952 but also "the traditional African armies of the past,"[56] the ghosts whose tramping feet and war cries Elias Tekwane hears at the moment of his death. La Guma aligns his characters' experience with the developing forms of resistance that characterized antiapartheid struggles in the 1960s and 1970s and the movement from the demand for freedom (*Mayibuye! iAfrika* "Let Africa return") to the demand for power (*Amandla!*).

Notes

1. Alex La Guma, *The Stone Country* (London: Heinemann, 1974), p. 96. All further references to this novel will be abbreviated as *SC* and included in the text.

2. Dieter Riemenschneider, "The Prisoner in South African Fiction," *ACLALS Bulletin*, vol. 5, no. 3, 1980, pp. 144–145.

3. Alex La Guma, *In The Fog of the Seasons' End* (London: Heinemann, 1972), p. 9.

4. Robin Cohen has identified four fundamental structures of apartheid. These are the monopoly of centralized (White) political power, the ordering of spatial relations (as with the Group Areas Act of 1950), the regulation of the labor supply and the maintenance of urban social control. See *Endgame in South Africa?* (London: UNESCO/James Currey, 1986), p.8.

5. David Lloyd, "Race Under Representation," *Oxford Literary Review*, vol. 13, 1991, p. 68.

6. Etienne Balibar and Emmanuel Wallerstein, *Race, Nation, Class: Ambiguous Identities* (London: Verso, 1991), pp. 41–43.

7. For a discussion of this issue, see, for example, Mokgethi Motlhabi, *Challenge to Apartheid: Toward A Moral National Resistance* (Grand Rapids, Michigan: Eerdmans Publishing Co., 1988), p. 12.

8. Dr. D. F. Malan quoted in D. T. Moodie, *The Rise of Afrikanerdom: Power, Apartheid and Afrikaner Civil Religion* (Berkeley: University of California Press, 1980), p.47.

9. Edward Said, *The World, the Text and the Critic* (London: Vintage, 1991), p. 11.

10. Joe Forster has analyzed apartheid's links with capitalism: "South Africa's history has been characterized by great repression and the major political and ideological *instrument* for this repression has been *racism*. Yet the major effect of this repression has been to very rapidly establish a large capitalist economy . . . Capital did its very best to keep in the political background and as a result this helped prevent the creation of capital's logical political opposite which is a working-class (*sic*) political movement. However, of crucial significance was that capital was growing rapidly and changing its very nature into a more monopolistic, technologically advanced and concentrated form. Its links internationally were growing as was its importance for international capital . . . We find, therefore, that behind the scenes of the great battle between the apartheid regime and its popular opponents that the capitalist economy has flourished and capital emerges now as a powerful and different force." Joe Forster, "The Workers' Struggle—Where does FOSATU Stand?," *South African Labour Bulletin*, vol. 7, no. 8, pp. 71–73, quoted in Michael Vaughan "Literature and Populism in South Africa: Reflections on the Ideology of *Staffrider*," pp. 198–199 in Georg M. Gugelberger, ed., *Marxism and African Literature* (Trenton, NJ: Africa World Press, 1986), pp. 195–220.

11. Cecil A. Abrahams, *Alex La Guma* (Boston: Twayne Publishers, 1985), p. 87.

12. Alex La Guma, *Time of the Butcherbird* (London: Heinemann, 1979), p. 80.

13. D. M. Zwelonke, *Robben Island* (London: Heinemann, 1973), p. 40.

14. Zwelonke, *Robben Island*, p. 14.

15. Kathleen Balutansky, *The Novels of Alex La Guma: The Representation of a Political Conflict* (Boulder, Colorado: Lynne Riennier Publishing, Inc., 1990), p. 76. Interestingly, Samuel Asein sees the cat and mouse episode as relating

directly to the prisoners: "On the individual level, the cat bears a symbolic relation to Butcherboy Williams . . . while the rat . . . comes to stand for any one of the 'little men' in the prison," p. 113. See S. O. Asein, *Alex La Guma: The Man and His Work* (Ibadan: New Horn Press/Heinemann, 1987).

16. Michel Foucault, *Discipline and Punish: The Birth of the Prison* (London: Penguin, 1979), p. 108.

17. Foucault, *Discipline and Punish*, pp. 77–78.

18. Homi Bhabha, "Signs Taken for Wonders: Questions of Ambivalence and Authority Under a Tree Outside Delhi, May 1817" in *The Location of Culture* (London: Routledge, 1994), pp. 102–122.

19. Mikhail Bakhtin, *Problems of Dostoevsky's Poetics,* ed. and tr. Caryl Emerson (Manchester: Manchester University Press, 1984), pp. 122–23.

20. Bakhtin, *Problems of Dostoevsky's Poetics*, p. 123.

21. Terry Eagleton, *Walter Benjamin: Towards a Revolutionary Criticism* (London: Verso, 1981), p. 148, as quoted in Peter Stallybrass and Allon White, *The Politics and Poetics of Transgression* (London: Methuen, 1986), p. 13.

22. Bakhtin, *Problems of Dostoevsky's Poetics*, p. 124.

23. Foucault, *Discipline and Punish*, p. 10.

24. Foucault, *Discipline and Punish*, p. 11.

25. Alex La Guma, *A Walk in the Night* (London: Heinemann, 1967), p. 10.

26. Abrahams, *Alex La Guma*, p. 92.

27. La Guma, *Time of the Butcherbird*, p. 75.

28. Samuel Asein, "The Revolutionary Vision in Alex La Guma's Novels," in *Lotus: Afro-Asian Writings*, nos. 24–25, April-September 1975, p.18.

29. Mikhail Bakhtin, *The Dialogic Imagination,* ed., M. Holquist, trs. Caryl Emerson and M. Holquist (Austin: University of Texas, 1981), p. 353.

30. Ioan Davies, *Writers in Prison* (Oxford: Blackwell, 1990), pp. 16–17.

31. Davies, *Writers in Prison*, p. 18.

32. La Guma, *In the Fog of the Seasons' End*, p. 172.

33. See Davies, *Writers in Prison,* p. 71, for an exploration of how writers as dissimilar as John Bunyan and Breyten Breytenbach use metaphor in prison writing and his conclusion "Inscribing the Everyday," pp. 219–240. See also Harold Barratt's article on symbols and motifs in La Guma's fiction, "South Africa's Dark Night: Metaphor and Symbol in La Guma's Fiction," *The Literary Griot*, vol. 3, no. 2, Fall 1991, pp. 28–36; William Carpenter, "'Ovals, Spheres, Ellipses, and Sundry Bulges': Alex La Guma Imagines the Human Body," *Research in African Literature*, vol. 22, pt. 4, Winter 1991, pp. 79–98.

34. See, for example, Michael Wade's "Art and Morality in Alex La Guma's *A Walk in the Night*" in Kenneth Parker, ed., *The South African Novel in English* (London: Macmillian, 1978) and Cecil A. Abrahams, "Alex La Guma" in Robert L. Ross, ed., *International Literature in English: Essays on the Major Writers* (New York and London: Garland Publishing Inc., 1991).

35. Davies, *Writers in Prison*, p. 127.

36. Davies, *Writers in Prison*, p. 141.

37. Riemenschneider, "The Prisoner in South African Fiction," p. 149.

38. La Guma, *In the Fog of the Seasons' End*, p. 180.

39. Vernie A. February, *Mind Your Colour: The "Coloured" Stereotype in South African Literature* (London: Kegan Paul International, 1981), p. 157.

40. Bakhtin, *The Dialogic Imagination*, p. 402.

41. Bakhtin, *The Dialogic Imagination*, p. 403.

42. Bakhtin, *The Dialogic Imagination*, p. 403.

43. Bakhtin, *The Dialogic Imagination*, p. 365.

44. Bakhtin, *Problems of Dostoevsky's Poetics,* p. 287.

45. David Maughan-Brown, "Adjusting the Focal Length: Alex La Guma and Exile," *English in Africa*, vol. 18, October 1991, pt. 2, p. 21. In calling the jail Roeland Street, Maughan-Brown conflates La Guma's experience with George Adams's since La Guma was himself an inmate at Roeland Street.

46. Sheila Roberts, "South African Prison Literature," *Ariel,* vol. 16, no. 2, 1985, p. 65.

47. Barbara Harlow, *Resistance Literature* (London: Methuen, 1987), pp. 28–29. See p. 120 for her position on "prison writing" and "prison memoirs."

48. Susan R. Suleiman, *Authoritarian Fictions: The Ideological Novel as a Literary Genre* (New York: Columbia University Press, 1983), p. 7, quoted in Lennard J. Davis, *Resisting Novels: Ideology and Fiction* (New York: Methuen, 1987), p. 25.

49. Pierre Macherey, *A Theory of Literary Production* (London: Routledge, 1992), p. 60.

50. For a fuller discussion, see Karl Marx and Frederick Engels, *The German Ideology,* ed., C. J. Arthur (London: Lawrence and Wishart, 1989), especially pp. 52–53.

51. See Michele Barrett, *Women's Oppression Today: Problems in Marxist Feminist Analysis* (London: Verso, 1986). Historically Marx and subsequently critics including Michele Barrett have appropriated slavery as a term with which to metaphorically describe hierarchical structures within the family as well as labor relations. Metaphorical use of "slavery" does not, of course, acknowledge the physical as well as ideological realities of the institution of slavery and the structures of slavocracies.

52. Balutansky, *The Novels of Alex La Guma*, p. 78.

53. Balutansky, *The Novels of Alex La Guma*, p. 76.

54. See Oliver Tambo, "Call to Revolution" (pp. 17–23) and Vincent Goabakwe Matthews, "The Development of the South African Revolution" (pp. 163–175) together with the ANC's "Strategy and Tactics of the South African Revolution," all in Alex La Guma, ed., *Apartheid* (London: Lawrence and Wishart, 1972).

55. ANC, "Strategy and Tactics," in La Guma, ed., *Apartheid*, p. 187.

56. La Guma, ed., *Apartheid*, p. 187.

Chapter 5
▼▼▼▼▼▼▼▼▼▼

Making History: Politics and Violence in
In the Fog of the Seasons' End

In the Fog of the Seasons' End is La Guma's most overtly political novel. In it he discernibly develops the elements of political consciousness raising that had characterized his earlier novels and pushes them towards their logical conclusion: resistance to apartheid regardless of the cost. The nascent community of *And a Threefold Cord* has become in *In the Fog of the Seasons' End* the resistance cell that focuses predominantly on the activities of Elias Tekwane, Beukes and Isaac, but also incorporates, almost in cameo, the part played by whites and Indians in the resistance struggle. While this disparate group of individuals remains a marginal community, it nevertheless promotes and highlights the multi-ethnic constituency of South Africa.[1] La Guma moves beyond the presentation of "men and women who don't talk about apartheid: [who] bear its weals, so that its flesh and blood meaning becomes a shocking, sensuous impact."[2] In this novel, more directly than in La Guma's earlier novels, the regime's mask is ripped from its face and the protagonists appreciate the importance of speaking about and resisting their lived reality under apartheid.

Critical responses to *In the Fog of the Seasons' End* vary dramatically from praise to outright dismissive comments on the value of its political and aesthetic contribution to South African literature. For example, David Rabkin represents the latter view. Believing the characters are representative of the author and delimited as such, he argues that the "heuristic functions of the novel become redundant" and the "artifices of fiction" obscure what would serve better as documentary.[3] Rabkin goes so far as to state that "whatever one may think of La Guma's analysis of the political situation, it is clearly not one which will assist the novelist's art."[4] This

view, which clearly borders on the "art for art's sake" argument, aligns
Rabkin with Lewis Nkosi's "to put it bluntly nothing stands behind the
fiction of black South Africans."[5] Neither view is particularly useful and
both critics seem to be questioning the credentials of South African freedom fighters as creative cultural producers. La Guma's apartheid narratives
are grounded in the "political situation" that Rabkin surprisingly, given his
own involvement in the ANC, dismisses so blithely.[6] A slightly more balanced response is voiced by Adrian Roscoe whose assessment of *In the Fog
of the Seasons' End* in relation to the earlier novels includes the following:
"the prose is slacker, the rich poetic quality of earlier writing giving way to
a more discursive mode, energised only occasionally by figurative touches
as if, perhaps, the artist feels guilty of wallowing in verbal aesthetics when
the cause is so urgent." Roscoe contends that La Guma has become "im-
patient with the subtleties of high art and must spell everything out." He
detects "set speeches from both sides of the struggle" and compares these
adversely to the "delicate suggestiveness" of his short stories.[7] Since La
Guma's fiction was banned inside South Africa, it may have led to the
desire to provide "set speeches from both sides of the struggle" in an effort
to jolt readers into awareness of the daily and deadly cat-and-mouse activities of the oppressors and oppressed. It is clearly a matter of opinion as to
whether the text in question lacks the poetic quality of the earlier novels
or whether the prose is slacker. I, for one, would find it hard to agree with
Roscoe on either point and would suggest that a closer reading of the
novel, particularly of the sections dealing with the Sharpeville massacre
and the issuing of pass books, shows La Guma at his aesthetic best.[8]

At the other end of the spectrum we find critics such as Leonard
Kibera, who sees the novel as reinforcing "a basic historical truth" that
"the oppressed inevitably fight back at some point no matter how dim,
or foggy the future." In his view it is the novel's awareness of history
and the author's own recognition of "the complexities of revolutionary
commitment" that make *In the Fog of the Seasons' End* a major achievement.[9] This view comes closer to La Guma's own ideological stance.
Indeed, La Guma in an interview with Cecil Abrahams stated in quite
emphatic terms that:

> the novel presents an attitude that we have now protested enough
> and that we should now fight. Well, I believe that I had earlier set
> down to a certain extent anyway the situation in our country. All
> of us have bewailed this situation and others will continue to do
> so. But, as I say, trying to convey a picture of South Africa one
> must also realize that apart from people bewailing their fate, there

are also people struggling against it, and that the political and revolutionary movement in South Africa was a part of the South African scene and that one way or another people have always been fighting against this situation. The political and revolutionary movement has to appear somewhere in the picture and I hope *In the Fog of the Seasons' End* is a start. I tried to present the underground struggle against the regime as part of the picture of South Africa.[10]

In my view, in *In the Fog of the Seasons' End* we are taught in a relatively didactic manner that the positions that underpin and that reject apartheid ideology are diametrically opposed and that the only open means of resistance to apartheid is to move from a peaceful Gandhian passive resistance to a campaign that encompasses sabotage and that will inevitably involve risk to life. *In the Fog of the Seasons' End* is essentially the story of an underground resistance cell and the main narrative follows Beukes's activities over a period of approximately five days. But this narrative is framed by another: the narrative of Elias "Hazel" Tekwane and his memories of "freedom" as he is captured and finally tortured to death by the security forces. The novel opens with a Prologue in which we are introduced to the unnamed prisoner, later revealed to be Elias, during his first encounter with "the Major." The Prologue functions to state the two ideologically divergent positions with the Major saying:

> "Look what we, our Government, have done for your people. We have given you nice jobs, houses, education. Education, *ja*. Take education for instance. We have allowed you people to get education, your own special schools, but you are not satisfied. No, you want more than what you get. I have heard that some of your young people even want to learn mathematics. What good is mathematics to you? You see, you people are not the same as we are. We can understand these things, mathematics. We know the things which are best for you. We have gone far to help you, do things for you. Yet you want to be like the Whites. It's impossible. You want this country to be like Ghana, the Congo. Look what they did in the Congo. You people will never be able to govern anything. But we understand that you must have certain things, rights, so we have arranged for you to have the things you need, under our supervision."[11]

This speech exemplifies clearly and rigorously the paternalistic mode of operation that, in La Guma's analysis, underpins apartheid: The blacks are inferior. Therefore they must be governed as children are governed, but they must also be punished when they overstep the mark and begin thinking for themselves. Elias Tekwane is not dissuaded by the rhetoric of the Major's fervent speech, however:

> The prisoner looked at him and thought, he believes he is making a speech, pleading with me to understand. For an instant he wanted to laugh . . . The prisoner ignored him and said to the Major, "You want me to co-operate. You have shot my people when they have protested against unjust treatment; you have torn people from their homes, imprisoned them, not for stealing or murder, but for not having your permission to live. Our children live in rags and die of hunger. And you want me to co-operate with you? It is impossible" (*Fog*, pp. 4–6).

From this opening La Guma launches us into the erratic life of a revolutionary freedom fighter, Beukes. There is no romanticizing of Beukes's role. In fact, La Guma is at pains to show that his existence, and that of his fellow revolutionaries, is characterized by their marginality from others in their designated racial group. Abdul JanMohamed has suggested that "by opting for voluntary marginality the oppressed South African finds a form of liberation in recognition of his own imprisonment."[12] This is an accurate summary of a particular subject position but it does not take into account the psychological effects or repercussions for the individual. As can be determined from the Major's speech, the "ideal" product of apartheid is a nonperson, a nonperson who knows that he or she—or it—belongs at the bottom of the pile; a nonperson who should be satisfied with whatever sustenance the state is prepared to provide in its magnanimity.

Across his fiction, La Guma demonstrates that the overcoming of this subject-position is necessary for real liberation of the individual psyche: only when self-worth and self-affirmation are achieved will one progress to a condition in which one may stand up for one's rights and the rights of others. Elias Tekwane sacrifices his life for the cause; Beukes inhabits the margins in an almost paranoid state, forfeiting ordinary life with his wife and child for the greater good. Even the future of Isaac—who manages to escape South Africa in order to receive military training—remains uncertain. I concur with JanMohamed that the actions of these men allow them a degree of freedom, but it is a limited freedom, achieved, if at all, by the grotesque subordination of the masses, for if the mass population stood up and rebelled, that rebellion would be far easier to quash

than that of the "invisible" few. Here I refer specifically to the pass protest at Sharpeville where sixty-seven innocent people died, while one hun-
dred and eighty-seven more were wounded.[13] The task of Beukes and
others like him is to educate the people and, when necessary, to mobilize them through the exchange of information, and to recruit new members to the resistance cell. Therefore, I find it difficult to understand
why Abrahams is satisfied with making such a blanket statement as the
following: "Like the artisans and the lower middle classes that have succeeded in rising slightly above the living standards of the majority of
their compatriots in the urban slums and ghettoes, many of the oppressed
care little about the plight of the majority and instead wrap themselves
inside a cocoon of unreality."[14] Abrahams' comments are premised on
the scene in which Bennett, an acquaintance of Beukes, lets him down
when he proves unable to provide him with safe lodging as promised.
But I would argue that the character of Bennett is represented as more
thoughtful than Abrahams gives him credit for being. Bennett actually
tries to do Beukes a favor, and this is of particular import when we re-
member that the problem lies with Bennett's wife. In a culture where
unannounced searches by the security forces and the widespread practice
of informing were commonplace, there will inevitably be the paranoid
fear of punishment at the hands of the security forces for those who aid
the resistance. Indeed, the Major tells Elias that "We know all about
you. You see, man, it is no use, because we have people working for us,
for the good of your people, and they co-operate with us" (*Fog*, p. 5).
Furthermore, the majority population is discriminated against at every
level so it would seem spurious to suggest that those who do not openly
participate in the resistance struggle are somehow living "inside a cocoon of unreality."

La Guma goes to some lengths to demonstrate the regular encroachment of what many might consider "fiction" into the territory of "reality."
Two instances demand particular attention. The first is where Beukes is in
a taxi and notices the taxi driver's reading material—a gangster novel—
which prompts him to think:

> It's like a bloody gangster picture itself. Life had become mysteri-
> ous rides, messages left in obscure places, veiled telephone conver-
> sations. The torture chambers and the third degree had been trans-
> ferred from celluloid strips in segregated cinemas to the real world
> which still hung on to its outward visible signs of peace: the shop-
> pers innocently crowding the sidewalks, the racing results, the Sat-
> urday night parties, the act of love.

> Beukes remembered the electrode burns on the hands of pris-
> oners. Behind the picture of normality the cobwebs and grime
> of a spider reality lay hidden. Men and women disappeared
> from sight, snatched into the barred cells of the security police,
> into the square rooms with the Public Works Department tea-
> cups and the thin-lipped, red faced men with mocking eyes
> and brutal minds, into the world of clubbed fists and electric
> instruments of torture, the days and nights of sleeplessness, the
> screams (*Fog*, p. 25).

Although the passage might read like a treatment for a film, it is more accurately an evocation of the realities of those who are oppressed by apartheid. On the surface, life carries on as "normal," within the confines of the restrictive apartheid laws, but scratch beneath the surface and an alternative reality is discovered. The second incident is linked to the first in that after Beukes has been shot in the arm, while making his escape from the raid that results in Elias Tekwane's arrest, he thinks "Dammit, it's like a bladdy Western movie" (*Fog*, p. 147). Taken together, the two scenes neatly show how the resistance fighters live on the edge of a reality that blurs into fiction. La Guma aligns the majority population with Native American Indians, poorly organized and armed in the face of the white frontiersmen and the cavalry; they are flies trapped on the web of apart-heid. But more than this, these two scenes are indicative of the painful treatment that those who transgress the monologic world of apartheid can expect.

After the initial shock of being captured, Elias Tekwane is told "No more lawyers. Those times are past. We don't give a bogger for them. We even keep the magistrates away now" and that the security forces, as rep-resented by the two officers, will "make you shit" (*Fog*, p. 2). He is then sent sprawling into a cell. La Guma here alludes to the fact that the security police had been granted massive powers with the General Law Amendment Act of 1963. It allowed them to hold suspects indefinitely without necessarily charging them at all, since the suspects had no re-course to legal representation of any kind. This is obviously a civil liberty issue but the state did not concern itself with the civil liberties of those it considered to be agitators and saboteurs. The act was passed as a result of the infamous 1956–61 Treason Trial, and as a reaction to the increase in nonviolent, passive antipass campaigns that culminated in the PAC-orga-nized demonstrations at Langa and Sharpeville. Once in the cell nursing his grazed face, Elias Tekwane is jolted into comprehension of the speci-ficities of his situation:

He had been anticipating a test of endurance for a long time, but now he realized that he did not really know what was going to happen to him. Behind the ugly mask of the regime was an even uglier face which he had not yet looked on. You went through the police charges in the squares, the flailing clubs, the arrogant rejection of all pleas and petitions, blood dried on the street like spilled paint where a shot body had lain, but here, behind the polished windows, the gratings and the Government paintwork, was another dimension of terror (*Fog*, p. 3).

Elias comes to a shocking realization of what lies ahead of him: a terror the like of which he has never before encountered. He is thrown into a situation where he will struggle to survive, where he will be tortured in order to betray the members of his resistance cell. Elias and the Major's henchmen will be the human embodiments of the cat and mouse that the reader encounters in *The Stone Country*; unfortunately, the mouse will die.

Frantz Fanon's statement in *Black Skin, White Masks* that "only for the white man the Other is perceived on the level of the body image, absolutely as the not-self—that is, the unidentifiable, the unassimilable" is an adequate summary of the position adopted by the enforcers of apartheid rule in their ideology.[15] My contention is grounded in the equation whiteness = superiority. Whiteness is a self-perpetuating term; ostensibly transparent, it colonizes normality and designates all "others" as racially marked. The sportsman and his young colleague think nothing of beating Elias Tekwane or of labeling him a baboon, an animal. Yet the Major can acknowledge that "He is no baboon. He is one of the 'big shots,' the 'top brass' in these parts" (*Fog*, p. 6) and his view, acerbically couched as it is, is indicative of the growing realization that the identity of his prisoner is not as static a construct as he might wish. In his "Foreword: Remembering Fanon" Homi Bhabha argues that "it is not the Colonialist Self or the Colonized Other, but the disturbing distance in-between that constitutes the figure of colonial otherness—the White man's artifice inscribed on the black man's body. It is in relation to this impossible object that emerges the liminal problem of colonial identity and its vicissitudes."[16] This is a key liberatory aspect of the self/other relationship. Bhabha takes it further to suggest that identification is "always a production of an 'image' of identity and the transformation of the subject in assuming that image." In this dialogic formation of identity it is the "return" of an image which "bears the mark of splitting in that 'Other' place from which it comes."[17] This is precisely what the apartheid regime attempted to curb. For the regime to survive, it had to mark the black population with its monologic stamp and reinforce the notion of black inferiority. As a result, the hybrid other, the black man as a product of white society, was marked as a mimic man, the man who questions the ideology of "separate but equal." Mimicry unsettles colonial discourse, undermining its authority through a complex strategy. In Bhabha's terms it is a process of disavowal: "Mimicry is thus the sign of a double articulation" that "'appropriates' the Other as it visualizes power. Mimicry is also the sign of the inappropriate, however, a difference or recalcitrance which coheres the dominant strategic function of colonial power, intensifies surveillance, and poses an immanent threat to both 'normalized' knowledges and disciplinary powers."[18] The question that arises for the regime is that of how to stamp out subversive behavior, behavior that inevitably asks questions, disturbs and makes demands of the State. Such questioning is necessarily met with force and, in the case of *In the Fog of the Seasons' End*, with torture, and death.

Interrogators seek neither elucidation nor clarification, as J. U. Jacobs argues, but "a pre-established result, which is to make other people see eye to eye with themselves."[19] This point is extremely telling in the South African apartheid context, for the interrogators maintained their belief in their infinite superiority over the black man. His status remained that of an animal, albeit an intelligent one, and it was their job to break him down, to make him talk and confess all. Ironically, in *In the Fog of the Seasons' End*, the interrogators only succeed in killing Elias and therefore lose any opportunity they might have had to obtain the information they ostensibly required. This action reinforces the idea that those who torture are not finally as interested in gaining information, as they are in their own sadomasochistic enjoyment of the act of torture itself. The issues are played out intimately and succinctly in the following exchange:

> "Everything. I want you to tell us the names of all who work with you, where you meet, and so on. Who is your contact with the central committee or the high command—is that what you call it? If you speak now, you will be okay, you will save yourself a lot of trouble. If you don't talk now, you will later on, but then all the trouble that you go through, and the damage, will have been for nothing. You know we need not bring you to court; we can hold you indefinitely, merely on suspicion."
>
> The prisoner smiled a little and said: "But if, as you say, we are wrong and only making trouble, and that nobody believes us, why are you so concerned with us?" (*Fog*, p. 5).

It is quite clear that the Major's view is entirely myopic since Elias Tekwane's response is met first with verbal violence and then with physical violence and, consequently, the pain that prefigures his death.

Despite the shocking impact of the torture on Elias, La Guma's representation of it is controlled and restrained; he is tempted neither to sensationalize nor to sanitize. The reader is presented with the simple facts and is allowed space in which to judge the interrogators' methods. What is especially pertinent in this scene is the way in which La Guma draws the elements of what is termed the DDD syndrome together and permits each of the specific elements to dominate in turn. In his study of detention and torture in South Africa, which draws on the findings of Farber, Harlow and West, Don Foster summarizes DDD: "Debility is produced by semi-starvation, fatigue, disease, constant humiliation and chronic physical pain through beatings and other physical abuses . . . Dependency is the product of the totalitarian regime imposed by the captors and is demonstrated to the captives by deprivation of those factors needed to maintain sanity and life . . . Dread is simply the state of chronic fear induced by captors through a range of threatening devices."[20] Taking debility first, Elias is subjected to the humiliation of being urinated on by the sportsman before being battered by each of them in turn:

> The prisoner fought for breath and struggled to avoid the blows. He could smell his own vomit and the detective's urine on his clothes. Strength drained from his body like water from a burst bottle. The young one drew his revolver and struck at the prisoner's writhing shins with the barrel. Pain sprang through his legs with the stab of skinning-knives. His legs went numb and he hung by the manacles while the young man smacked him with the pistol barrel. He cried out in pain—pain from his legs, from his battered body, from the manacled wrists by which he dangled (*Fog*, p. 7).

Subsequently, in a reminder that there will be no relief, Elias is warned, "There will be more to come, you *donder*. You will talk" (*Fog*, p. 7). This is the element of dread, the gnawing recognition that the ritual of punishment has only just started. Debility and dread have the immediate effect of throwing Elias's mind into a panic, wherein he finds himself remembering an incident in which he almost drowned: "Far away, he was suddenly a child again and he had fallen into the dam and was drowning, smelly water filling his nose, while his companions ran up and down the bank in terror" (*Fog*, p. 7). This moment functions most precisely as a premonition that this time he will not be saved; he will die at the hands of his tormentors who are the terror. By the end of the Prologue, the reader has been introduced to the ugliest aspect of apartheid and can only assume that the prisoner will be unable to endure the suffering inflicted upon him and will eventually crack and recount for the authorities what they wish to hear.

The reader is not allowed back into Elias's cell until the penultimate chapter of the book as witness to his brave silence while he is electrocuted. There are two significant points that I would like to make here, related to Elias's desire to talk but not to tell, and to his recollection of his ancestors. Taking the former, it is clear that in this representation the pain inherent in the act of torture has the effect of destroying language. Most specifically in the South African context, "torture also mimes (objectifies in the external environment) this language-destroying capacity in its interrogation." In fact, language is destroyed, demolished or, as Elaine Scarry has it, "reversed or uncreated" through and in torture.[21] Elias's response to pain is simple: He screams—"He had anticipated violence, but not this, not this. Talk, talk, talk his mind told him while his body jerked and jigged like a broken puppet on badly-manipulated strings" (*Fog*, p. 173)—but he cannot speak; he has become inarticulate, voiceless. The regime has achieved one of its primary aims; it has succeeded in silencing a subversive element. However, within this silent resolve a desire for a dignified death prevails. Elias is taken back in history to a time when his ancestors fought the first white oppressors, the colonists. The pain of torture is mixed with the memory of those brave soldiers who, with their inferior weapons, stood their ground. This recalls for Elias the fact that between that war and the one he is fighting there is a historical continuity. The generations that have passed and the generations that will follow will not rest until South Africa is free of the oppressor and extricated from the continuity of resistance. In this Elias reenacts what Fanon describes in the following terms: "the memory of the anti-colonial period is very much alive in the villages, where women still croon in their children's ears songs to which the warriors marched when they went out to fight the conquerors. At twelve or thirteen years of age the village children know the names of the old men who were in the last rising, and the dreams they dream in the *douars* or in the villages are . . . dreams of indentification with some rebel or another, the story of whose heroic death still today moves them to tears."[22] The representation of Elias at this juncture also recalls Nelson Mandela in his statement at the Rivonia trial. He refuted the State's claims that outside agitators had influenced the development of the anti-apartheid struggle: "among the tales they related to me were those of wars fought by our ancestors in defence of the fatherland. . . . I hoped then that life might offer me the opportunity to serve my people and make my own humble contribution to their freedom struggle."[23]

La Guma's reconfiguration of an African ancestral past has prompted some rather misinformed responses from his critics. For example, Kathleen Balutansky believes that Elias's final victory over his tormentors comes as a result of his "transcendence of all the physical reality into the mythical realm of African history in which he joins his glorious ancestors."[24] Her point echoes Abdul JanMohamed's statement that because Elias has been "exposed through folklore and myth to the oral history of his ancestors who fought with the initial Afrikaner and British invaders," La Guma "uses the African past, *which is more powerful because it is a mythic past,* to sustain a character's dignity and beliefs in his present task and in the future community."[25] The problem with these two related positions is that they each seek to demean the function and impact of the original anticolonial soldiers, without whose sacrifice and courage overt anticolonial struggle would not have existed in modern South Africa. Official South African history of the apartheid era is inextricable from its efforts to diminish the achievements of the first African freedom fighters and from its focus upon the victories of the white armies. Terms such as "mythical" and, even worse, the "mythical realm of African history" do little more than reproduce colonialist discourse with its attendant aim of writing African history out of reality. The implication is that the first warrior/fighters are imaginary figures who did not in fact exist.

La Guma is at pains to take the first warriors out of an anthropological exhibition in a museum and make their concerted historical efforts count explicitly within a South African historical world view. Throughout the narrative, reference is made to these "first ones" and the impact their actions now have contiguously on the so-called terrorists, the modern resistance fighters. As Beukes wanders through the museum for his rendezvous with Isaac, he approaches an exhibit where he sees that "Bushmen had hunted with bows and tiny arrows . . . red-yellow dwarfs with peppercorn hair and beady eyes. Beukes had thought sentimentally that they were the first to fight" (*Fog,* p. 14). Like La Guma, Fanon, in another context, is aware of the importance attached to ancestors: "the people make use of certain episodes in the life of the community in order to hold themselves ready and to keep alive their revolutionary zeal." Most significantly, they make use of the role played by resistance figures at the time of conquest, "the great figures of the colonized people are always those who led the national resistance to invasion." For Fanon, they "all spring again to life with peculiar intensity in the period which comes directly before action." Ancestors are understood as portentous, their presence precipitating contemporary resistance: "This is the proof that the people are getting ready to begin to go forward again, to put an end to the static period begun by colonization, and to make history."[26] For the apartheid State, South Africa was an empty space that could be written into existence, an existence that reflected the role and the needs of the white man at the expense of the indigenous population. The importance of history cannot be underestimated, and it underpins any reading of *In the Fog of the Seasons' End*. For the apartheid regime, history began with their conquest of South Africa and with the arrival of Jan van Riebeeck. Indeed, Flotman tells Beukes that the regime's strict monitoring of the educational syllabus demands that lecturers tell their students that "everything that happens is ordained by God and that it's no use, even sinful, trying to change the order of things. The Boer War was a sort of holy crusade, evolution is heresy and nobody existed in this country before Jan van Riebeeck arrived" (*Fog*, p. 86). The centrality of history in postcolonial theory should not be overlooked, especially when certain applications of that theory have tended to obscure its significance. Anne McClintock and Aijaz Ahmad have most usefully theorized the ways in which conceptualizing history via the triadic periodizing phases— precolonial, colonial and postcolonial—"privileges as primary the role of colonialism as the principle of structuration in that history." This is to diminish precolonial history so that "whatever comes after can only be lived as infinite aftermath."[27] In another context, Bill Ashcroft *et al.* also concede the importance of history to the (once) colonized people when they argue that its significance lies in its origins as a discourse and discipline "coterminous with the rise of modern colonialism, which in its radical othering and violent annexation of the non-European world, found in history a prominent, if not *the* prominent, instrument for the control of subject peoples."[28] This may invest too much in the power of discourse, as evidently Peter Childs and Patrick Williams believe when they ask whether history is "'the prominent instrument for control of subject peoples'—rather than, for example, armies, police forces, bureaucracies, laws or economic policies."[29] However, the role of history in resistance struggles is particularly significant and apt to be overlooked, and it is this last point that La Guma reiterates throughout *In the Fog of the Seasons' End*.

If we accept that history is constructed of a series of epistemes, then oppressive ideologies such as apartheid are guilty of perpetuating what Gayatri Spivak has described as "epistemic violence." It is generally agreed that epistemic violence is "an interested construction," rather than "the disinterested production of facts."[30] What this means for the colonized is that "the project of imperialism is violently to put together the episteme that will 'mean' (for others) and 'know' (for the self) the colonial subject as history's nearly-selved other."[31] This construction leads to hegemony, whereby the colonizer is the central figure and the colonized is pushed to the boundary; once marginalized, the colonized subject may be represented without any recourse to reality at all.[32] The centrality of history in *In the Fog of the Seasons' End* has been underestimated by many critics. David Rabkin and Piniel Viriri Shava, by choosing to focus on the ways in which the characters' "histories" are deployed, ignore the much more significant aspect of reclaiming history in order that it might play a part in the modern resistance struggle. By this I do not suggest that history is deployed by La Guma as the idyllic return to the past, which Anthony Chennells appears to suggest.[33] Rather, the emphasis on African traditions may be seen to offer possibilities of resistance, in the way that Bhabha has discussed:

> The "right" to signify from the periphery of authorized power and privilege does not depend on the persistence of tradition; it is resourced by the power of tradition to be reinscribed through the conditions of contingency and contradictoriness that attend upon the lives of those who are in "the minority." The recognition that tradition bestows is a partial form of identification. In restaging the past it introduces other, incommensurable temporalities into the invention of tradition.[34]

In this way, tradition may be mobilized. For Elias Tekwane the memory of his ancestors opens his historical understanding of the ill treatment he received at the hands of his white employer, Wasserman, and contextualizes some of the quotidian inequalities that he and his peers have faced. This, in turn, instigates his militancy as can be witnessed in his participation in the laundry strike and his eventual entry into resistance politics.

The apartheid state's paranoid fear of "the black man" was exemplified through the means by which it controlled and restricted the avenues a black subject might take towards what might be termed "enlightenment." Education was one such avenue, but black people were debarred from fulfilling the inherent aim of education, to develop one's individual and collective claims to self-knowledge. It is clear that the restrictive social conditions did not allow for development, but forced the black person to the social margins. The education system necessarily mirrored the apartheid ideology of separate development and therefore forced the differently designated racial groups to attend different schools in order to perform their separately allotted social functions. Linked to this notion of separate development was the controlling element of curriculum management. In the Major's speech, the superficially simple question of whether black South Africans should have access to a subject such as mathematics is a highly emotive political issue. As Minister of Native Affairs, H. F. Verwoerd argued during the Second Reading of the Bantu Education Bill in 1953: "What does it help to design a curriculum for the African child which is, in the first place, European?. . . . What does it help to teach a Bantu child maths, something which he could not use practically . . . People should be educated according to the life chances of the spheres within which they live. Some Natives would have to be educated to serve their own people in the higher occupations . . . But apart from these people who can be employed in their own communities, others would have to receive education according to their life chances."[35] In establishing and maintaining apartheid the State demanded that the education of blacks be inferior to that of whites and that it serve no other purpose than a utilitarian one, delimiting the "life chances" of individuals and groups.

Education is not the accumulation of knowledge, in its wider sense, but rather a pragmatic necessity that might then be utilized to delimit other blacks. What this process does is to prevent the development of thinking individuals, although, paradoxically, as Beukes remembers, it may also serve to open the minds of young blacks to the oppressive way in which education is managed. On his way to meet Flotman, Beukes recalls his first visit to a white school: "That was really the first time that the little boy had realized that children called 'White' attended separate schools" (*Fog*, pp. 83–84). The impact of this childhood realization is not lost on the adult whose activism relates specifically to the policy of separate development that remains tenable only while there is a South Africa in which groups of South Africans are treated differently. In short, inherent in a divisive education system is the intention to indoctrinate the authochthonous population into believing in their inferior status. As Aletta J. Norval has argued, the introduction of a bill that addressed "Bantu" education served two purposes. First, "the reversal of contemporary trends associated with an egalitarian and universalist missionary education which fostered individualism and undermined tribal bonds" and second, "the consolidation of the key role of the Afrikaner as the guardian of the African people."[36]

The first element or function is clearly one that required the African to maintain an attitude of tribal affiliation that would enable the State to control the individual through the group in the person of the tribal chief.

Furthermore, communal responsibilities necessarily militated against individual ambitions, and placing tribal lands under threat of confiscation, under the aegis of the Native Land Act, forced Africans into a cycle of precarious readjustment to an increasingly tenuous geosocial position within the apartheid state. When people are relocated in *Time of the Butcherbird*, or the lands are too poor to sustain a family, then the younger members are forced into urban environments—as Elias is—in order to support the rest of the family, and are made to feel their marginalization. This is a point to which I shall return, but one of the abiding functions of apartheid was the supposed maintenance of "the" African's "authenticity," that is, to keep the individual grounded in his or her perceived culture, with no real opportunity for economic advancement in any case, since the survival of an economically viable "tribal" group is constantly under threat. To this end, the regime began to make distinctions between "good" and "bad" black people, where the "good" black knew his or her place. The argument advocated that the majority of blacks were "good" but were nevertheless susceptible to the influence of the "bad." In contriving such an image the government was able to lay the blame for the Sharpeville pass protest at the feet of the African National Congress and the Pan Africanist Congress and use the Unlawful Organisations Act (1960) to ban the ANC and PAC. The regime's propaganda contended that trouble in rural areas was largely due to the urban-based ANC and PAC, and to this end it declared that it would quash the "reign of terror" the two organizations had supposedly conducted. The ANC and PAC were labeled terrorists by the apartheid government, which alleged that "cruel and barbaric intimidation," including assault and threats to "innocent" people, was the method used by the resistance to mobilize the people.[37] Apart from the occasional police raid, the country dwellers of South Africa were left to fend for themselves, except when the Land Act required them to leave their homes and be relocated. The reasoning behind this was simply a question of economics: There were too many mouths to feed and the land was too poor to sustain a mass population, so in order to survive one was forced to try to find employment in an urban area, which suited the regime perfectly as it ensured a cheap and constant supply of labor. The point was not lost on La Guma: "The young men were forced to contract themselves, for the debts with the shopkeepers had grown and the land did not provide enough to pay them and feed the families" (*Fog*, p. 80).

The move to the city has been schematized by a number of liberal writers in their deployment of the "Jim comes to Jo'burg trope."[38] If, as some critics have argued,[39] Elias in *In the Fog of the Seasons' End* is representative of "Jim comes to Jo'burg," then we must also acknowledge how

this trope is subtly inverted in the novel. Elias comes to the city in order
to work and to support his mother, who remains in the country. But in
coming to the city, he is also exposed to the reality of the struggle against
the hegemony of the apartheid government. He remembers going back to
the country after having spent three years in the city and thinking: "There
was ignorance in the countryside too; in that part of the land one did not
see any meetings like the ones which were held in the city. In the cities it
was not easy to avoid the movement. The people stirred under the weight
of tyranny, then went to the meetings in the squares, halls, houses, to
listen to the speakers" (*Fog*, p. 132). For Elias the experience of urban
living is not alienating, but rather adds weight to his growing awareness of
the inequities between blacks and whites. As a young man he was sacked
from his job in a white man's shop, because he dared to attempt to sign up
to fight against the Germans in World War II. His dismissal from such
menial employment forces him back onto the land where "anger grew
inside him like a ripening seed and the tendrils of its burgeoning writhed
along his bones, through his muscles into his mind. Why, he thought,
why, we are as they are, except that their lands are bigger and they have
more money, and all we do is work for them when we are not trying to
make a little corn grow among the stones of our own patches" (*Fog*, p.
79).

Elias's first encounter with white authority comes about through the
issuing of his pass. He is humiliated at an early age, but he needs the
pass in order to leave the countryside. In this context the countryside
bears little resemblance to the agrarian idyll that has characterized South
African literature from the Afrikaans farm novel on, but is presented as a
wasteland that forces the economically disenfranchised out and away to
discover those other and different forms of economic wasteland allocated
to them on the edges of the cities, in camps and shantytowns. In sustained and evocative rhetoric, La Guma explains how apartheid functions
to write Africans into existence in its own terms and terminology, therefore continuing the practice of colonial discourse and epistemic violence.
The ironic undertone belies the fact that this insidious practice is little
more than an overt form of surveillance: "When African people turn six-
teen they are born again or, even worse, they are accepted into the mys-
teries of the Devil's mass, confirmed into the blood rites of a servitude
as cruel as Caligula, as merciless as Nero. Its bonds are the entangled
chains of infinite regulations, its rivets are driven in with rubber stamps,
and the scratchy pens in the offices of the Native Commissioners are
like the branding irons which leave scars for life" (*Fog*, p. 80). La Guma
outlines explicitly how the authorities can stop and demand sight of a

pass, and demonstrates the function of that pass: it is required for the purpose of travel, work, visits to and from the family home, to indicate right of abode in a district other than the district where one was born, to assign one existence. Without the pass one can expect harsh treatment, including imprisonment, "or all permits cancelled so that you cease to exist. You will be nothing, nobody, in fact you will be decreated. You will not be able to go anywhere on the face of this earth, no man will be able to give you work, nowhere will you be able to be recognized; you will not eat or drink; you will be as nothing, perhaps even less than nothing" (*Fog*, p. 82). The black man is in this way written into existence as a ward of the apartheid state and this form of epistemic violence finds its zenith in the pass book that all black people were compelled to carry.

La Guma's representations are sharply pragmatic even when rhetoricized via metaphor and simile. Simon Gikandi contends that gnosis and praxis are closely linked concepts in *In the Fog of the Seasons' End* and cites Elias Tekwane and Beukes as examples of characters who clearly perceive this link, while he suggests that Beattie and Tommy do not, as "knowledge demands some kind of action."[40] The need for praxis is articulated by Beukes, who prefers to act on his beliefs rather than remain a victim of apartheid even though his actions mean that he leads a fragmentary life, constantly on the move, making contacts and distributing leaflets. But this existence opens the vista of resistance to him and makes him an active participant in his own history and the history of his country. In this way he and Isaac, who is portrayed as the most militant of the three activist characters, and Elias Tekwane substantiate their avowed intent to topple the racist regime and implement in its place an egalitarian power structure intended to meet the needs of *all* South Africans. Through Isaac the short-term myopia of the regime is articulated. He demolishes the false assumptions of white supporters of apartheid, those "stupid idiots who cherished the idea that they were God's Chosen just because they had white skins":

> The silly bastards, he thought, they had been stupefied into supporting a system which had to bust one day and take them all down with it; instead of permanent security and justice, they had chosen to preserve a tyranny that could only feed them temporarily on the crumbs of power and privilege. Now that the writing had started to appear on the wall, they either scrambled to shore it up with blood and bullets and the electric torture apparatus or hid their heads in the sand and pretended that nothing was happening (*Fog*, pp. 114–115).

Isaac is made indelibly aware that gnosis and praxis must be aligned in the fight against apartheid and, unlike Flotman who only talks of revolution, Isaac is prepared to stake his life for a South Africa that will be free of the tyranny of apartheid. Isaac's unequivocal alertness to his situation prompts him to speak out against his white bosses when he considers that their actions lead to injustices and grossly unfair treatment. Isaac has "nerve," and this is not lost on his white employers, one of whom, in his organizing of the staff social, sees Isaac as "a surly sort of bugger . . . Always on about not being anybody's servant and passing remarks about equality and higher wages" while his peers, the other "boys," knew their place in the scheme of things (*Fog*, p. 113). Isaac, a satirical development of the "bad" black, should also be read as providing a point of departure between the students and the active resistance fighters. Flotman's students have taken to "surreptitious reading of the theories of guerilla warfare under the flaps of their desks" and Beukes promises to supply them with material of a political kind, "prohibited stuff" (*Fog*, p. 88). This is only a preliminary measure since, as Michel Foucault has argued, knowledge and power are interdependent and "there is no point of dreaming of a time when knowledge will cease to depend on power." However, it is essential to educate the young people who will, like Isaac, be prepared to put into practice the teachings of resistance warfare, because if "it is not possible for power to be exercised without knowledge, it is impossible for knowledge not to engender power."[41]

La Guma is faced with a tremendous problem with this novel, namely, the range of issues that he attempts to address. Due to this integral diversity, *In the Fog of the Seasons' End* is open to reductive readings—a number of which I have already alluded to—but La Guma's inclusivity of divergent points of view functions as a coherent whole to demonstrate, by example, why the apartheid regime believed in its own superiority, and what remained to be achieved in order to attain freedom outside of the regime's formulations. To this end, the novel incorporates short speeches that function to elucidate a range of perspectives. For example, the doctor who treats Beukes for his gun shot wound states that "if the community is given the opportunity of participating in making the law, then they have moral obligation to obey it . . . But if the law is made for them, without their consent or participation, then it's a different matter. . . . if the law defends injustice, prosecutes and persecutes those who fight injustice, then I am under no obligation to uphold it . . . Injustice prevails, and there are people who have the nerve enough to defy it. Perhaps I have been waiting for the opportunity to put my penny in the hat as well" (*Fog*, p. 161). The doctor's politicization, in the face of what he could lose by openly espousing such a position, and Flotman's encouraging words to Beukes serve to illustrate the ways in which the professional classes might participate, albeit indirectly, in the struggle for freedom. Even the politically uninterested Tommy is willing to risk imprisonment in order to collect the subversive pamphlets for his friend Beukes. *In the Fog of the Seasons' End* represents the cumulative efforts of a series of brave individuals who are either directly involved in the resistance cell or are genuine sympathizers. Genuine commitment is of the utmost importance as it is set against those who are willing to betray the cause for the sake of individual gain, and it is one such person who betrays Elias, Isaac and Beukes. Ultimately, and presciently, La Guma indicates that the desire to replace a monologic system of government with a dialogic model will prove difficult, particularly when the security forces continue their insidious activities of ensuring that spies and informants are co-opted to infiltrate the ranks of the freedom fighters. The closing pages of *In the Fog of the Seasons' End* suggest that, despite the regime's best efforts, the new dawn will bring about change in South Africa: "What the enemy himself has created, these will become battle-grounds, and what we see now is only the tip of an iceberg of resentment against an ignoble regime, the tortured victims of hatred and humiliation. And those who persist in hatred and humiliation must prepare. Let them prepare hard and fast—they do not have long to wait" (*Fog*, pp. 180–181).

In *In the Fog of the Seasons' End* La Guma presents the reader with a broad account of the monologic tendency of apartheid, accenting the avenues that are open to those who oppose it. Each of the characters encountered is well aware of the liminal existence they have chosen and each is cognizant of the risks that their actions will invariably entail. But the essential point here is that it is no longer possible to endure subjugation under apartheid. The key issue remains that apartheid was monologic and that monologism in such an extreme form denies that outside itself there might exist a consciousness with equal rights and responsibilities. In Bakhtinian terms, extrapolating on his definitions of a monologic approach, monologue is "finalized and deaf to the other's response, does not expect it and does not acknowledge in it any *decisive force*. Monologue pretends to be the *ultimate word*. It closes down the represented world and represented persons."[42] La Guma advocates an alternative, dialogic future for South Africa through those who would participate in that future and, consequently, in "the dialogic nature of human life itself." In a Bakhtinian sense this is to open a restricted discourse of freedom out into dialogue: "the single adequate form for *verbally expressing* authentic human life is the *open-ended dialogue*. Life by its very nature is dialogic. To live means to participate in dialogue: to ask questions, to heed, to respond, to agree, and so forth. In this dialogue a person . . . invests his entire self in discourse, and this discourse enters into the dialogic fabric of human life, into the world symposium."[43] In the last instance La Guma's protagonists are, as Flotman states, aware that they have "talked about the revolution among ourselves too long" (*Fog*, p. 90) and that the time has come to act, to move beyond interpretation towards making change.[44] La Guma charts the evolution of political ideas out of conflict in *In the Fog of the Seasons' End*. This is essentially true of La Guma's *oeuvre*, for his characters very clearly move from a position of unfocused individualism to collective strength, from impotent anger to oblique theorizing about their subordinate positions, before finally arriving at the epiphanic realization that tyranny must be met with collective resistance, even violent resistance, but that it must be met head on.

Notes

I would like to thank Roger Field for his comments on an earlier version of this chapter.

1. David Maughan-Brown concurs with my view when he states in "Adjusting the Focal Length: Alex La Guma and Exile" that *In the Fog of the Seasons' End* "locates revolutionary activity firmly in the economic and social conditions of the people rather than in the individual's reaction to his or her personal experience of oppression." See "Adjusting the Focal Length: Alex La Guma and Exile," *English in Africa*, 18, October 1991, pt. 2, p. 21.

2. Nadine Gordimer, "English-Language Literature and Politics in South Africa" in Christopher Heywood, ed., *Aspects of South African Literature* (London: Heinemann, 1976), p. 111.

3. David Rabkin, "La Guma and Reality in South Africa," *The Journal of Commonwealth Literature*, viii:1, June 1973, pp. 60–61.

4. Rabkin, "La Guma and Reality in South Africa," p. 60.

5. Lewis Nkosi, *Home and Exile and Other Selections* (London: Longman, 1965, 1983), p. 131.

6. See Maughan-Brown, "Adjusting the Focal Length," p. 33.

7. Adrian Roscoe, *Uhuru's Fire: African Literature East to South* (Cambridge, Cambridge University Press, 1977), pp. 253–54.

8. Alex La Guma, *In the Fog of the Seasons' End* (London: Heinemann, 1972). See, for example, pp. 97–105 for the representation of the Sharpeville massacre and pp. 123–127 for La Guma's portrayal of the issuing of pass books.

9. Leonard Kibera, "A Critical Appreciation of Alex La Guma's *In The Fog of the Seasons' End*," *Busara,* 8:1, 1976, p. 68.

10. Abrahams, *Alex La Guma* (Boston: Twayne Publishers, 1984), p. 100.

11. La Guma, *In the Fog of the Seasons' End*, p. 4. All further references to this novel will be abbreviated as *Fog* and included in the text.

12. Abdul JanMohamed, *Manichean Aesthetics: The Politics of Literature in Colonial Africa* (Amherst: University of Massachusetts Press, 1983), p. 254.

13. See Mbulelo Vizikhungo Mzamane, "Sharpeville and Its Aftermath: The Novels of Richard Rive, Peter Abrahams, Alex La Guma, and Lauretta Ngcobo," *Ariel,* 16:2, 1985, p. 32.

14. Abrahams, *Alex La Guma*, p. 110.

15. Frantz Fanon, *Black Skin, White Masks* (London: Pluto Press, 1991), p. 161.

16. Homi Bhabha, "Remembering Fanon: Self, Psyche and the Colonial Condition," foreword to *Black Skin, White Masks*, p. xvi.

17. Bhabha, "Remembering Fanon," p. xvi.

18. Homi Bhabha, *The Location of Culture* (London: Routledge, 1994), p. 86.

19. J. U. Jacobs, "Confession, Interrogation and Self-interrogation in the New South African Prison Writing" in Kirsten Holst Petersen and Anna Rutherford, eds., *On Shifting Sands: New Art and Literature from South Africa* (Coventry, UK and Portsmouth, New Hampshire: Dangaroo Press and Heinemann, 1992), p. 120. Jacobs quotes Noica from "Pity for the Powerful," *Times Literary Supplement*, 4:259, 19–25, January 1990, pp. 61–62.

20. Don Foster, with Dennis Davies and Diane Sandler, *Detention and Torture in South Africa: Psychological, Legal and Historical Studies* (London: James Currey, 1987), p. 79.

21. Elaine Scarry, *The Body in Pain: The Making and Unmaking of the World* (Oxford: Oxford University Press, 1985), pp. 19–20.

22. Frantz Fanon, *The Wretched of the Earth* (London, Penguin, 1990), pp. 90–91.

23. Nelson Mandela, *The Struggle Is My Life* (London: International Defence and Aid Fund for Southern Africa, 1986), p. 161.

24. Kathleen Balutansky, *The Novels of Alex La Guma: The Representation of a Political Conflict* (Boulder, Colorado: Lynne Rienner Publishers, Inc., 1990), p. 100.

25. JanMohamed, *Manichean Aesthetics*, p. 256. Emphasis added.

26. Fanon, *The Wretched of the Earth*, p. 54.

27. Aijaz Ahmad, "The Politics of Literary Postcoloniality," *Race and Class*, 36:3, 1995, pp. 6–7. See also Anne McClintock, "The Angel of Progress: Pitfalls of the Term 'Post-colonialism,'" *Social Text* 31/32: 1992.

28. Bill Ashcroft, Gareth Griffiths and Helen Tiffin, eds., *The Post-Colonial Studies Reader* (London: Routledge, 1995), p. 355.

29. Peter Childs and Patrick Williams, *An Introduction to Post-Colonial Theory* (Hemel Hempstead: Harvester, 1997), p. 9.

30. Childs and Williams, *An Introduction to Post-Colonial Theory*, p. 165.

31. Gayatri Spivak quoted in Childs and Williams, *An Introduction to Post-Colonial Theory*, p. 165.

32. See, for example, Robert Young, *White Mythologies: Writing History and the West* (London: Routledge, 1990), p. 158, where he reads Spivak's assertion as "history is not simply the disinterested production of facts, but is rather a process of 'epistemic violence' . . . an interested construction of a particular representation of an object, which may . . . be entirely constructed with no existence or reality outside its representation. Where such history does not take the form of a representation, Spivak argues that it generally consists of a historical narrative, usually one written from the perspective and assumptions of the West or the colonizing power."

33. See Anthony Chennells, "Pastoral and Anti-Pastoral Elements in Alex La Guma's Later Novels" in Emmanuel Ngara and Andrew Morrison, eds., *Literature, Language and the Nation* (Harare, Zimbabwe: Association of University Teachers of Literature and Language and Baobab Books, 1989), especially pp. 39–41.

34. Homi Bhabha, *The Location of Culture*, p. 2.

35. H. F. Verwoerd quoted in Aletta J. Norval, *Deconstructing Apartheid Discourse* (London: Verso, 1996), p. 133. Verwoerd's speech addresses the education of black South Africans but was applied in a modified form to Indian and colored educational policy, too.

36. Norval, *Deconstructing Apartheid Discourse*, p. 133.

37. Norval, *Deconstructing Apartheid Discourse*, p. 167.

38. For example, J. M. Coetzee, in an otherwise thoughtfully argued piece, falls prey to colonialist thinking of this sort with his statement that "the young Tekwane comes out of Paton's *Cry, the Beloved Country* and Doris Lessing's 'Hunger,' and is thereby saddled with a freight of tragic connotation, religious and naturalistic," which suggests that La Guma follows a politically liberal aesthetic. See J. M. Coetzee, "Man's Fate in the Novels of Alex La Guma," *Studies in Black Literature*, 5:1, 1974, p. 22.

39. See, for example, Balasubramanyam Chandramohan, *A Study in Trans-Ethnicity in Modern South Africa: The Writings of Alex La Guma* (Lewiston/ Lampeter: Mellen Research University Press, 1992), p. 138.

40. Simon Gikandi, *Reading the African Novel* (London: James Currey/ Heinemann, 1987), p. 31.

41. Michel Foucault, *Power/Knowledge: Selected Interviews and Other Writings 1972–1977* (Hemel Hempstead: Harvester Wheatsheaf, 1980), p. 52. See also Simon Gikandi, *Reading the African Novel*, who argues that in relation to

In the Fog of the Seasons' End "knowledge or consciousness is a double-edged weapon that opens the minds of the characters to the possibilities of the life and beauty which the regime has denied them, but also exposes them to the violent tentacles of the police state," p. 132.

42. Mikhail Bakhtin, *Problems of Dostoevsky's Poetics,* trs. Caryl Emerson (Manchester: Manchester University Press, 1984), pp. 292–293.

43. Bakhtin, *Problems of Dostoevsky's Poetics*, p. 293.

44. See, for example, Karl Marx and Frederick Engels, "Theses on Feuerbach" in *The German Ideology* (London: Lawrence and Wishart, 1989), p. 123.

Chapter 6

Conceptualization and Contextualization: Time of the Butcherbird

In sharp contrast to the incessant rain that opens *And A Threefold Cord*, in *Time of the Butcherbird* the landscape of the novel is a dry, arid plain across which people with "the look of scarecrows" move. The land is "not even good enough to be buried in" and the drought is stressed through the description of a water tank full of dusty and brackish water that stands in the middle of the parched plain.[1] From the first, La Guma details the abiding endurance of those Africans who are to be removed from their land, the land of their ancestors, and relocated here. It is their resilience in the face of dispossession in accordance with the Promotion of Bantu Self-Government Act—commonly known as the "Removals Act"—of 1959 that leads La Guma to dedicate the novel to "the dispossessed": "I believe that one of the most serious social problems of South Africa is that of the mass removal of millions of African people from their well-established homes and the government program to establish or reinforce 'Bantustans.'"[2]

Those designated to speak to the Bantu Commissioner on behalf of the black people are the first African characters to be dismissed in their efforts to communicate across the social barriers represented in this novel. With their failure, the focus shifts suddenly to a nameless black man who has returned to the area and to his "home" but who has refused to register his presence with the Commissioner as required of him by law. His weariness is shot through with a determination for revenge that motivates each step across the plain and propels him towards a bitterly satisfying end: "I am finished with Bantu Commissioners now, and with white people. I will do this one thing and then I shall be finished with all people" (*TB*, p. 16). Precisely what motivates the young man—the cause of the "old rage" that "nagged at his guts"—is left unsaid and unexplained for much of the novel and the retardation devices employed again bespeak the ongoing resistance that La Guma takes as his subject matter.

"Home" and culture are floating signifiers in *Time of the Butcherbird*. Metaphors that La Guma has used to symbolic and heightened political effect elsewhere, like Mma Tau's declaration that "The whole country is a prison"(*TB,* p. 80), which resonates throughout *The Stone Country* and crackles with meaning in *In the Fog of* the *Seasons' End,* are present in this last novel but compounded by La Guma's attention to issues of land and belonging as they affect the black characters through the enforced mass removals and the subsequent and spurious 1959 Promotion of Bantu Self-Government Act. Here a different tranche of South African life is explored. Coloreds and Africans live together in *And A Threefold Cord* and they fight the same fight in *The Stone Country.* Though George Adams and Jefferson Mpolo are separated in jail as are Elias and Beukes in *In the Fog of the Seasons' End,* Elias will not give up his colleagues, one of whom is Beukes. Characters connect across markedly different experiences to accentuate the range of positions within a politics of resistance, as in exchanges between George Adams and Yusuf the Turk or the Casbah Kid, many of which are profoundly moving. La Guma opens the range still further in *Time of the Butcherbird* to expose the reductive "reasoning" of Afrikaner and English protagonists through the seasons of apartheid. Cecil Abrahams believes that La Guma succeeds in satirizing the myth that "the so-called liberal, English-speaking white South African has a 'better', more 'meaningful' attitude to blacks." He goes further to allege that "the English settler has since taken a disinterested back seat in solving the racial problems of South Africa, preferring instead to mock the Afrikaners' approach and to blame all disharmony on the government. Meanwhile, English settler businessmen have played and continue to play a major role in the economic success that South Africa enjoys."[3] Complicit in upholding apartheid ideology in this way, La Guma's Edgar Stopes of Universal Products—"Anything From a Needle to an Anchor"—traveling through the Karroo on a less-than-successful sales pitch to the Afrikaners has his liberalism unmasked. Also disclosed is the racism that underpins the Barends family's relationships with their customers prior to the Group Areas Act. In their tiny shop in an urban area populated by blacks, words like "kaffir" and "coon" are commonplace as the Barends keep their daughter Maisie away from neighborhood children, and Barends cannot conceive of what he might talk about to "a damn applesammy" (*TB,* p. 30). The flow of everyday racism is left unchecked and the level of political understanding conveyed by the working- and lower-middle-class whites is low, as when

Elizabeth Barends disdains "politics" as "awright for the government and the kaffirs" (*TB*, p. 32) and Stopes comments loosely about boycotts: "Look at these stupid natives, refusing to ride their bloody buses . . . They got their own buses and then they go an' boycott them because of fares" (*TB*, p. 36).

For the writer, *Time of the Butcherbird* is a progression in his depiction of the wider South African scene.[4] The colored community so central in the earlier novels also recedes as Africans like Shilling Murile and Mma Tau are brought to the fore to stand firm in opposition to the policies of the National Party on the allocation of "homelands" and to white-on-black violence, as exemplified in the death of the young boy Timi Murile. Shilling Murile is the name of the lone figure on the Karroo who, once recognized by a member of his community, is tied into the landscape of the novel despite his reluctance to align himself with anything other than his own anger: "Making his way through the dust, the man once again identified scanty landmarks which he had known a long time ago" (*TB*, p. 14). He has come from "that place," the white man's jail where "there were people . . . who had also been put there by the white man who said we should fight on. I used to listen to them talking" (*TB*, p. 19). Shilling does not talk much himself, however, and the extent to which his mission for revenge has been fueled by such talk is unclear to the reader and to the character himself until very far into the novel.

Shilling Murile is no straightforward example of one whose political consciousness has been awakened to resistance through the stories or the observations of others. La Guma examines in this book, and in *And A Threefold Cord*, the extent to which resistance, violent or otherwise, may lie dormant and untested in the gut of the individual until the occasion when, like bile, it rages through the system and rushes out in a stream of urgent retaliation or insurgency. Murile believes he has lost his place in the Karroo: "There is no home now" (*TB*, p. 19). His return is motivated, he believes, by the single act of revenge for his brother's death eight years previously, an act that will invert the roles of violator and victim. For Murile, killing Hannes Meulen will vent the anger that he has carried within and, in contrast to Michael Adonis in La Guma's first novel who nurses his anger like a toothache,[5] in this novel the hatred of the oppressor that usually remains implicit is made explicit. It is a "special hatred" that Mma Tau feels should be harnessed to the fight for the land (*TB*, p. 83).

Location is of salient but ambivalent importance in this novel. In *And A Threefold Cord* the material and social poverty miniaturized in Windermere gives rise to an unprecedented response on the part of Charlie Pauls who punches a police officer. At this moment it is made clear that there can be no escape for any individual from the deleterious effects of the system, which locates them in direct relation to violence and oppression. In relation to *Time of the Butcherbird*, it is precisely the means of "locating" the novel—in the Karroo, in a rural "community" of Afrikaners and Africans—that has given rise to most of the discussion around this novel's potential flaws. David Maughan-Brown is the critic whose reading relates most directly to La Guma's exile from South Africa, and to the foreignness of the veld from his predominantly urban experience in any case.[6] The detail with which Mbulelo Mzamane and Maughan-Brown challenge La Guma's geographically or linguistically erroneous or anomalous descriptions is not to be brooked. However, it is not finally the geographical or anthropological accuracy of the novel's composite landscape that is at stake here but whether inaccuracies detract from the political and ideological statement that the book intends and whether that statement is communicated to best effect.

In fact, La Guma has deployed such landscapes in previous work. In the short story "Coffee for the Road," an Indian mother drives her two children from Johannesburg to Cape Town through a landscape of red dust and scorched, flat country and low, flat hills dotted with sheep. The car passes the colored and the African locations and stops in a small town, "just some place in the Karroo," very much like the unnamed town in *Time of the Butcherbird*, where the woman is refused coffee to refill their flask and is finally stopped at a roadblock where officials wait to escort her out of the area, back the way she has come. Entering a café rather than waiting outside has made of her an "agitator."[7] This story is described by La Guma as "based on a true account given to me by an Asiatic South African woman" but "having made the trip myself at some time or other, I was able to portray the journey and the scenery as it appears in the story."[8] In actuality, in 1955 La Guma was detained by the police in the Karroo on his way to the Congress of the People in Kliptown. La Guma seems to take Maughan-Brown's view that to "go there is to know there," to borrow Zora Neale Hurston's famous phrase, but at the same time to disprove some of the critic's points about his delineation of the landscape. It is not a delineation at all: "I collected enough scenes of South Africa— 'Bantustans,' praying for rain, people in the desert, and then I wrote."[9]

To discuss La Guma's writing process and intentionality in this way is to risk becoming embroiled in a discourse of realism, of the significance of documentary-style recording and mimetic reflection, and to argue the synecdochic importance of the part to the whole. Chandramohan works through an elaborate investigation as to whether the novel may be said to take place in the Eastern or Western Karroo, despite his assurance that the setting is symbolic and that the Karroo (instead of the prison) "stands as a metaphor for South African society as a whole."[10] It is of little importance exactly where the action takes place since the "homelands" policy that is so crucial to this text affected a total of 260 "small and separate areas scattered throughout the country," which the government intended to amalgamate into eight defined and designated "homelands." Govan Mbeki dedicated himself to analyzing the Bantustan policy in *South Africa: The Peasants' Revolt* (1964)—living as a political outlaw when not in prison or living as a banned person within the confines of his home. He provides a context for what he terms "South Africa's backwaters": "primitive rural slums, soil-eroded and under-developed, lacking power resources and without developed communication systems. They have no cities, no industries, and few sources of employment. They are congested and permanently distressed areas where the inhabitants live on a narrow ledge of starvation, where a drought . . . leads inevitably to famine." Such areas are socially deprived; the men are forced to find work away from their families—on white-owned farms or in the mines—and those who remain in the Karroo—women and the elderly—"pursue a primitive agriculture incapable of providing even subsistence."[11] It is with this broad context that La Guma engages in *Time of the Butcherbird* and with the government's plans to administer Africans. Disallowing them from setting up family homes in urban areas ensures they become migrant laborers whose only hope lies with the government-operated Bantustan policy to be administered ostensibly by disenfranchised tribal "headmen," formerly chiefs, like Hlangeni in this novel, a "dwindling old man" with "fallen shoulders" (*TB*, p. 85), fearful and apprehensive of resisting the engines of apartheid.

Critics of La Guma generally agree that a developing political consciousness is represented incrementally and chronologically through the sequence of novels via their black protagonists. Abrahams adjudges this to be the case and Chandramohan also discusses the increasing emphasis on symbolism in La Guma's work, seeing its apotheosis in *Time of the Butcherbird*. While most critics are quick to support the idea of progression and development, some difficulties arise when they read this final novel, as David Maughan-Brown's argument makes clear. To view La Guma's exile as debilitating to his writing, and therefore his "focal length" as inevitably shortsighted, may block other critical and political perspectives on this novel. But, to celebrate symbolism as the mainstay of this novel's success is to risk missing the import of its ideological pertinence when that symbolism is not tied directly to its overall cogency.

Symbolism and its reliance on metaphor is hardly the most politically expedient literary technique of which to avail oneself. This is not to say that symbolism is redundant as a technique for developing political analysis: Chandramohan's thesis whereby interethnicity shifts to transethnicity in the later works is paralleled, he believes, by a movement in style from "near-naturalism to symbolism and allegory" so that "history" is allegorized.[12] The thesis is clear but exactly why the use of symbolism should be commended in this specific context is never fully elaborated. Chandramohan describes symbolism as "unavoidable," taking his lead from La Guma.[13] But the inevitability detected in the change of stylistic emphasis across the books is not analyzed beyond specific examples of symbols at work in this text. The same is true of Kathleen Balutansky's thesis, which points to the "metaphoric structure" and "symbolic framework" of the *Time of the Butcherbird*.[14] Literature is inevitably figurative in its textuality, and some literary critics have celebrated the political turn of symbolism, notably feminist critics who argue that it may challenge the dominant patriarchal discourse.[15] However, rigorous analysis of symbolism as methodology and counterstrategy has not been forthcoming in the case of La Guma.[16]

The discussion as to the effectiveness of La Guma's symbolism is one element of particular interest to critics of this book, but the possible repercussions of his exile from South Africa on his writing are mooted as an equally significant problem by David Maughan-Brown and others. While the effects of exile and displacement on cultural productions and on cultural producers have been discussed and debated at length,[17] it is difficult to decide where La Guma may sit in the debate. Only his final published novel was conceived and written outside of South Africa and he can hardly be considered acculturated. Film critic Zuzana M. Pick captures the nuances of the dialectical process that is, or may be, cultural production in exile: "If displacement is a signifier of loss, it is also affected by a reconstructive process of belonging . . . the subjectivity of exile is constantly reinventing itself in a labouring process of decantation."[18]

In many ways, La Guma's *Time of the Butcherbird* is interesting precisely because it engages in the process that Pick describes: Displacement and belonging are the very issues that La Guma draws out through a cast of South African characters whose relationships to State, nation and citizenship are tenuous and strained. This is not an autobiographical novel; as La Guma states, many of the characters in his previous works were drawn from people he knew, whereas the manner of representation in *Time of the Butcherbird* is less naturalistic and more disjunctive. He configures and manipulates the very disjunctions in the work that worry certain critics to accentuate what seem to be insurmountable differences between individuals and groups. In adjusting the focal length, to borrow Maughan-Brown's phrase, La Guma adjusts the pace, rhythm and structuring of this novel to provide spaces in the text—ellipses—that function to break the text down analytically into component parts and to control the time of the action of the novel. A total of twenty separate sequences combine to create a panoptic vision of quotidian life across two days.

To take the fifth segment as indicative of its wider structuring and to read it closely is to acknowledge the heterogeneity of voices and subject-positions that La Guma incorporates. On his first evening in the village, Edgar Stopes tries the hotel bar. He has complained virulently about the fact that the "houseboy" Fanie neglected to deliver a beer to his room and his tirade against Fanie has been warmly supported by the Afrikaner couple who run the place, the Kroners. Before entering the bar to indulge his desire for a beer, Stopes joins with other white characters in roundly debasing Fanie, indulging in the classically racist paradigms of infantilism and "othering" to do so: "They're not like us, you have to take them by the hand all the time, show them what to do" (*TB,* p. 24). Nevertheless, the environment of the bar itself arouses the English-speaking South African's own set prejudices against the "backward Dutchmen as dumb as the sheep they raise," with whom he finds himself sharing a dorp in the Karroo. What Stopes says to the Afrikaners he meets and what he thinks about them are presented as two separate discourses, externally produced and internally realized, which jangle discordantly as Stopes manages the time he must spend in the Karroo waiting for his car to be fixed:

> Kroner the barman came up and Edgar Stopes said, "Brandy, a double brandy." The man who had his back to him turned at the sound of an unfamiliar voice and looked at Edgar Stopes. He looked away again at the other man and their voices dropped, as if they were reminded that what they were discussing was very private. Edgar Stopes felt again the feeling of rejection, so that he quickly wrapped the armour of worn cynicism about himself, telling them in his mind to shove their bloody sheep and sermons because it was a lot of eye-wash, anyway (*TB,* pp. 25–26).

He is a stranger and he feels himself made strange, defamiliarized and alienated, and so he internalizes such feelings: "Christ, one would think one was a bloody nigger, them and their bloody ox-wagons and ploughs. Who's running the country anyway?" (*TB,* p. 24). The bar "scene" is symptomatic—and consequently diagnostic—of the problems of divisive instability that beset South African society. It forms a set piece in which the narrator pushes behind the conscious façade the individual builds against the rest of the world—against "these people"—and punctures it to reveal the fears and anxieties that underpin such belligerent racism and intraracial antagonisms.

In the bar Stopes meets Hannes Meulen; the novel is carefully patterned and arranged so that lives touch and circumstances intersect. Meulen talks precisely of the importance of contact between English-speaking South Africans and Afrikaners "in dangerous times," since they should unite against the Africans. With hindsight, the irony of what will befall these two, chance-met a second time facing the barrel of Murile's gun, is not lost but neither is the fact that Meulen carries on this conversation in Afrikaans. Who *is* running the country? Meulen is standing for election on a National Party ticket and the sole analogy Stopes can contrive to express his discomfort in the taproom is to align himself with the disenfranchised "nigger" he castigated only moments before. In effect, although the bar is socially engineered to exclude blacks, Verwoerd's "honoured guests" in white South Africa,[19] Murile is present in Kroner's rendition of the story of citizen Meulen's rise: "Some years ago there was trouble with a kaffir and he got a suspended sentence, but it was really a small matter and nobody around here thinks about it" (*TB*, p. 29). In many ways, the novel turns on precisely this incident that nobody seems to think about, whereby the gun with which the Murile boys are threatened, and with which Shilling is knocked out, will be taken and turned on Meulen and, then, taken up once more to arm the Africans for the fight ahead.

The separate sequences work to destabilize the whole. La Guma does not intend to produce an aesthetics of coalition in *Time of the Butcherbird* but rather to reproduce the circumstances in which the actions and movements of separate and unequal subjects are orchestrated to depict a society fractured and fractious at the point of breakdown. The twenty sections or sequences juxtapose fragments of an inconsistent society in which apartheid's grand segregationist design cannot obtain while blacks are required to work across the color line. Whites in city bungalows live in "paranoia of perpetual siege": "Bungalows where nervous ladies viewed the black houseboys and kitchenmaids as potential outriders to hordes of rampaging barbarians" (*TB*, p. 49); Afrikaners believe they came to South Africa "like the followers of Joshua. Any other conception was anathema" (*TB*, p. 58) but they depend almost exclusively on black servants, as Oupa Meulen does on Koos; a nameless black woman with her baby simply pauses on the street to sit in the shade for a moment only to be moved on by a police patrolman who prods the woman with a club (*TB*, p. 52); an Afrikaner attracted to the "coloured" maid who attends his sick mother keeps their relationship secret and persists in seeing the woman as a "she-animal" with "quivering dugs" (*TB*, p. 99). Such contradictions are the axiomatic starting point for an exploration of the inexorable pull towards the next stage of South Africa's struggle: violent confrontation following Sharpeville and the spiraling down the 1970s to the Soweto uprising of 1976, in what Norval calls "The Roots of an Expanding Imaginary."[20]

La Guma draws the faultlines in the society, and internal coherence is a problem for critics whose readings appear to strain towards a single effect, while undermining the novel's potential to achieve it through its form. Perhaps JanMohamed in his relatively short treatment of the novel comes closest to articulating the internal inconsistencies he perceives. JanMohamed reads the orchestration of characters and groups as marred by "coincidences" through which they intersect. For him there is a problem of internal coherence, as there is for Maughan-Brown who feels that "the novel 'pulls'" in "contradictory directions."[21] There is much to be considered in what each of these critics notes and neither sets out to undermine the final work of a political novelist whose novels have given rise to admiration and debate. But, there is another way of reading the tensions that they perceive before deciding the extent to which they work to best effect.

Those critics who place the pull towards inclusivity over the depiction of parallel lives lived at odds lose the effect of events occurring simultaneously, jarring the reader into recognition of the orchestration of sectarian groups and individuals within a sectional society. Agnes Sam has addressed a similar problem: She could not find a publisher for her novel *What Passing Bells,* which was "impressionistic, it's [*sic*] form suggestive of a fractured society, of people in an apartheid system isolated from each other . . . It's [*sic*] purpose was to frustrate the reader's need for continuity because this is precisely how we are frustrated."[22] Any study of cinematic cross-cutting will demonstrate how in a film text the editing together of separate sequences may establish cause and effect but may also point up discontinuities as well as parallels. In short, "in most cases, crosscutting gives us a range of knowledge greater than that of any one character."[23] La Guma cross-cuts Afrikaner with African, English-speaking South African with Afrikaner, Afrikaner with Afrikaner, in a Bantu Commissioner's office, in a bar of a hotel, at a wedding, on the street, at the dinner table, in order to convey the discordancies and to distill their effects into a self-consciously created cross-section of South Africans living precariously under apartheid. At the Steens' dinner table, Rina's project to preserve the wild flowers of the veld is mooted without regard to the Africans who are to be cleared from the very same land in the same trucks she wishes to use to transport cycads and orchids to more fertile ground:

"Hannes," Rina said as they ate, "You must help me . . . there are hundreds and hundreds of wild flowers out in the veld and they will die from thirst if they are not moved to places where they can be preserved . . . "

"Altogether a good idea. I've read about it. So you're overseeing things here?" . . .

"The thing is," Rina said, dabbing her mouth, "We need lorries, Land Rovers, you know? You must donate us a couple of lorries, Hannes. Will you?"

"Trucks I can lend you," Meulen said while the rest of the meal was brought in. "When you're ready. But at the moment some of the trucks have taken sheep over to where there is more water, and I have promised two lorries to the Commissioner to transport the kaffirs tomorrow" (*TB*, pp. 62–63).

La Guma refines the structuring of this novel in order to contemplate the complex relationships within the South Africa he has been forced to leave behind. Since it is widely agreed that, until this novel, there could be discerned a consistent and carefully staged development on the part of his characters towards conscious resistance, is it, as David Maughan-Brown would attest, lost in this final work? I believe that *Time of the Butcherbird* is the work in which its author pauses and, with the added dimension of geographical distance from his subject to aid him, decants the antagonisms, the distrust, the misalliances between people into a study of rural *and* urban South Africa. Gathered together are the inequities, the rage and the dysfunction of the bitter, the dispossessed, and those living with fear "like an itch in the groin of the continent" (*TB*, p. 49), in country and in city, at home and on the road. As Maureen Whitebrook has argued, "Narrative form has a distinctive characteristic of potential benefit to political theory, that of its capacity for enabling reflection and speculation." She sees the potential within novels to clarify political choices: "novels are particularly good at showing the necessity of making choices, the psychological pressures on the individuals who face them, the moral dilemmas involved and the consequences of choice, the political effects of reactions to those problems."[24] Philosophers working at the interface of literature and politics are beginning to address the ways in which the novel form, traditionally noted for its emphasis on individual characters, which would seem to make it "ill-suited to describe a culture or ideology in which individuality matters less than it does in Western liberal democracies," produces some of the most powerful representations of politically motivated writing. Bakhtinian readings, and indeed critics like Catherine Belsey within the Western tradition, have efficaciously deconstructed the idea of a single and coherent subject-position.[25]

Comparing *Time of the Butcherbird* unfavorably with *And A Threefold Cord*, Abdul JanMohamed persists with a reading that rests with representative protagonists and finds the final novel unsubtle in its triptych of three main characters made to represent three major groups. He believes that the inevitability of white complicity (i.e., Stopes is shot because he is talking to Meulen at the point Murile assassinates him) and the continued but violent black and white struggle are undermined by the coincidences he so abhors, which relate directly to the representation of individual characters. That is to say, for example, Jaap Opperman's death from a snake bite and Murile's perceptible shift (though JanMohamed argues an "unknowing" one) towards communal resistance.[26] The criticism is carefully argued in the limited space JanMohamed allows, but it rests on the understanding that only three main characters carry the ideological impetus of the novel and that the final "winds of change" rely exclusively on Shilling Murile's repositioning in the text. My reading of the structuring of *Time of the Butcherbird* and its characterizations is more open and dialogic than JanMohamed's. The very structuring of the text militates against the assumption that the novel may be adequately read according to three main protagonists.

It is certainly the case that Murile, Stopes and Meulen serve significantly as representative of different factions within the system of apartheid, and Stopes's position as witness or bystander is indicative of La Guma's analysis of the more ambiguous position of English-speaking whites. But the structuring is such that a number of other characters and subject-positions also receive particularized and sustained attention in the novel. Rather than reduce the "main characters" to three, I would challenge the usefulness of "main" as a designation in a novel where communities and groups are described in so much detail.[27] David Maughan-Brown, in arguably the most informed reading of the novel to date, specifies five "focuses of interest" across the narrative and a broader sense of the community than JanMohamed.[28] He quotes La Guma's own comments on the novel in conversation with Cecil Abrahams on the importance of "the various communities in the country and their relationship," and of characters as hopefully "representative of the South African scene." However, he argues that the title of the novel itself gives weight to any reading that places Shilling Murile and his revenge at the forefront.[29] Abrahams himself follows this line and talks of "major stories" and "minor stories" in his version of the novel's various emphases and narrative shifts. A reading of the novel must also engage with the debates and discussions between Hlangeni and Mma Tau, which underpin the black community's evolution into a resistant force against the removals. It should also engage with the gender dynamics within Stopes's relationship with his wife Maisie and Meulen's with his fiancée Rina, for example. The first couple's marriage is failing on a number of levels, not least at the level of communication across differing experiences that La Guma posits as central to his vision of social breakdown. The draconian patriarchal principles by which Meulen reads his fiancée, and according to which they each prepare for their life together, are delimiting and ultimately reductive:

> She would make a good wife, he thought happily. He loved her and she would bear his children. They would live at the farm and go travelling about the country, of course, when his public duties allowed him to take her with him. Otherwise she would oversee the farm, potter about in the kitchen garden and grow flowers— she loved flowers—or experiment with new recipes, make rusks, *biltong* and preserves, or turn the house upside down with spring-cleaning (*TB,* p. 59).

Rina's hopes are remarkably similar and formulated in the same terms: "she would stand by him, in everything he wished to do. That was her duty. Her college education would be an asset to him too. She would be his good wife and the mother of his children, live under his protecting arm, and she would watch him grow to something in this community, and her heart fluttered with pride" (*TB,* p. 65). Juxtaposing these thoughts and opening up such debates involves differences of perspective. But it is clear that Rina's dismissal of politics as "the affairs of the men" (*TB,* p. 65) differs little from Elizabeth Barends's debunking of "politics," despite the differences of class and culture that divide the two white women. Ultimately, in this novel it is differences that dominate and it is the process of distinguishing between and across different discourses that preoccupies La Guma.

A plethora of perceived differences are alluded to and maintained by the characters. It is in this novel that La Guma pits his wits against the structure of social encounters between individuals across nineteenth- and twentieth-century South African life. It could be argued, in fact, that problems lie in the fact that this remains a novella rather than becoming a bigger novel of epic sweep. The economy of La Guma's style and his general preference for the novella have received critical attention but little detailed analysis. Ironically perhaps, it is in this novel and through critics' discussion of its possible flaws, that the structuring is revealed to be at its most politically astute and critically apposite. La Guma issues what one might term an aesthetic attack in this novel. He creates a montage of scenes across which the reader travels through the text. He designates a broad cast of South African characters, which attests to his conviction that individuals cannot stand outside of the discourse according to which their group affiliation is read.[30] The novel is at its most *affective* when disaffected individuals clash or interact: Emotionally charged and embittered, Murile is affected by the old shepherd who seems to follow him around and by Mma Tau's call for him to join a collective protest, despite himself. Emotionally stunted, Maisie finds in the last futile moments of her adulterous fling with Wally the recognition that her life with Edgar may be her last best hope. Her realization will be undercut by the news of his untimely death. However, the novel is at its most *effective* when one considers that the schema of relations in *Time of the Butcherbird* is such that individuals and the groups to which they belong, or to which they are assigned in South Africa of the 1960s, cohere in a constellation of contradictory discourses that have at their center the imperative to perceive and maintain differences between individuals and across groups. Edgar Stopes drives across the veld with a "nigger doll" gently swaying in the middle of his windscreen. Like the doll, the black "help," Fanie at the hotel, barely edges into his consciousness except when a beer is not delivered to his room. Stopes considers blacks a resource he may command; interrecognition is not required; misrecognition is the order of the day, as is commodification, as the doll signifies.[31] The clerk at the Bantu Commissioner's office behaves in accordance with the stereotype that "all Kaffirs smelled" and the narrator interjects that he overlooks the fact that his visitors have walked through the heat for miles, preferring a false justification as to why he should make "these people" wait. The Commissioner will not hear what they say, describing their careful if cryptic warning that Africans cannot be annulled since their connections to the land of their ancestors can never be broken as "nonsense."

The Africans, boxed in at every turn, must pit themselves against what Gayatri Spivak terms "epistemic violence," which is closely linked in my analysis to what Bakhtin would call "authoritative discourse." Authoritative discourse is the discourse that demands that we acknowledge it. In this context, it is the pervasive ideology of apartheid that "binds us, quite independent of any power it might have to persuade us internally; we encounter it with its authority already fused to it. The authoritative word is located in a distanced zone, organically connected with a past that is felt to be hierarchically higher. It is, so to speak, the word of the fathers. Its authority was already acknowledged in the past. It is a

prior discourse."[32] Closely linked to the concept of authoritative discourse—but distinct from it—is "internally persuasive discourse." In
Bakhtin's analysis the two different discourses have the potential to act
as push and pull forces. In order to come to consciousness of self and
context, the two discourses must be acknowledged, but the first will
attempt to act as the "supra" term to relegate the latter to a position of
ideological powerlessness. However, if the internally persuasive discourse
is urged to the forefront, then it is possible to avoid the damning glare
and debilitating mental chains of authoritative discourse. It is this that
Mma Tau achieves in mobilizing her people. Shilling Murile is subject
to both of these positions at different points in the text. At first, the
white man's authoritative discourse is a violent assault on his subject-
position, but this occurs while he is young and unprepared, or not yet
ready to face his ideological position. Subsequently, in prison, in the
liminal space of the text that the reader does not witness, a process that
involves the "struggle and dialogic interrelationship of these categories"
is enacted and informs and determines his newly forming ideological
consciousness.[33] Interestingly, a similar process occurs for Mma Tau during
her spell in the "white city" (*TB*, p. 83). Mma Tau's understanding of
authoritative discourse is of a different type, namely, that it is passed
down through the oral history of the tribe and contrasts directly with
the discourse of the old Afrikaners, who believed that they made history
in their victory over the Africans. Those critics who find problems with
Murile's joining with the "she-lion" in that more consequential of causes—
freedom from tyranny for all—fail to grasp the idea that "the semantic
structure of an internally persuasive discourse is *not finite*, it is *open*; in
each of the new contexts that dialogize it, this discourse is able to reveal
ever newer *ways to mean*."[34] What is represented through Mma Tau and
Hlangeni in their public struggle is a conflict between centripetal and
centrifugal forces in which they distinguish and discriminate between
two possible positions:

> "You yourself have said, this is our land. Your own words asked, is
> it so terrible to love one's home? Were not our ancestors leaders
> before you? Are you not descended from warriors?"
> "The times are different," Hlangeni cried. "*They* rule us now."
> The woman nodded. "Yes, the times are different. There is
> meaning in what you say, even though you do not know it. But I
> say this clearly, I shall not go from this land. This is what the
> times mean for me."
> "Who will stay with you, to defy them?"

> "Listen my brother, there are those who will follow my word, and there are those who will follow yours. It has come to that" (*TB,* p. 48).

Mma Tau rejects the hegemony of apartheid discourse out of hand while Hlangeni, her brother, maintains his belief in its overwhelming effects.

Divisions and perceived differences are heightened and maintained in daily exchanges. References the white characters make to "those people . . . they're not like us," reinforce at a linguistic level how keenly cherished and ingrained the falsely constituted hierarchy of South African social relations has become. However, it is not unassailable, as this novel shows. The constellation of voices and positions that is *Time of the Butcherbird* is elucidated through a Bakhtinian reading of the novel whereby "the novel orchestrates all its themes, the totality of the world of objects and ideas depicted and expressed in it, by means of the social diversity of speech types" and by "the differing individual voices that flourish under such conditions."[35] The key factor here is that the apartheid regime has failed to prevent its ideology from being diluted and altered. Bakhtin's assertion that "when someone else's ideological discourse is internally persuasive for us and acknowledged by us, entirely different possibilities open up" has important implications in terms of group resistance.[36] In this context, La Guma ensures that characters like Mma Tau and Murile hone their responses to apartheid and discriminate the ways in which authoritarianism may be parried or withstood; in Bakhtin's terms: "consciousness awakens to independent ideological life precisely in a world of alien discourse surrounding it, and from which it cannot initially separate itself."[37]

The philosophical debate about politicized realism is perhaps conducted with the most sharply defining edges in critical work on cinema and by those like Sergei Eisenstein, Andre Bazin and Christopher Williams, who have pursued the extent to which the ideology of revolution may be served by cinematographic techniques. What I have called the faultlines in South African society as drawn by La Guma in his most complicated structuring of an apartheid narrative, Eisenstein would see as the process of polyphonic montage: "the several interdependent lines virtually resemble a ball of vari-coloured yarn, with the lines running through and binding together the entire sequence of shots."[38] The cinematographic language reworks a Bakhtinian philosophy of the novel's heteroglot function but again it is in its miniaturization—in the pithy telling of memories and encounters—through which its overall impact as an overarching apartheid narrative is achieved. It is through memory—replaying and reconstructing the past—that La Guma achieves the sweep across generations and locations, political stances and social discrepancies, Boer history and African struggles through history in this novel. It is Oupa Meulen, so old he remembers the Boer War and battles at Eslin Hoogte and Modderrivier (*TB*, p. 96), and so centered in his pain at the loss of life that his dreams disturb and dismay, through whom La Guma conveys the long-established beliefs in white destiny in his nation's complicated history. Through Jaap Opperman and his mother who, "when it came to the special powers of black witch-doctors, medicine-men, diviners, . . . cast her race prejudice aside" (*TB*, p. 97), La Guma encodes the cultural cross-overs that are inevitably thrown up in even the most segregated of societies. In many ways the novel's general outlook is conceptually based rather than contextually driven. La Guma posits a philosophy of intraracial tensions and cross-racial discord in a panoptic vision of the country, its bitter and bloody past, its factions and its cross-fertilizations, and its inevitably strife-ridden future.[39]

JanMohamed commends the "exquisite descriptions" in this as in *And A Threefold Cord* but does not see them as "systematic or consistent emblems of apartheid,"[40] thereby marginalizing their contribution to a *coherent* presentation of a community living under and engaging with apartheid in its quotidian forms. It is true that the barren and unwelcoming landscape itself exists outside of apartheid but the value of the land is set by the regime. The price the government sets on the land is its designated "value" in a sense that cuts across the value it holds for those who live on it. In Fanonian terms, "for a colonized people the most essential value, because the most concrete, is first and foremost the land: the land which will bring them bread and, above all, dignity."[41] In fact, characters who inhabit the land are often at odds with it in ways that those who "belong" to it can understand. But Opperman's fear of the Kloof is Mangonele's respect for it, "a dry wound in the earth that was held in mysterious respect by folk" (*TB*, p. 116). When it becomes the scene of Opperman's death by snake-bite, it is bound up inextricably with Opperman's fear and guilt over his part in the death of Timi Murile. He is driven to dismiss his fear of the place and of the Africans whose stories it holds, but Mangonele approaches the hill with those very stories and legends in mind. The story he tucks away "in the folds of his mind until such time as he was able to sit quietly by the fire of contemplation" (*TB*, p. 116) is, one imagines, the story that derives from the incident that no one thought much about in Kroner's taproom, which comes to climax in the drought-ridden two days covered in this novel; it is a sequence in the continuing saga of stories that cut through the landscape of South African history.

The shepherd, in a novel that La Guma has maintained relies on symbolism *as much as* character and action, is key to the philosophy mooted by La Guma. "Minor" in Abrahams' sense, Mangonele's presence fortifies Murile in his quest for violent redress. The man is undernourished but resilient, wretchedly thin, in fact, described as skeletal, living on the "narrow ledge of starvation" and pursuing the primitive agrarian lifestyle that Mbeki describes: "He had a skeleton-thin body that looked tough nevertheless, dried and stringy and lasting as jerked meat, and his small wizened face criss-crossed with wrinkles that had caught up the dust of the land so that he looked as if he had been drawn all over with red lines" (*TB*, p. 17). He is charged, however, with as much political meaning as the three protagonists who have received much more considered critical attention. Murile's disaffected pronouncement that he no longer has a familial connection to the place, or to the group to which he has been affiliated from birth, is countered by the old shepherd with "we are all your brothers" and "you have forgotten that fatherless children belong to everybody" (*TB*, p. 20). Mangonele's intention to return from the hills the first night in time for the council meeting indicates that he retains his faith in the tribe and its ways. Fanon recognizes the political role played by the rural population: "in the colonial countries the peasants alone are revolutionary, for they have nothing to lose and everything to gain." He contends that the peasant, starving on the edges of the class system "is the first among the exploited to discover that only violence pays."[42] Mangonele and Murile converge with Mma Tau in this realization of the "collective debt" (*TB*, p. 80) to be paid to the populace.

Whether Mangonele's presence as a potential catalyst for Murile's shift towards group identification and action irks critics and therefore receives little serious attention from those who assess the novel's success according to its effective deployment of symbols and tropes, or whether his relative silence on specific issues of political expediency seems to render him ineffectual, is unclear. Nevertheless, Mangonele is not only or simply an old man who follows Murile around for tobacco: his progress through the novel is patterned to coincide with Murile's own. Murile's action is contingent upon his subsequent understanding of his position in relation to others. In reference to the task that he must complete, Murile like other of La Guma's characters—Charlie Pauls, for example, in his spirited but unpremeditated attack on an officious police officer—discovers that for the individual engaged in an individualistic act, violence can be "a cleansing force." In Fanon's assessment, it is a preliminary stage in the more epistemologically complex mechanisms of concerted group resistance: "It frees the native from his inferiority complex and from his despair and inaction; it makes him fearless and restores his self-respect."[43] Only once this restoration has taken place can Murile accept that he might have a part to play in the collective restoration of the dignity of his people in the face of the apartheid regime.

In 1962 when Patrick van Rensburg published his personal account of his movement away from his country's diplomatic service to a thoroughgoing critique of the effects of apartheid on blacks themselves and on fearful whites, one of the most groundbreaking visceral realizations he comes to in *Guilty Land* is that he had "failed to realize that African group assertion had become an end in itself; if Africanists did not themselves bring about their own liberation they would go on for ever to be tortured with the need to assert the African personality, to 'prove themselves' and disprove the White myth that the black man is inferior."[44] My Fanonian reading of La Guma's work fulfills a kind of diagnostic function: The crisis in South Africa is analyzed but the analysis is taken up in the form of the novel itself, in so far as its structuring stirs up a variegated and unremitting politically committed narrative

Shilling Murile is the "native" whom Fanon describes as ready to "exchange the role of quarry for that of the hunter" and, therefore, to live out what has been his "permanent dream," to "become the persecutor."[45] Murile has become rebel and persecutor; he has made his destiny the persecution and destruction of the white "baas" whose cruelty resulted in his brother's death. His behavior structures an accusation at a regime that imprisons him for attempted murder when he lashes out ineffectually and angrily at one of his brother's aggressors but which rewards those aggressors with a "severe reprimand and a stiff fine" (*TB,* p. 77). These characters mean so much more than themselves or the sum of their actions: they reflect a system at work that elevates whites in order to negate blacks. Consequently, Murile makes of himself an invisible man in order to wreak revenge; unregistered and disregarded, he appears unrecognized before Hannes Meulen and carries out a calm and carefully prepared execution. As Fanon describes the moment:

> All the new, revolutionary assurance of the native stems from it. For if, in fact, my life is worth as much as the settler's, his glance no longers [*sic*] shrivels me up nor freezes me, and his voice no longer turns me into stone. I am no longer on tenterhooks in his presence; in fact, I don't give a damn for him. Not only does his presence no longer trouble me, but I am already preparing such efficient ambushes for him that soon there will be no way out but that of flight.[46]

In her discussion of "rebels and realists," Gail M. Gerhart states that the strategy of violent confrontation and ambush is that which appeals to "the mentally healthy African whose self-confidence had never been undermined by white 'training,' for whom the redressing of wrongs by violent means is a 'natural reaction.'"[47] The violence is clean, the moment of death contrasting markedly with the agony Timi, and indeed Shilling Murile himself, experienced. Tortured for accidentally letting Meulen's sheep out of a pen, they are pinioned, chained to a fence through the long night in its cold bitterness. Taking revenge—taking on the role of the "butcherbird" who hunts and impales his victims—Murile enacts the kind of representative vengeance that Mma Tau recognizes as prefatory to the larger fight and struggle that will take place in the wider zone of contact. Alex La Guma's characters inhabit what Gayatri Spivak describes as subject-positions, which are "epistemically fractured": "The so-called private individual and the public citizen . . . can inhabit widely different epistemes, violently at odds with each other yet yoked together by everyday ruses of *pouvoir-savoir*."[48] In Bakhtin's analysis Spivak's epistemes correlate with what he calls the "zone of contact." The zone of contact is where everyday life and ideologies intermingle, which is a zone that authoritative discourse attempts to avoid.[49] It is the zone that La Guma's "butcherbirds" inhabit, and in my reading the idea of the cleansing butcherbird does not begin and end with Shilling Murile but shifts and mutates through the places and spaces in the text. The collective struggle to clear the society of racism and oppression is beginning as the novel ends, in the hills above the dusty plain of the Karroo and in the cities. But it is a struggle that continues into "the yellowing afternoon light" (*TB*, p. 119), and that continued beyond the death of Alex La Guma in 1985. It is with his writing as foundational to the hopes and fears that characterize the "new South Africa" in a post-apartheid era that I concern myself in the conclusion.

Notes

1. Alex La Guma, *Time of the Butcherbird* (London: Heinemann, 1979), p. 1. All further references to this novel will be abbreviated as *TB* and included in the text.

2. Cecil A. Abrahams, *Alex La Guma* (Boston: Twayne, 1985), p. 115.

3. Abrahams, *Alex La Guma*, pp. 131–132.

4. Alex La Guma, "The Real Picture: Interview with Cecil Abrahams" in Cecil A. Abrahams, ed., *Memories of Home: The Writings of Alex La Guma* (Trenton, NJ: Africa World Press, 1991), p. 27.

5. Alex La Guma, *A Walk in the Night* (London: Heinemann, 1986), p. 1.

6. David Maughan-Brown, "Adjusting the Focal Length: Alex La Guma and Exile," *English in Africa*, 18:2 (October 1991), pp. 19–38.

7. Alex La Guma, "Coffee for the Road" in Jane Leggett and Roy Blatchford, eds., *It's Now or Never: Unwin Hyman Short Stories* (London: Unwin Hyman, 1988), pp. 70–79.

8. See Leggett and Blatchford, eds., *It's Now or Never*, p. 79.

9. Abrahams, *Alex La Guma*, p. 117.

10. Balasubramanyam Chandramohan, *A Study in Trans-Ethnicity in Modern South Africa: The Writings of Alex La Guma* (Lampeter: Mellen Research University Press, 1992), p. 162. The discussion of the significance of the Karroo runs from pp. 159–163. Chandramohan draws out interesting points as to the prevalence of "literature of the Karroo" in the South African literary tradition, from Olive Schreiner's *The Story of an African Farm* (1883) to Dan Jacobson's *A Dance in the Sun* (1956).

11. Govan Mbeki, *South Africa: The Peasants' Revolt* (London: International Defence and Aid Fund for Southern Africa, 1984), p. 16.

12. Chandramohan, *A Study in Trans-Ethnicity*, p. 149 and p. 179.

13. Chandramohan, *A Study in Trans-Ethnicity*, especially pp. 49–51.

14. Kathleen Balutansky, *The Novels of Alex La Guma: The Representation of a Political Conflict* (Boulder, Colorado: Lynne Rienner Publishers, Inc., 1990), pp. 105–106.

15. See, for example, Sandra M. Gilbert and Susan Gubar's discussion of the "metaphor of literary paternity" that begins in *The Madwoman in the Attic: The Woman Writer and the Nineteenth-Century Imagination* (New Haven and London: Yale University Press, 1979) and is followed through the *No Man's Land* trilogy of texts, which focus on the twentieth century. See also, Avril Horner and Sue Zlosnik, *Landscape of Desire: Metaphors in Modern Women's Fiction* (Hemel Hempstead: Harvester Wheatsheaf, 1990). In the context of African writing, Karla F. C. Holloway pushes her discussion of symbolism to more satisfying conclusions. Allowing that studies of metaphor and figurative language are complex and risk becoming unwieldy, she discusses three areas: revision, remembrance and recursion and the figurative strategies West African and African American writers deploy across a range of texts. See *Moorings and Metaphors: Figures of Gender in Black Women's Literature* (New Brunswick, NJ: Rutgers University Press, 1992).

16. To exemplify this point, see Theodora Akachi Ezeigbo, "'A Sign of the Times': Alex La Guma's *Time of the Butcherbird*," *Literary Half-Yearly*, 32:1, 1991, pp. 100–114. Ezeigbo turns to the study of symbols to "consider the way La Guma uses symbols to explore the socio-political dislocation that is inherent in his country." But her reading results in oversimplification and generalization: the Boers are "befogged by the dust of conservatism and short-sightedness" and "muddle-headed as regards the cause of the drought that is ravaging the whole country"; the heatwave is indicative of the smouldering of the black people; and all the symbols work as "signs of the times." See pp. 107–114. If anything, the effect of La Guma's vision of the country in the novel is weakened by this method of "ac-

counting" for each symbol in this way and the strategic politicized effects remain uninterrogated.

17. See, for example, in the South African context, Chapter One of Ursula A. Barnett, *A Vision of Order* (London: Sinclair Browne Ltd., 1983) and Hilda Bernstein's *The Rift: The Exile Experience of South Africans* (London: Jonathan Cape, 1994).

18. Zuzana M. Pick, "The Dialectical Wanderings of Exile" in *Screen: Over the Borderlines, Questioning National Identities,* 30:4 (Autumn 1989), p. 48.

19. Hendrick Frensch Verwoerd's words as recorded by Sir John Maud, British High Commissioner to South Africa 1959–1963, as quoted in Brian Lapping, *Apartheid: A History* (London: Paladin, 1988), p. 182.

20. Aletta J. Norval, "The Roots of an Expanding Imaginary: From Separate Development to Plural Society" in *Deconstructing Apartheid Discourse* (London: Verso, 1996), pp. 101–218.

21. Abdul JanMohamed, "Alex La Guma: The Generation of Marginal Fiction" in *Manichean Aesthetics: The Politics of Literature in Colonial Africa* (Amherst: University of Massachusetts Press, 1983), pp. 260–261, and Maughan-Brown, "Adjusting the Focal Length," p. 24.

22. Agnes Sam, "South Africa: Guest of Honour Amongst the Uninvited Newcomers to England's Great Tradition" in Kirsten Holst Petersen and Anna Rutherford, eds., *A Double Colonization: Colonial and Post-Colonial Women's Writing* (Mundelstrup, Denmark: Dangaroo Press, 1986), p. 94.

23. David Bordwell and Kristin Thompson, *Film Art: An Introduction* (New York: Alfred A. Knopf, 1986), p. 218. See Chapter 7, "The Relation of Shot to Shot: Editing" for an accessible exemplification of film theorizing in this area, pp. 199–231. For an application of such ideas in another African context, see my "Sembene Ousmane and 'Rhetorical Film Form'" in *Wasafiri,* 22 Africa '95 issue (Autumn 1995), pp. 49–53.

24. Maureen Whitebrook, "Taking the narrative turn: What the novel has to offer political theory," pp. 43 and 47, in John Horton and Andrea T. Baumeister, eds., *Literature and the Political Imagination* (London and New York: Routledge, 1996), pp. 33–52.

25. Susan Mendus, "'What of soul was left, I wonder?': The narrative self in political philosophy," p. 65 in Horton and Baumeister, *Literature and the Political Imagination.* Catherine Belsey, *Critical Practice* (London and New York: Methuen, 1980).

26. JanMohamed, *Manichean Aesthetics,* pp. 225–262.

27. Theodora Akachi Ezeigbo reads the novel as inclusive of the oppressors as well as the oppressed in the apartheid system but still persists with the idea that the novel has only three protagonists: see "'A Sign of the Times,'" pp. 102–106.

28. Maughan-Brown, "Adjusting the Focal Length," pp. 19–38.

29. Maughan-Brown, "Adjusting the Focal Length," pp. 22–23. He quotes La Guma's explanation of the title: "The title of the novel comes from African

folklore. One of the riddles from the oral tradition indicates that the butcherbird represents something which not only cleanses the cattle but also cleanses the society . . . What I'm trying to say is that conscious resistance of the people heralds the time when the butcherbird will cleanse South Africa of racism, oppression, and so on," p. 23.

30. Alex La Guma in interview with Robert Seramuga in 1966 responds in these terms to Seramuga's observation that South African writers do not create individuals so much as figures within a situation: "I think that it's inevitable—having to live in a society based on racial discrimination, one where people are set virtually into compartments . . . Whatever opinion they have to express becomes involved with the impact of this situation, this colour situation, on them." See Dennis Duerden and Cosmo Pieterse, *African Writers Talking* (New York: Africana Publishing Corporation, 1972), p. 92.

31. Frantz Fanon, *Black Skin, White Masks* (London: Pluto Press, 1986), pp. 161–163. In the context of American civil rights in the 1960s, Richard H. King makes a similar point discussing Lacan's mirror stage as deployed by Fanon at this stage of his analysis in his chapter "Violence and Self-respect: Fanon and Black Radicalism." See Richard H. King, *Civil Rights and the Idea of Freedom* (New York and Oxford: Oxford University Press, 1992), pp. 178–179.

32. Mikhail Bakhtin, *The Dialogic Imagination,* ed. M. Holquist, trans. C. Emerson and M. Holquist (Austin: University of Texas, 1981), p. 342.

33. Bakhtin, *The Dialogic Imagination,* p. 342.

34. Bakhtin, *The Dialogic Imagination,* p. 346.

35. Bakhtin, *The Dialogic Imagination,* p. 263.

36. Bakhtin, *The Dialogic Imagination,* p. 263.

37. Bakhtin, *The Dialogic Imagination,* p. 345.

38. Sergei Eisenstein, *The Film Sense* (1943) (London and Boston: Faber and Faber, 1977), p.65.

39. Louis Tremaine comes nearest to this position when he reads *Time of the Butcherbird* as a movement away from analytical fiction to "speculative fiction." See "Ironic Convergence in Alex La Guma's *Time of the Butcherbird,*" *Journal of Commonwealth Literature,* 29:2, 1994, pp. 31–44. Balutansky in *The Novels of Alex La Guma* appears to move towards a similar reading but her conclusion (which focuses on the "bisecting roads" in this novel as discussed by Cecil Abrahams and others) is that La Guma's "optimism" transcends the alienating effects of apartheid. This novel "offers a glimpse" into a "land from which the curse of apartheid has been lifted," see pp. 121. Balutansky projects the novel beyond its conceptualization and its context.

40. JanMohamed, *Manichean Aesthetics,* p. 260.

41. Frantz Fanon, *The Wretched of the Earth* (London: Penguin, 1990), p. 34.

42. Fanon, *The Wretched of the Earth*, p. 47.

43. Fanon, *The Wretched of the Earth*, p. 74.

44. Patrick van Rensburg, *Guilty Land* (London: Penguin, 1962), p. 161.

45. Fanon, *The Wretched of the Earth*, p. 41.

46. Fanon, *The Wretched of the Earth*, p. 35.

47. Gail M. Gerhart, *Black Power in South Africa: The Evolution of an Ideology* (Berkeley: University of California Press, 1978), p. 42. See her discussion of "rebels and realists," pp. 39–44.

48. Gayatri Spivak, "More on Power/Knowledge" in Donna Landry and Gerald MacLean, eds., *The Spivak Reader: Selected Works of Gayatri Chakravorty Spivak* (New York and London: Routledge, 1996), p. 163.

49. Bakhtin, *The Dialogic Imagination*, p. 345.

Chapter 7
▼▼▼▼▼▼▼▼▼

Towards Post-Apartheid Narratives

Alex La Guma's writing was committed to the cause: to bringing down the oppressive structure of South African apartheid, which was refined and expanded from the British-implemented model of segregation. In this book I have explored how La Guma describes the role of the writer in the same terms as the revolutionary freedom fighter, willing to give his life for a political cause that will emancipate all those subjugated by the racist ideologies of white oppressors. In his fiction there is the discernible voice of one who is prepared to give vent to the inequalities of life for the masses under apartheid, but there is also the authorial distance of one who clearly sees that not every individual is able to participate in the struggle in the same way. Hence, there is no sense of his passing judgment in his fiction: the characters he represents are often drawn from the communities he knew, or was intensely aware of, as in the case of the Afrikaners of the Karroo in his final published work. In this way he is able to present the reader with a cross-section of society that includes the disaffected, like Foxy and his gang in *A Walk in the Night,* and the apathetic, like Tommy from *In the Fog of the Seasons' End,* as well as those politically committed to the destruction of apartheid like Mma Tau, as set against the regime's intermediaries like Constable Raalt or the politician Hannes Meulen.

Those committed to the struggle for a free and democratic South Africa participated in the struggle in whichever ways lay open to them. But the role of the writer was also that of reporter in apartheid South Africa, fully prepared to report events in an unflinching manner, no matter how gory or unpalatable those events might prove to be. Indeed, in his address to the delegates at the 1986 Stockholm Conference for African Writers, Sipho Sepamla—renowned for incisive works like the "Soweto" novel *Ride on the Whirlwind* (1981)—made it quite clear that the South African writer under apartheid was "confronted with such devastating material" that he or she had no need to "embellish it by exaggeration."[1] What we uncover in La Guma's fiction might be termed the testimonies of ordinary people, those people struggling through their daily existence to survive the horrors of apartheid and even to plot ways of overthrowing the regime. La Guma's novels are examples of what Njabulo Ndebele calls protest fiction, but it is difficult to agree with his assertion that this genre is specifically characterized by the "spectacular." For Ndebele the spectacular documents: "it indicts implicitly; it is demonstrative, preferring exteriority to interiority; it keeps the larger issues of society in our minds, obliterating the details; it provokes identification through recognition and feeling rather than through observation and analytical thought; it calls for emotion rather than conviction; it establishes a vast sense of presence without offering intimate knowledge; it confirms without necessarily offering a challenge." In short, he describes the spectacular as "the literature of the powerless." The powerless simply identify the factors that conspire to ensure their powerlessness.[2] Ndebele's assumption, here, is that this type of writing is all flat surfaces; it lacks the substance to empower. My reasons for bringing Ndebele into this debate are precisely because he analyzes La Guma's short story "Coffee for the Road" to exemplify his argument (originally presented as a conference paper in 1984), some five years after the publication of La Guma's final novel *Time of the Butcherbird*.

It is germane, then, to point to the fact that his analysis is made to fit "Coffee for the Road," for an examination of La Guma's novels would have clearly identified a depth that Ndebele finds so lacking in what I have termed apartheid narratives. Ndebele examines three short stories, which he considers exemplificatory of a rejection of the "spectacular" because they attest to his notion of "rediscovering the ordinary"—the opposite of the "spectacular." Ndebele commends the "ordinary" for its "sobering rationality," investing in the delineation of the quotidian.[3] He calls for fiction that addresses everyday realities as the basis for social transformation, as distinct from novels that protest, in his view, but fail to challenge the overarching apartheid system. La Guma's novels clearly attest to the "ordinary," the everyday intransigence of poverty and marginalization in a dialectical relationship to "the spectacular moral wrong." In an interview with Cecil Abrahams, La Guma succinctly expressed his views on this feature of his writing:

> I have always tried to avoid idealizing the South African scene. I
> don't try to present a picture where all black people are good and
> all white people are bad. That is not a consideration at all. The
> effect of black and white is purely circumstantial and there is more
> to it than that. So that when I portray the life of South Africa I
> try to show it as it actually is, as people actually are.[4]

As I have shown, La Guma's characters are neither one-dimensional nor
flat but ordinarily multifaceted individuals who, through their exchanges
with others, grow and develop politically, gradually coming to a consciously
politicized understanding and realization of their social predicament. Ndebele
demands an analysis of the apartheid situation, and La Guma provides it
through his carefully crafted novels, if not quite so demonstrably in the
cameos reconfigured in his short stories.

In *Culture and Imperialism*, Edward Said argues that it is not possible to examine the work of politically committed writers like Alex
La Guma without taking into account that such work is "embedded
in its political circumstances, of which the history of imperialism and
resistance to it is surely one of the most important."[5] He believes that
it is "harder to render invisible the politics of African culture"[6] and
that Alex La Guma's achievement lies precisely in his ability to render
visible the daily frustrations of an oppressed people, while also keeping his international audience keyed to the horrors that black South
Africans endured as direct result of apartheid policies. One need only
recall the mechanical sacking of Michael Adonis, which ultimately re-
moves him from the economy of labor in *A Walk in the Night*; or the
treatment of Isaac who, though a grown man, is still referred to as a
"boy" by his white colleagues in *In the Fog of the Seasons' End*; or, in
the same novel, the unnamed old woman who is left on the streets
with her belongings because she is too poor to maintain her accommodations. Across his fiction, La Guma conveys the minutiae, decanting
the details into the "bigger picture" of life under apartheid. While it
is true to say that La Guma occasionally falls into polemics, he is
generally assured in his portrayal and analysis of the injustices inflicted
upon his fellow "citizens" by his fellow citizens. Accepting Said's idea
that resistance is a two-part action whereby the first part is "primary
resistance" defined as "literally fighting against outside intrusion," it
is possible to see how literary works like La Guma's attempted to
present a counterideology, an open democratic dialogical model, in
opposition to the hegemony represented as apartheid. This counterideology performs the second part of the resistance equation, which
Said characterizes, via Basil Davidson, as encompassing a reconstitu-

tion of a "shattered" community, in order to "save or reinforce the sense and fact of community against all the pressures of the colonial system."[7]

Through characters like George Adams, Yusef the Turk and Solly in *The Stone Country*, La Guma indicates that it is possible to resist in a system where intraracial violence is sanctioned by the state in an effort to erode solidarity, just as it is possible to retain a sense of dignity and community in the face of disgusting and dehumanizing living conditions, as exemplified by the party scene in *And A Threefold Cord*. Resistance that inevitably moves from a pacifist model to a violent one is shown to be the inevitable final resort in *In the Fog of the Seasons' End* and *Time of the Butcherbird*. There is clearly a discernible shift from a politics that combines the will to survive with a resigned apathy in which apartheid is accepted, towards a gradual understanding of state-sanctioned oppression that incorporates a move towards action on the part of the characters: a politics of resistance.

In the most banal of definitions, nations bound "together in independence and nationalist groupings" are based in an identity-formation—whether ethnic, religious, or communal—that opposes Western interference and encroachment.[8] The point cannot be overstated that in apartheid South Africa, the Nationalist Party's policies after 1948 existed to cement segregation into the national fabric of the republic. To this end the existence of small "political" groups like the Coloured Peoples' Organisation or the Indian Congress was not perceived as a *major* threat to South Africa—unlike the Communist Party of South Africa, which was disbanded before it could be banned in 1950. It was only with the Congress of the People that the government saw the real danger of mass mobilization, so it sought to hinder the meeting, allowing the three thousand delegates and speakers a platform only on the first day, before moving in on the second day to arrest those involved and seize all papers. The function of Congress of the People was primarily for organizations representing formerly discrete racial groups to ratify the Freedom Charter in Congress and to accept it as a manifesto for *all* South Africans. In this they succeeded. This was an historically momentous event in 1955, expressing the real possibility that all oppressed South Africans and "democratic whites" could fight the racist government on a united front. The cataclysmic significance of this breakthrough in anti-apartheid ideology and action is revealed in La Guma's fiction, where he incorporates the roles played by Indian, African and colored peoples in resistance to the dominant racist ideology. In both *And A Threefold Cord* and *In the Fog of the Seasons' End,* La Guma presents the reader with characters who are willing to risk their lives for the greater freedom of all South Africans, regardless of race.[9]

In February 1990, F. W. de Klerk claimed that "The season of violence is over. The time for reconstruction and reconciliation has arrived."[10] It was at this point that Nelson Mandela's release from jail was announced and de Klerk intended his statement as an endorsement, perhaps, of the fact that South Africa had indeed battled through the fog at the end of many seasons of apartheid policy. However, while the structure that was apartheid was beginning to be dismantled, important questions about culture in the new South Africa were being asked. Indeed, Kenneth Parker writing his "Apartheid and the Politics of Literature" in 1986 was then clear that apartheid was soon to be replaced but believed that "the manner of replacement" would prove crucial.[11] Parker uses inverted commas around "South Africa" throughout his article in order to illustrate that the region had always been a white construct and that the appellation had never reflected the fragmented "communities" that the term sought to contain. Critics now are loath to remove their inverted commas from the "new South Africa" until it has proved its existence in more than words. It is still uncertain what the "new South Africa" will entail but discussions have already opened up debates as to the role of literature post-apartheid. A 1990 conference entitled "Literature in Another South Africa" looked to the future of South African writing. The editors of the collected papers note the continuing threat of "internecine violence, even civil war" and consider how "to give concrete shape to a post-apartheid culture while remaining interrogative and dialogic about our projections."[12]

The debate about the centrality of a literature of commitment continues and Albie Sachs has added his thoughts to those of Ndebele. In "Preparing Ourselves For Freedom,"[13] Sachs advocated at an in-house ANC seminar that the slogan "Culture as a Weapon of Struggle" be banned together with all culturally symbolic uses of guns and spears (the spear is one of the symbols of the ANC itself, of course). Sachs has been consistent over the years in his desire to emphasize nonviolent alternatives in struggle.[14] But, his paper elicited an unprecedented range of responses that coincided with the ANC announcing the official suspension of the armed struggle, after Mandela's release in 1990. The problem remains as to the extent to which the oppressors' violent suppression of blacks and their consequent armed resistance to that violence can fade easily into the background with the end of apartheid. Apartheid was not ended by armed resistance alone but came about incrementally through a gradual wearing away and crumbling of the architecture of the system—although murders, massacres, confrontations, demonstrations and assassinations preceded its demise. Fanon almost seems to have predicted the difficulties Mandela and the ANC government would face when he argues in "Concerning Violence" that "the young independent nation evolves during the first years in an atmosphere of the battlefield, for the political leader of an underdeveloped country looks fearfully at the huge distance his country will have to cover."[15] The "new South Africa" is certainly not underdeveloped in all areas but ideas of equitably redistributing status and wealth and restructuring social systems peacefully and yet effectively have been impossible to enact without first recognizing that the developing people's culture of the "new South Africa" can itself become a weapon of struggle. Pitika Ntuli provides a response to Albie Sachs that has influenced some of my thinking and that deploys Fanon's example of national reconstruction as more workable or achievable than Sachs' formulations: "Each generation must, out of relative obscurity, discover its mission, fulfil it or betray it."[16] Abstract intentions are still to be legislated into concrete realities, and Sachs is understandably worried as to the potential "role" for cultural products in a post-apartheid South Africa for, as Graham Pechey has argued, "writing in South Africa has always existed in, and been implicitly or explicitly informed by, a certain relationship to fighting."[17]

Writing in South Africa has developed an extremely close relationship with anti-apartheid politics and policies, but it has never had an immediate or uncomplicated impact on the outside world, a factor that reflects the complicity of many governments', not least Britain's, reluctance to support the oppressed masses in South Africa. Literature of the apartheid era, like the literature of any number of decolonizing nations, has not enjoyed universal critical acclaim. In Edward Said's words, "Westerners have assumed the integrity and the inviolability of their cultural masterpieces, their scholarship, their worlds of discourse; the rest of the world stands petitioning for attention at our windowsill."[18] The greatest achievement of La Guma's writing lies in its attempt to smash the windows to which Said refers and in so doing to throw light on the atrocities of the apartheid era.

La Guma would no doubt relish the irony of the Truth and Reconciliation Commission chaired by Archbishop Desmond Tutu. In an effort to ensure the smooth transition of power and to maintain healthy relations with the former colonizers, the new government attempted to heal the rifts between the majority population and its former oppressors. This process was intended to be cathartic and to provide a public platform that would work to ensure that such atrocities would be avoided in the future. In fact, Fanon foresaw such a move when he stated that the new government of a formally subjugated state expects: "from those who for centuries have kept it in slavery . . . that they will help it to rehabilitate mankind, and make man victorious everywhere, once and for all." But he warns: "we are not so naive as to think that this will come about with cooperation and the goodwill of the European governments" but they "must realize that in the past they have often joined the ranks of our common masters where colonial questions were concerned. To achieve this, the European peoples must first decide to wake up and shake themselves, use their brains, and stop playing the stupid game of the Sleeping Beauty."[19] The "new South Africa" must wait and see what the future holds in the twenty-first century, as the descendants of European settlers finally begin to co-exist with their African counterparts. The only certainty is that the nation has started on the long road to rehabilitation that follows colonial conquest and rule. The country now welcomes back those "dissidents" and freedom fighters who were exiled, but sadly, one important figure will not return, though La Guma's legacy lives on in his fiction and in his criticism of the apartheid era in his country's history.

This book has examined how the novels of Alex La Guma are clearly impacted by the institutional violence of apartheid but, with the dismantling of its structures, violence remains an undertow in the situation. Even at the moment of the first democratic elections, the extreme Right threatened "to mobilise 60,000 armed men and disrupt the transition,"[20] and Inkatha and the Freedom Alliance's unwillingness to register prior to the 1994 Elections signaled an early possibility of strife that materialized in a demonstration and shootings on March 28 in Johannesburg.[21] Throughout this book I have argued that La Guma's apartheid narratives painstakingly bear witness to the atrocities of the long night of apartheid but that he achieves much more; his novels chart the move towards ideological and violent resistance. La Guma memorably conveys the struggle with violence that inevitably characterized the transition to a multiracial democratic "new South Africa." It will now be the task of contemporary writers to create out of the "new South Africa." Only time will tell whether fighting and violence will prove to be appropriate subject matter or whether guns and spears will become the symbols of South Africa's past.

Notes

1. Sipho Sepamla, "To What Extent Is the South Africa Writer's Problem Still Bleak and Immense?," p. 187 in Kirsten Holst Petersen, ed., *Criticism and Ideology: Second African Writers' Conference, Stockholm 1986* (Uppsala: Scandinavian Institute of African Studies, 1988), pp. 186–192.

2. Njabulo Ndebele, "The Rediscovery of the Ordinary: Some New Writings in South Africa" in his *South African Literature and Culture: Rediscovery of the Ordinary* (Manchester: Manchester University Press, 1994), p. 49.

3. Ndebele, "The Rediscovery of the Ordinary," p. 53.

4. Cecil A. Abrahams, ed., *Memories of Home: The Writings of Alex La Guma* (Trenton, NJ: Africa World Press, 1991), p. 26.

5. Edward Said, *Culture and Imperialism* (London: Chatto and Windus, 1993), p. 288.

6. Idem.

7. Said, *Culture and Imperialism*, pp. 252–253.

8. Said, *Culture and Imperialism*, p. 263.

9. For a fuller discussion of this feature of La Guma's fiction, see Balasubramanyam Chandramohan, *A Study in Trans-Ethnicity in Modern South Africa: The Writings of Alex La Guma* (Lewiston/Lampeter: Mellen Research University Press, 1992).

10. F. W. de Klerk quoted in Jo-Anne Birnie Danzker, "Organizational Apartheid," *Third Text*, no. 13, Winter 1990/1991, p. 85.

11. Kenneth Parker, "Apartheid and the Politics of Literature," *Red Letters*, vol. 20, 1986, p. 12.

12. Elleke Boehmer, Laura Chrisman, Kenneth Parker, eds., *Altered State? Writing and South Africa* (Yorkshire: Dangaroo Press, 1994), pp. vii–viii.

13. Albie Sachs's paper and responses to it are collected in Ingrid de Kok and Karen Press, eds., *Spring Is Rebellious: Arguments About Cultural Freedom by Albie Sachs and Respondents* (Cape Town: Buchu Books, 1990).

14. See, for example, his discussion of violence in Albie Sachs, *The Jail Diary of Albie Sachs* (London: Paladin, 1990), pp. 102–105.

15. Frantz Fanon, *The Wretched of the Earth* (London: Penguin, 1990), p. 75.

16. Frantz Fanon quoted in Pitika Ntuli, "Fragments Under a Telescope: A Response to Albie Sachs," p. 73, *Third Text*, no. 23, Summer 1993, pp. 69-77.

17. Graham Pechey, "Post-apartheid Narratives" in Francis Barker *et al.*, *Colonial Discourse/Postcolonial Theory* (Manchester: Manchester University Press, 1994), p. 162.

18. Said, *Culture and Imperialism*, p. 313.

19. Fanon, *The Wretched of the Earth*, p. 84.

20. Gillian Slovo, "The Hope and the Fear," *Weekend Guardian*, 26 March 1994, p. 6.

21. See, for example, John Carlin's report "Modern Times" in the *Independent Magazine*, 9 April 1994, p. 13.

Bibliography

Abrahams, Cecil A. *Alex La Guma*. Boston: Twayne Publishers, 1985.

————. "Alex La Guma." In *International Literature in English: Essays on the Major Writers*, edited by Robert L. Ross. New York and London: Garland Publishing Inc., 1991: 193–204.

————. *Essays on Literature*. Toronto, Canada: AFO Enterprises, 1986.

————, ed. *Memories of Home: The Writings of Alex La Guma*. Trenton, NJ: Africa World Press, 1991.

————. "The South African Writer in a Changing Society." *Matatu* 3–4 (1988): 32–43.

Adam, Ian, and Helen Tiffin, eds. *Past the Last Post: Theorizing Post-Colonialism and Post-Modernism*. Hemel Hempstead: Harvester Wheatsheaf, 1993.

Ahmad, Aijaz. "The Politics of Literary Postcoloniality." *Race and Class* 36:3 (1995): 1–20.

Althusser, Louis. *Essays on Ideology*. London: Verso, 1984.

Alvarado, Manuel and John O. Thompson, eds. *The Media Reader*. London: BFI, 1990.

Arendt, Hannah. *On Violence*. London: Allen Lane/Penguin Press, 1970.

Asein, Samuel. "The Revolutionary Vision in Alex La Guma's Novels." *Lotus: Afro-Asian Writings* 24–25 (April–September 1975): 9–21.

————. *Alex La Guma: The Man and His Work*. Ibadan: New Horn/Heinemann, 1987.

Ashcroft, Bill, Gareth Griffiths, and Helen Tiffin, eds. *The Empire Writes Back: Theory and Practice in Post-colonial Literatures*. London: Routledge, 1989.

————. *The Post-Colonial Studies Reader*. London: Routledge, 1995.

Bakhtin, Mikhail. *The Dialogic Imagination.* Edited by M. Holquist, translated by Caryl Emerson and M. Holquist. Austin: University of Texas, 1981.

———. *Problems of Dostoevsky's Poetics.* Introduced and translated by Caryl Emerson. Manchester: Manchester University Press, 1984.

Balibar, Etienne, and Immanuel Wallerstein. *Race, Nation, Class: Ambiguous Identities.* London: Verso, 1991.

Balutansky, Kathleen. *The Novels of Alex La Guma: The Representation of a Political Conflict.* Boulder, CO: Lynne Rienner Publishers Inc., 1990.

Barker, Francis, Peter Hulme, and Margaret Iverson, eds. *Colonial Discourse/ Postcolonial Theory.* Manchester: Manchester University Press, 1994.

Barnett, Ursula A. *A Vision of Order.* London: Sinclair Browne Ltd., 1983.

Barratt, Harold. "South Africa's Dark Night: Metaphor and Symbol in La Guma's Fiction." *The Literary Griot: International Journal of Black Oral and Literary Studies* 3:2 (1991): 28–36.

Barrett, Michele. *Women's Oppression Today: Problems in Marxist Feminist Analysis.* London: Verso, 1986.

Baudrillard, Jean. *America.* London: Verso, 1988.

Beier, Uli, ed. *Introduction to African Literature.* London: Longman, 1967.

Bell, Bernard W. *The Afro-American Novel and Its Tradition.* Amherst: University of Massachusetts Press, 1987.

Belsey, Catherine. *Critical Practice.* London and New York: Methuen, 1980.

Benjamin, Andrew, and Peter Osbourne, eds. *Walter Benjamin's Philosophy: Destruction and Experience.* London: Routledge, 1994.

Benjamin, Walter. *Illuminations.* London: Fontana, 1992.

Bernstein, Hilda. *The Rift: The Exile Experience of South Africans.* London: Jonathan Cape, 1994.

———. "Schools for Servitude." In *Apartheid,* edited by Alex La Guma. London: Lawrence and Wishart, 1972: 43–79.

———. *The World That Was Ours: The Story of the Rivonia Trial.* London: SAWriters, 1989.

Bhabha, Homi. *The Location of Culture.* London: Routledge, 1994.

———. "The Other Question: The Stereotype and Colonial Discourse." *Screen* 24: 6 (1983): 18–36.

———. "Representation and the Colonial Text: A Critical Exploration of Some Forms of Mimeticism." In *The Theory of Reading,* edited by Frank Gloversmith. Brighton: Harvester, 1984: 93–122.

Boehmer, Elleke, Laura Chrisman, and Kenneth Parker, eds. *Altered State? Writing and South Africa.* Yorkshire: Dangaroo Press, 1994.

Bordwell, David, and Kristin Thompson. *Film Art: An Introduction.* New York: Alfred A. Knopf, 1986.

Breytenbach, Breyten. "Vulture Culture: The Alienation of White South Africa." In *Apartheid,* edited by Alex La Guma. London: Lawrence and Wishart, 1972: 137–148.

Brookes, Edgar H. *Apartheid: A Documentary Study of South Africa.* London: Routledge and Kegan Paul 1968.

Bulhan, Hussein Abdilahi. *Frantz Fanon and the Psychology of Oppression.* New York and London: Plenum Press, 1985.

Carlin, John. "Modern Times." *Independent Magazine* (London), April 9, 1994, 13.

Carpenter, William. "'Ovals, Spheres, Ellipses, and Sundry Bulges': Alex La Guma Imagines the Human Body." *Research in African Literatures* 22:4 (Winter 1991): 79–98.

———. "The Scene of Representation in Alex La Guma's Later Novels." *English in Africa* 18:2 (October 1991): 1–18.

Carusi, Annamaria. "Post, Post and Post. Or Where Is South African Literature In All This?" In *Past the Last Post: Theorizing Post-Colonialism and Post-Modernism,* edited by Ian Adam and Helen Tiffin. Hemel Hempstead: Harvester Wheatsheaf, 1991: 95–108.

Caute, David. *Fanon.* London: Fontana, 1970.

Chandramohan, Balasubramanyam. *A Study in Trans-Ethnicity in Modern South Africa: The Writings of Alex La Guma.* Lampeter: Mellen Research University Press, 1992.

Chapman, Michael. *Southern African Literatures.* London and New York: Longman, 1996.

Chennells, Anthony. "Pastoral and Anti-Pastoral Elements in Alex La Guma's Later Novels." In *Literature, Language and the Nation,* edited by Emmanuel Ngara and Andrew Morrison. Harare, Zimbabwe: Association of University Teachers of Literature and Language [ATOLL] and Baobab Books, 1989: 39–49.

Childs, Peter, and Patrick Williams. *An Introduction to Post-Colonial Theory.* Hemel Hempstead: Harvester Wheatsheaf, 1997.

Clingman, Stephen, ed. *Nadine Gordimer: The Essential Gesture.* London: Penguin, 1988.

Cock, Jacklyn. *Maids and Madams: A Study in the Politics of Exploitation.* Johannesburg: Ravan Press, 1980.

Coetzee, J. M. "Alex La Guma and the Responsibilities of the South African Writer." In *New African Literature and the Arts, vol. iii,* edited by Joseph Okpaku. New York: The Third Press: Joseph Okpaku Publishing Co., 1973: 116–124.

———. "Man's Fate in the Novels of Alex La Guma." *Studies in Black Literature* 5:1 (1974): 16–23.

———. *White Writing: On the Culture of Letters in South Africa.* New Haven and London: Yale University Press, 1988.

Cohen, Robin. *Endgame in South Africa?* London: UNESCO/James Currey, 1986.

Collits, Terry. "Theorizing Racism." In *De-scribing Empire: Post-colonialism and Textuality,* edited by Chris Tiffin and Alan Lawson. London: Routledge, 1994: 61–69.

Dailly, Christophe. "The Coming of Age of the African Novel." *Presence Africaine* 130:2 (1984): 118–131.

Dalton, Dennis. *Mahatma Gandhi: Nonviolent Power in Action.* New York: Columbia University Press, 1993.

Danzker, Jo-Anne Birnie. "Organizational Apartheid." *Third Text* 13 (Winter 1990/1991): 85–95.

Davenport, T.R.H. *South Africa: A Modern History.* London: Macmillan, 1992.

Davies, Ioan. *Writers in Prison.* Oxford: Blackwell, 1990.

Davis, Lennard, J. *Resisting Novels: Ideology and Fiction.* New York: Methuen, 1987.

Davis, Rob, Dan O'Meara, and Sipho Dlamini. *The Struggle for South Africa: A Reference Guide, Volume One.* London: Zed Books, 1984.

de Jongh, James. *Vicious Modernism: Black Harlem and the Literary Imagination.* Cambridge: Cambridge University Press, 1990.

de Kok, Ingrid, and Karen Press, eds. *Spring Is Rebellious: Arguments About Cultural Freedom by Albie Sachs and Respondents.* Cape Town, South Africa: Buchu Books, 1990.

Derrida, Jacques. "But, Beyond . . . " In *"Race," Writing and Difference,* edited by Henry Louis Gates. Chicago: University of Chicago Press, 1986: 354–369.

———. "Racism's Last Word." In *"Race," Writing and Difference,* edited by Henry Louis Gates. Chicago: University of Chicago Press, 1986: 329–338.

Duerden, Dennis, and Cosmo Pieterse, eds. *African Writers Talking.* New York: Africana Publishing Corporation, 1972.

du Plessis, Phil. "White Blood, Black Fire." *Contrast (South African Journal)* 16 (July 1987): 35–41.

Eisenstein, Sergei. *The Film Sense.* London and Boston: Faber and Faber, 1977.

Ezeigbo, Theodora Akachi. "'A Sign of the Times': Alex La Guma's *Time of the Butcherbird.*" *Literary Half-Yearly* 32:1 (1991): 100–114.

Fanon, Frantz. *Black Skin, White Masks.* London: Pluto Press, 1986.

———. *The Wretched of the Earth.* London: Penguin, 1990.

February, Vernie A. *Mind Your Colour: The "Coloured" Stereotype in South African Literature.* London: Kegan Paul International, 1981.

Foster, Don (with Dennis Davies and Diane Sandler). *Detention and Torture in South Africa: Psychological, Legal and Historical Studies.* London: James Currey, 1987.

Foucault, Michel. *Discipline and Punish: The Birth of the Prison.* London: Penguin, 1979.

———. *Power/Knowledge: Selected Interviews and Other Writings 1972–1977,* edited by Colin Gordon. Hemel Hempstead: Harvester Wheatsheaf, 1980.

Freire, Paulo. *The Pedagogy of the Oppressed*. London: Penguin, 1972.

Fuss, Diana. "Interior Colonies: Frantz Fanon and the Politics of Identification." *Diacritics* 23:2, 3 (1994): 20–42.

Futcha, Innocent. "The Fog in *In the Fog of the Seasons' End*." *Ngam* 1 and 2 (1977): 78–92.

Gates, Henry Louis, ed. *"Race," Writing and Difference*. Chicago: University of Chicago Press, 1986.

Gendzier, Irene L. *Frantz Fanon: A Critical Study*. London: Wildwood House, 1973.

Gerhart, Gail M. *Black Power in South Africa: The Evolution of an Ideology*. Berkeley: University of California Press, 1978.

Gikandi, Simon. *Reading the African Novel*. London: James Currey/Heinemann, 1987.

Gilbert, Sandra M., and Susan Gubar. *The Madwoman in the Attic: The Woman Writer and the Nineteenth-Century Imagination*. New Haven and London: Yale University Press, 1979.

Girard, Rene. *Violence and the Sacred*. Translated by Patrick Gregory. Baltimore and London: Johns Hopkins University Press, 1977.

Gloversmith, Frank, ed. *The Theory of Reading*. Brighton: Harvester, 1984.

Gordimer, Nadine. "English-Language Literature and Politics in South Africa." In *Aspects of South African Literature,* edited by Christopher Heywood. London: Heinemann, 1976: 99–120.

Green, Robert. "Alex La Guma's *In the Fog of the Seasons' End*: The Politics of Subversion." *UMOJA* 3:2 (1979): 85–93.

———. "Chopin in the Ghetto: The Short Stories of Alex La Guma." *World Literature Written in English* 20:1 (1981): 5–16.

Griffiths, Gareth. "The Myth of Authenticity." In *De-scribing Empire: Postcolonialism and Textuality,* edited by Chris Tiffin and Alan Lawson. London: Routledge, 1994: 70–85.

Gugelberger, Georg M., ed. *Marxism and African Literature*. Trenton, NJ: Africa World Press, 1986.

Hall, Stuart. "Cultural Identity and Diaspora." In *Identity: Community, Culture, Difference,* edited by Jonathan Rutherford. London: Lawrence and Wishart, 1990: 222–237.

———. "The Whites of Their Eyes: Racist Ideologies and the Media." In *The Media Reader,* edited by Manuel Alvarado and John O. Thompson. London: BFI, 1990: 7–23.

Hamacher, Werner. "Afformative Strike: Benjamin's 'Critique of Violence.'" In *Walter Benjamin's Philosophy: Destruction and Experience,* edited by Andrew Benjamin and Peter Osbourne. London: Routledge, 1994: 110–138.

Harlow, Barbara. *After Lives: Legacies of Revolutionary Writing*. London: Verso, 1996.

———. *Resistance Literature*. New York and London: Methuen, 1987.

Heywood, Christopher, ed. *Aspects of South African Literature*. London: Heinemann, 1976.

Holloway, Karla, F. C. *Moorings and Metaphors: Figures of Gender in Black Women's Literature*. New Brunswick, NJ: Rutgers University Press, 1992.

Holt, Elvin. "Confronting Apartheid in Alex La Guma's *A Walk in the Night*." *Griot: Official Journal of the Southern Conference on Afro American Studies* (Fall 1990): 39–43.

Honderich, Ted. *Three Essays on Political Violence*. Oxford: Blackwell, 1976.

Horn, Andrew, and George E. Carter, eds. *American Studies in Africa*. Lesotho: University Press of Lesotho and the Ford Foundation, 1984.

Horner, Avril, and Sue Zlosnik. *Landscape of Desire: Metaphors in Modern Women's Fiction*. Hemel Hempstead: Harvester Wheatsheaf, 1990.

Horton, John, and Andrea T. Baumeister, eds. *Literature and the Political Imagination*. London and New York: Routledge, 1996.

Jacobs, J. U. "Confession, Interrogation and Self-interrogation in the New South African Prison Writing." In *On Shifting Sands: New Art and Literature from South Africa,* edited by Kirsten Holst Petersen and Anna Rutherford. Coventry, UK and Portsmouth, NH: Dangaroo Press and Heinemann, 1992: 115–127.

JanMohamed, Abdul R. "The Economy of Manichean Allegory: The Function of Racial Difference in Colonialist Literature" *Critical Inquiry* 12, (1985): 59–87.

———. *Manichean Aesthetics: The Politics of Literature in Colonial Africa*. Amherst: University of Massachusetts Press, 1983.

July, Robert. "The African Personality in the African Novel." In *Introduction to African Literature: An Anthology of Critical Writing,* edited by Uli Beier. London: Longman, 1967: 218–233.

Ketrak, Ketu H. "Decolonizing Culture: Toward a Theory of Postcolonial Women's Texts." *Modern Fiction Studies* 35:1 (Fall 1989): 157–179.

Kibera, Leonard. "A Critical Appreciation of Alex La Guma's *In The Fog of the Seasons' End*." *Busara* 8:1 (1976): 59–68.

King, Richard H. *Civil Rights and the Idea of Freedom*. New York and Oxford: Oxford University Press, 1992.

Klima, V., et al. *Black Africa: Literature and Language*. Prague: Czechoslovakian Academy of Sciences, 1976.

Kunene, Mazisi. "Revolutionary Challenges and Cultural Perspectives." In *New African Literature and the Arts, vol. iii,* edited by Joseph Okpaku. New York: The Third Press and Joseph Okpaku Publishing Co., 1973: 49–56.

La Guma, Alex. "African Culture and National Liberation." In *New African Literature and the Arts, vol. iii,* edited by Joseph Okpaku. New York: The Third Press and Joseph Okpaku Publishing Co., 1973: 58–61.

———. *And A Threefold Cord.* London: Kliptown Books, 1988.

———, ed. *Apartheid.* London: Lawrence and Wishart, 1972.

———. "At the Portagee's." In *A Walk in the Night*: 108–113.

———. "Blankets." In *A Walk in the Night*: 121–124.

———. "Coffee for the Road." In *It's Now Or Never,* edited by Jane Leggett and Roy Blatchford. London: Unwin Hyman, 1988: 70–79.

———. "The Condition of Culture in South Africa." *Presence Africaine* 80 (1971): 113–122.

———. "Culture and Liberation." *World Literature Written in English* xviii:18 (1979): 26–36.

———. "The Gladiators." In *A Walk in the Night*: 114–120.

———. "A Glass of Wine." In *Quartet: New Voices From South Africa,* edited by Richard Rive. London: Heinemann, 1971: 91–96.

———. *In the Fog of the Seasons' End.* London: Heinemann, 1972.

———. "The Lemon Orchard." In *A Walk in the Night*: 131–136.

———. "A Matter of Taste." In *A Walk in the Night*: 125–130.

———. "Nocturne." In *Quartet: New Voices From South Africa,* edited by Richard Rive. London: Heinemann, 1971: 111–116.

———. "On A Wedding Day." In *Memories of Home: The Writings of Alex La Guma,* edited by Cecil Abrahams. Trenton, NJ: Africa World Press, 1991: 81–95.

———. "Out of Darkness." In *Quartet: New Voices From South Africa,* edited by Richard Rive. London: Heinemann, 1971: 33–38.

———. "Slipper Satin." In *Quartet: New Voices From South Africa,* edited by Richard Rive. London: Heinemann, 1971: 67–73.

———. *The Stone Country.* London: Heinemann, 1974.

———. "Tatto Marks and Nails." In *A Walk in the Night*: 97–107.

———. *Time of the Butcherbird.* London: Heinemann, 1979.

———. "The Time Has Come." *Sechaba.* 1, no. 3 (1967): 14–15; no. 4 (1967): 13–14; no. 5 (1967): 14–16; no. 6 (1967): 15–16.

———. *A Walk in the Night and Other Stories.* London: Heinemann, 1967.

———. "The Writer in a Modern African State." In *The Writer in Modern Africa,* edited by Per Wastberg. Uppsala: Scandinavian Institute of African Studies, 1969: 21–24.

Landry, Donna, and Gerald MacLean, eds. *The Spivak Reader: Selected Works of Gayatri Chakravorty Spivak.* New York and London: Routledge, 1996.

Lapping, Brian. *Apartheid: A History.* London: Paladin, 1988.

Lazarus, Neil. *Resistance in Postcolonial African Fiction.* New Haven and London: Yale University Press, 1990.

Leggett, Jane, and Roy Blatchford, eds. *It's Now or Never.* London: Unwin Hyman, 1988.

Lessing, Doris. *Five.* London: Penguin, 1960.

Lloyd, David. "Race Under Representation." *Oxford Literary Review* 13 (1991): 62–94.

Macherey, Pierre. *A Theory of Literary Production.* London: Routledge, 1992.

Machor, James L., ed. *Readers in History: Nineteenth Century American Literature and the Contexts of Response.* Baltimore: The Johns Hopkins Press, 1993.

Mandela, Nelson. *The Struggle Is My Life.* London: International Defence and Aid Fund for South Africa, 1986.

Marx, Karl. "On the Jewish Question." In *The Early Writings* introduced by Lucio Colletti. Harmondsworth: Penguin, 1992.

———. *Selected Writings,* edited by David McLellan. Oxford: Oxford University Press, 1990.

Marx, Karl, and Frederick Engels. *The German Ideology,* edited by C. J. Arthur. London: Lawrence and Wishart, 1989.

Matthews, Vincent Goabakwe. "The Development of the South African Revolution." In *Apartheid,* edited by Alex La Guma. London: Lawrence and Wishart, 1972: 163–175.

Maughan-Brown, David. "Adjusting the Focal Length: Alex La Guma and Exile." *English in Africa* 18:2 (October 1991): 19–38.

Mbeki, Govan. *South Africa: The Peasants' Revolt.* London: International Defence and Aid Fund for Southern Africa, 1984.

McClintock, Anne. "The Angel of Progess: Pitfalls of the Term 'Post-colonialism.'" *Social Text* 31/32 (1992): 1–15.

McClintock, Anne and Rob Nixon. "No Names Apart: The Separation of Word and History in Derrida's 'Le Dernier Mot du Racisme.'" In *"Race," Writing and Difference,* edited by Henry Louis Gates. Chicago: University of Chicago Press, 1986: 339–353.

Medvedev, P. N. *The Formal Method in Literary Scholarship: A Critical Introduction to Sociological Poetics.* Translated by Albert J. Wehrle. Baltimore and London: Johns Hopkins University Press, 1978.

Memmi, Albert. *The Colonized and the Colonizer.* London: Earthscan Publications, 1990.

Mendus, Susan. "'What of soul was left, I wonder?': The narrative self in political philosophy." In *Literature and the Political Imagination,* edited by John Horton and Andrea T. Baumeister. London and New York: Routledge, 1996: 53–69.

Miller, Christopher L. "Nationalism as Resistance and Resistance to Nationalism in the Literature of Francophone Africa." *Yale French Studies* 11:82 (1993): 62–100.

Mishra, Vijay and Bob Hodge. "What is post (-) colonialism?" *Textual Practice* 5 (1991): 399–414.

Mnthali, Felix. "Common Grounds in the Literatures of Black America and Southern Africa." In *American Studies in Africa,* edited by Andrew Horn and George E. Carter. Lesotho: University Press of Lesotho and the Ford Foundation, 1984: 39–54.

Moodie, D. T. *The Rise of Afrikanerdom: Power, Apartheid and Afrikaner Civil Religion.* Berkeley: University of California Press, 1980.

Moore, Gerald. *Twelve African Writers.* London: Hutchinson, 1980.

Motlhabi, Mokgethi. *Challenge to Apartheid: Toward a Moral National Resistance.* Grand Rapids, Michigan: Eerdmans Publishing Co., 1988.

Moyana, T. T. "Problems of a Creative Writer in South Africa." In *Aspects of South African Literature,* edited by Christopher Heywood. London: Heinemann, 1976: 85–98.

Mphahlele, Ezekiel. *Down Second Avenue.* London: Faber and Faber, 1971.

Muthien, Yvonne. *State and Resistance in South Africa, 1939–1965.* Aldershot: Avebury Press, 1994.

Mzamane, Mbulelo Vizikhungo. "Sharpeville and Its Aftermath: The Novels of Richard Rive, Peter Abrahams, Alex La Guma, and Lauretto Ngcobo." *Ariel* 16:2 (April 1985): 31–44.

Ndebele, Njabulo. "The Ethics of Intellectual Combat." *Current Writing* 1 (October 1989): 23–35.

———. "Redefining Relevance." *PREtexts* 1:1 (Winter 1989): 40–51.

———. "Rediscovery of the Ordinary: Some New Writings in South Africa." In *South African Literature and Culture: Rediscovery of the Ordinary* by Njabulo Ndebele, edited and introduced by Graham Pechey. Manchester: Manchester University Press, 1994: 41–59.

———. "The Writers' Movement in South Africa." *Research in African Literatures* 20:3 (Fall 1989): 412–421.

Ngara, Emmanuel. *Art and Ideology in the African Novel: A Study of the Influence of Marxism on African Writing.* London: Heinemann, 1985.

Ngara, Emmanuel, and Andrew Morrison, eds. *Literature, Language and the Nation.* Harare, Zimbabwe: Association of University Teachers of Literature and Language [ATOLL] and Baobab Books, 1989.

Ngugi wa Thiong'o. *Decolonising the Mind: The Politics of Language in African Literature.* London: James Currey/Heinemann, 1986.

———. *Moving the Centre: The Struggle for Cultural Freedoms.* London: James Currey/Heinemann, 1993.

———. *Writers in Politics.* London: Heinemann, 1981.

Nkosi, Lewis. *Home and Exile and Other Selections.* London: Longman, 1965, 1983.

———. *Tasks and Masks: Themes and Styles of African Literature.* London: Longman, 1981.

Norval, Aletta J. *Deconstructing Apartheid Discourse.* London: Verso, 1996.

Ntuli, Pitika. "Fragments From Under a Telescope: A Response to Albie Sachs." *Third Text* 23 (Summer 1993): 69–77.

Obuke, J. Okpure. "The Structure of Commitment: A Study of Alex La Guma." *Ba Shiru* 5:1 (1973):14–20.

Odendaal, Andre, and Roger Field, eds. *Liberation Chabalala: The World of Alex La Guma.* Bellville, South Africa: Mayibuye Books, 1993.

Okpaku, Joseph, ed. *New African Literature and the Arts, vol. iii.* New York: The Third Press: Joseph Okpaku Publishing Co., 1973.

Parker, Kenneth. "Apartheid and the Politics of Literature." *Red Letters* 20 (December 1986): 12–33.

———, ed. *The South African Novel in English.* London: Macmillan, 1978.

Parry, Benita. "Problems in Current Theories of Colonial Discourse." *The Oxford Literary Review* 5:1–2 (1987): 27–58.

Paton, Alan. *Cry, the Beloved Country.* London: The Reprint Society, 1949.

Pechey, Graham. "Post-Apartheid Narratives." In *Colonial Discourse/Postcolonial Theory,* edited by Francis Barker, Peter Hulme and Margaret Iversen. Manchester: Manchester University Press, 1994: 151–171.

Petersen, Kirsten Holst, ed. *Criticism and Ideology.* Uppsala: Scandinavian Institute of African Studies, 1988.

Petersen, Kirsten Holst, and Anna Rutherford, eds. *A Double Colonization: Colonial and Post-Colonial Women's Writing.* Mundelstrup, Denmark: Dangaroo Press, 1986.

———. *On Shifting Grounds: New Art and Literature from South Africa.* Coventry, UK and Portsmouth, NH: Dangaroo Press and Heinemann, 1992.

Pick, Zuzana M. "The Dialectical Wanderings of Exile." *Screen: Over the Borderlines, Questioning National Identities* 30:4 (1989): 48–64.

Plomer, William. *Turbott Wolfe.* Oxford: Oxford University Press, 1985.

Rabkin, David. "La Guma and Reality in South Africa." *The Journal of Commonwealth Literature* viii:1 (June 1973): 54–62.

———. "Ways of Looking: Origins of the Novel in South Africa." *The Journal of Commonwealth Literature* xiii:1 (August 1978): 27–44.

Riemenschneider, Dieter. "The Prisoner in South African Fiction." *ACLALS Bulletin* 5:3 (1980): 144–153.

Rive, Richard. *Quartet: New Voices From South Africa.* London: Heinemann, 1971.

Rivkin, Elizabeth Thaele. "The Black Woman in South Africa: An Azanian Profile." In *The Black Woman Cross-Culturally,* edited by Filomená Chioma Steady. Cambridge, MA: Schenkman Publishing Company, 1981: 215–229.

Roberts, Sheila. "South African Prison Literature." *Ariel* 16:2 (April 1985): 61–105.

Robinson, Cedric. "The Appropriation of Frantz Fanon." *Race and Class* 35:1 (1993): 79–91.

Roscoe, Adrian. *Uhuru's Fire: African Literature East to South.* Cambridge: Cambridge University Press, 1977.

Ross, Robert L., ed. *International Literature in English: Essays on the Major Writers.* New York and London: Garland Publishing Inc., 1991.

Rutherford, Jonathan, ed. *Identity: Community, Culture, Difference.* London: Lawrence and Wishart, 1990.

Sachs, Albie. *The Jail Diary of Albie Sachs.* London: Paladin Books, 1990.

Said, Edward. *Culture and Imperialism.* London: Chatto and Windus, 1993.

———. *Orientalism.* London: Penguin, 1991.

———. "Representing the Colonized: Anthropology's Interlocutors." *Critical Inquiry* 15 (1989): 205–225.

———. *The World, the Text and the Critic.* London: Vintage, 1991.

Sam, Agnes. "South Africa: Guest of Honour Amongst the Uninvited New-comers to England's Great Tradition." In *A Double Colonization: Colonial and Post-Colonial Women's Writing,* edited by Kirsten Holst Petersen and Anna Rutherford. Mundelstrup, Denmark: Dangaroo Press, 1986: 92–96.

Scarry, Elaine. *The Body in Pain: The Making and Unmaking of the World.* Oxford: Oxford University Press, 1985.

Sepamla, Sipho. *A Ride on the Whirlwind.* London: Heinemann, 1984.

———. "To What Extent Is the South African Writer's Problem Still Bleak and Immense?" In *Criticism and Ideology,* edited by Kirsten Holst Petersen. Uppsala: Scandinavian Institute of African Studies, 1988: 186–192.

Serote, Wally. "Power to the People: A Glory to Creativity." In *Criticism and Ideology,* edited by Kirsten Holst Petersen. Uppsala: Scandinavian Institute of African Studies, 1988: 193–197.

Sharp, Gene. *Gandhi as a Political Strategist.* Boston, MA: Porter Sargent Publishers, 1979.

Shava, Piniel Viriri. *A People's Voice: Black South African Writing in the Twentieth Century.* London: Zed Books, 1989.

Sivanandan, A. *A Different Hunger: Writing Black Resistance.* London: Pluto Press, 1991.

Slovo, Gillian. "The Hope and the Fear." *Weekend Guardian* (London), March 26, 1994, 6.

Sougou, Omar. "Literature and Apartheid: Alex La Guma's Fiction." *Bridges: A Senegalese Journal of English Studies* (December 1992): 35–47.

Soyinka, Wole. *Art, Dialogue and Outrage: Essays on Literature and Culture.* London: Methuen, 1993.

Spivak, Gayatri. "More on Power/Knowledge." In *The Spivak Reader: Selected Works of Gayatri Chakravorty Spivak,* edited by Donna Landry and Gerald MacLean. New York and London: Routledge, 1996: 141–174.

Stallybrass, Peter, and Allon White. *The Politics and Poetics of Transgression.* London: Methuen, 1986.

Steady, Filomená Chioma, ed. *The Black Woman Cross-Culturally.* Cambridge, MA: Schenkman Publishing Company, 1981.

Sumaili, Fanuel. "Literature and the Process of Liberation." In *Literature, Language and the Nation,* edited by Emmanuel Ngara and Andrew Morrison. Harare, Zimbabwe: Association of University Teachers of Literature and Language and Baobab, 1989: 3–12.

Tambo, Oliver. "Call to Revolution." In *Apartheid*, edited by Alex La Guma. London: Lawrence and Wishart, 1972: 17–23.

Tiffin, Chris, and Alan Lawson, eds. *De-scribing Empire: Post-colonialism and Textuality*. London: Routledge, 1994.

Tlali, Miriam. *Amandla*. Johannesburg, South Africa: Ravan Press/Miriam Tlali, 1986.

———. "The Dominant Tone of Black South African Writing." In *Criticism and Ideology*, edited by Kirsten Holst Petersen. Uppsala: Scandinavian Institute of African Studies, 1988: 198–202.

Tremaine, Louis. "Ironic Convergence in Alex La Guma's *Time of the Butcherbird*." *Journal of Commonwealth Literature* 29:2 (1994): 31–44.

Trump, Martin, ed. *Rendering Things Visible: Essays on South African Literary Culture*. Johannesburg: Ravan Press, 1990.

Turner, Lou, and John Alan. *Frantz Fanon, Soweto and American Black Thought*. Chicago, IL: News and Letters, 1986.

van Rensburg, Patrick. *Guilty Land*. London: Penguin, 1962.

Vaughan, Michael. "Literature and Populism in South Africa: Reflections on the Ideology of *Staffrider*." In *Marxism and African Literature*, edited by Georg M. Gugelberger. Trenton, NJ: Africa World Press, 1986.

Vološinov, V. N. *Marxism and the Philosophy of Language*. Translated by Ladislav Matejka and I. R. Titunik. Cambridge, MA and London: Harvard University Press, 1973.

Wade, Michael. "Art and Morality in Alex La Guma's *A Walk in the Night*." In *The South African Novel in English*, edited by Kenneth Parker. London: Macmillan, 1978: 164–191.

Wastberg, Per, ed. *The Writer in Modern Africa*. Uppsala: Scandinavian Institute of African Studies, 1968.

Watt, Ian. *The Rise of the Novel*. London: Hogarth Press, 1987.

Whitebrook, Maureen. "Taking the narrative turn: what the novel has to offer political theory." In *Literature and the Political Imagination*, edited by John Horton and Andrea T. Baumeister. London and New York: Routledge, 1996: 33–52.

Williams, Patrick. "Problems of Post-Colonialism." *Paragraph* 16:1 (March 1993): 91–102.

Williams, Patrick, and Laura Chrisman, eds. *Colonial Discourse and Post-Colonial Theory: A Reader*. Hemel Hempstead: Harvester Wheatsheaf, 1993.

Williams, Raymond. *The English Novel from Dickens to Lawrence*. London: Hogarth Press, 1984.

Woods, Donald. *Biko*. London: Penguin, 1987.

Wright, Richard. *Native Son*. London: Penguin, 1986.

———. *Rite of Passage*. New York: Harper Collins, 1994.

Young, Robert. *Colonial Desire: Hybridity in Theory, Culture and Race.* London: Routledge, 1995.

————. *White Mythologies: Writing History and the West.* London: Routledge, 1990.

Yousaf, Nahem. "Sembene Ousmane and 'Rhetorical Film Form.'" *Wasafiri* 22 (1995): 49–53.

Zahar, Renate. *Colonialism and Alienation: Concerning Frantz Fanon's Political Theory.* Benin City, Nigeria: Ethiopa Publishing Corporation, 1974.

Zwelonke, D. M. *Robben Island.* London: Heinemann, 1973.

Index

About the Author

Nahem Yousaf is Senior Lecturer in English at the Nottingham Trent University.

DATE DUE
